GRAND PRIX
REFLECTIONS

GRAND PRIX REFLECTIONS

FROM THE 2½-LITRE FORMULA 1 ERA 1954-60

ANTHONY PRITCHARD

Foreword by Sir Jack Brabham

PSL

Patrick Stephens Limited

First published in 1990

British Library Cataloguing in Publication Data
Pritchard, Anthony
  Grand prix reflections: from the 2½ litre Formula 1 era 1954-60.
  1. Formula 1 racing cars. Racing. Races: Grand Prix
  I. Title
  796.7'2

ISBN 1-85260-160-4

Patrick Stephens Limited, part of Thorsons, a division of the Collins Publishing Group, has published authoritative, quality books for enthusiasts for more than twenty years. During that time the company has established a reputation as one of the world's leading publishers of books on aviation, maritime, military, model-making, motor cycling, motoring, motor racing, railway and railway modelling subjects. Readers or authors with suggestions for books they would like to see published are invited to write to: The Editorial Director, Patrick Stephens Limited, Thorsons Publishing Group, Wellingborough, Northants, NN8 2RQ.

Patrick Stephens Limited is part of the Thorsons Publishing Group, Wellingborough, Northamptonshire NN8 2RQ, England.

Printed by Butler and Tanner Limited, Frome, Somerset.
Typesetting by MJL Limited, Hitchin, Hertfordshire.

10 9 8 7 6 5 4 3 2 1

Contents

Foreword

by Sir Jack Brabham

The years 1955-1960 have a special meaning for me so far as my racing career is concerned. In 1955 I came to Great Britain for the first time to try to break into Grand Prix Racing. The end of that era of 2½ litre Grand Prix racing coincided with my second victory in the Drivers' World Championship. When I first came to Great Britain I bought from Peter Whitehead his Cooper powered by an Alta engine. It was a car that was less than successful and I soon substituted a Bristol 2 litre engine and my obsolescent, but still very fast, Formula 2 Cooper soon became a familiar sight on British racing circuits. Perhaps because of my consistency in being successful I was accepted by the Cooper team and I soon became a member of the 'Cooper family'. In 1955 I built a special rear-engined Cooper sports car, powered by a Bristol engine, and it was only accepted for the British Grand Prix that year because I entered it as having an engine of 2.2 litres, whereas it was a standard 1971cc engine.

I ran this car in a number of British events as well as the British Grand Prix that year and I am delighted to see it illustrated in this book. By 1956 I was driving rear-engined Works Cooper sports cars and the following year, working with Rob Walker, the Cooper team entered Formula 1. That was the real turning point of my career and my first Formula 1 race with the rear-engined Cooper was the 1957 Monaco Grand Prix. That year was largely unsuccessful in Formula 1, because our cars were not fast enough or reliable enough. By 1958 both I and my team-mate Roy Salvadori were scoring successes in Formula 1. The following year with the new Coventry Climax engine of 2495cc Bruce McLaren and I were able to compete on even terms with the world's best — which at that time, following the retirement of Vanwall from racing, meant Ferrari. By racing rear-engined Grand Prix cars, Cooper had brought about a revolution in motor racing and I was glad to be part of it. I won the World Championship in two successive years and these were among the happiest of my motor racing career. Later of course, I left Cooper to start my own team, but look back with especial affection on those momentous years in Grand Prix racing when the domination by Ferrari became instead a domination by the British Racing Green. This superbly illustrated book brings back to me many happy memories and I am delighted to have contributed this Foreword.

Introduction

The years covered by this book were years of dramatic change in motor racing, not merely Grand Prix racing, but racing in its other forms. At the start of the 1954 season, no British car had won a Grande Epreuve since Segrave's victory with a Sunbeam in the 1923 French Grand Prix at Tours. Segrave also won the 1924 San Sebastian Grand Prix, but this was not a Grande Epreuve. The expression Grande Epreuve, now fallen into complete disuse, meant the classic national events, the French, Belgian, German, Italian, Swiss and Spanish Grands Prix, together with from time to time the British Grand Prix (or as it was known originally, the RAC Grand Prix), together with the Indianapolis 500 Miles race. By the 1950s the term usually meant the races that were qualifying rounds in the Drivers' World Championship.

Shortly before the commencement of the 2,500cc Grand Prix formula, Jaguar had become a major force in sports car racing, with victories at Le Mans in 1951 and 1953, following this up with a second place in 1954, together with wins in 1955, 1956 and 1957. The marque was of course not a suitable car for other rounds in the Sports Car World Championship and in these other events it was Aston Martin that waved the flag, racing consistently throughout the 1950s, finishing second at Le Mans in 1955 and 1956, winning the Tourist Trophy in 1953 (when it was a round in the Sports Car World Championship)

Ferrari's first Grand Prix car was the single-stage supercharged 1496cc Tipo 125, a team of three of which ran in the 1948 Italian Grand Prix held in Valentino Park, Turin. Raymond Sommer, seen here, was the sole finisher in third place.

but not making a real breakthrough until the team won at the Nür-burgring 1000km race in 1957-59 and not only winning at Le Mans in 1959, but also winning the Sports Car World Championship that year. Colin Chapman's young innovative and vigorous Lotus team won the 1100cc and 750cc classes at Le Mans in 1957, together with the Index of Performance, and Lotus cars were literally winning thousands of races worldwide.

During these years Britain also rose to become the major force in Grand Prix racing, but it was a difficult and much harder path to ascend. The small British HWM which raced all over the continent in Formula 2 races between 1950 and 1953 demonstrated what sheer enthusiasm, despite financial problems, could achieve. During the early 1950s HWM received little national publicity, but the team did much to awaken British enthusiasm in motor racing and much to encourage and develop the careers of some of Britain's finest drivers. At the same time BRM was struggling, with only very limited success, to make its complicated and expensive V-16 car raceworthy and competitive. The V-16 BRM was to prove a lost cause, but in 1955 Tony Brooks with a Connaught B-series car won the Syracuse Grand Prix, defeating a strong team of works Maseratis; the following year Tony Vandervell's efforts with the Van-wall bore fruit with a win by Stirling Moss in the International Trophy Race at Silverstone, not a Championship race, but a race with a Championship-class field; and the final breakthrough came when Moss won the 1957 European Grand Prix at Aintree for Vanwall. Vanwall won three Grands Prix in 1957, and with a further six championship Grand Prix victories in 1958 won the newly inaugurated Manufacturers' Championship, although Stirling Moss was pipped for the Drivers' Championship by Ferrari driver Mike Hawthorn. The rear-engined Coopers dominated Grand Prix racing over the next two seasons, with Lotus also a serious force.

These years brought about a British supremacy in Grand Prix racing and year after year British-based teams dominated racing, with only an occasional intervention from Ferrari. The years of the 2500cc Grand Prix formula also brought about the swing from racing being dominated by substantial manufacturers and industrial concerns to small highly innovative constructors, relying on proprietary engines and other components. During these years more and more British drivers appeared for major continental works teams and racing began to move perceptively towards the present state where it is so heavily dependent on commercial sponsorship. It was also the era in which the modern racing car was born.

To form a clear appreciation of the factors that moulded the 2500cc Grand Prix formula, it is necessary to turn back the clock and review briefly the factors that led to the formula coming into being.

After the early races during the first years of the century, Grand Prix racing, in real, harsh terms, had never amounted to very much. The efforts of the British Sunbeam cars apart, racing throughout the 1920s and the early 1930s was rather a parochial affair, first dominated by

Although the first cars had appeared as long ago as 1934, the ERAs could still surprise. This is T.C. 'Cuth' Harrison with R1B, the ex-Dick Seaman car, which he drove into fourth place in the 1948 British Empire Trophy held on the Isle of Man. (Guy Griffiths)

Delage, then Alfa Romeo, followed by a three-cornered fight between Bugatti, Alfa Romeo and Maserati. The introduction of the 750kg formula for 1934 changed all that. During the years 1934-1937, the Grand Prix formula was to all intents free, subject only to a maximum dry weight without wheels of 750kg and a minimum body width of 85cm. The appearance of the German Mercedes-Benz and Auto Union teams transformed racing into a major propaganda exercise, and at the same time ushered in one of the greatest and most spectacular eras in Grand Prix racing. Backed by state finance, not so much through direct payments but through industrial contracts, the two German teams dominated racing in a magnificent spectacle of power and speed. Alfa Romeo, the dominant marque in the early 1930s, struggled to stay abreast, but lacked the money, the technical resources and the organization to combat the ever-increasing German supremacy. Since 1921 there had been a 1500cc category for so-called *Voiturettes* consistently supported by Maserati, the British ERA team from 1934 onwards and, from 1938, by Alfa Romeo.

For 1938 there was a new Grand Prix formula which incorporated a scale of minimum weights corresponding with engine size for capacities from 666cc to 4500cc, with a maximum limit of 3000cc for cars with supercharged engines. Both upper limits of engine size had a minimum weight of 850kg including wheels and tyres and the 85cm minimum body width was retained. The formula in fact gave little incentive for constructors to build cars with smaller engines than 3000cc blown or 4500cc unblown, and to all intents and purposes the formula can simply be regarded as 3000cc blown/4500cc unblown. Mercedes-Benz and Auto Union continued to dominate; Alfa Romeo, despite trying a number of different engine designs, remained an also-ran and in 1938 introduced the Tipo 158 straight-eight *Voiturette*. During that year Alfa Romeo ran the car in only four races, all in Italy, and won two. The contemporary Maserati *Voiturettes* were intended primarily for private owners and these scored many successes in minor events. Despairing at the domination of Grand Prix racing by Germany, the Italian authorities decided that in 1939 all Grands Prix held on Italian soil would be to *Voiturette* rules. On 7 May 1939 the Tripoli Grand Prix was held on the Mellaha circuit, and as Libya was Italian-controlled, the race was held for 1500cc supercharged cars. What little was left of the Axis sporting accord was destroyed when Mercedes-Benz appeared with two new 1500cc supercharged cars, known as the W165, for Hermann Lang and Rudolf Caracciola and they scored a clear and unexpected victory. Pre-war Grand Prix racing ceased when Tazio Nuvolari (Auto Union) won the Yugoslav Grand Prix at Belgrade on 3 September, held in fact immediately after the outbreak of war.

What would have happened to Grand Prix racing if it had continued through 1940 and onwards is obviously a matter of speculation. It should be added that racing continued in Italy until Italy entered the war. However, there is evidence that both Italy and Germany were seeking a change in the Grand Prix regulations for 1940 onwards to limit cars to 1500cc supercharged. Indeed, it is known that Auto Union was working on a 1500cc supercharged car, but it is far from clear how far development progressed and what the exact relationship was between the Auto Union design studies and the DAMW car that is now in the Donington Museum. The full story of Mercedes-Benz and Auto Union during these turbulent years is told in *Racing The Silver Arrows*, and all Mercedes-Benz racing cars are authoritatively described in *Mercedes-Benz Racing Cars* (see 'Further reading' for details).

Once hostilities were over, racing quickly resumed and the first post-war race was the Paris Cup held in the Bois de Boulogne in September 1945, and won by Jean-Pierre Wimille with a 4.7-litre Bugatti. This was followed by a hill climb held near Naples in December 1945. Throughout 1946 the pre-war racing regulations continued, but most races were strictly Formule Libre, which meant 1500cc *Voiturettes*, unblown 4.5-litre cars (Talbots and Delhayes), various pre-war Bugattis and the odd blown 3-litre Alfa Romeo. Germany was banned from international motor racing until 1950. From 1947 the Grand Prix formula was changed to suit what existed, namely the *Voiturettes* and the 4.5-litre unblown cars.

Alfa Romeo had returned to racing in 1946. Although the Company had quite a range of pre-war designs which it could race, including the rear-engine flat-twelve Tipo 512 *Voiturette* which was never raced, it decided to revert to the Tipo 158 cars. In 1942 seven complete Alfettas, as the 158 had become known, were moved from garages at Monza together with the two rear-engined Tipo 512 cars to the village of Melzo, where the Alfa Romeo design department was working following evacuation from Milan and where the cars were put into store. Alfa Romeo first entered two 158s in the St Cloud GP, held in a Paris suburb in 1946, and although drivers Farina and Wimille led the race, both retired because of clutch problems. The change in the racing regulations meant that these former *Voiturettes* became Grand Prix cars in 1947 and over

Louis Chiron with his Ecurie France-entered Talbot in the 1949 Jersey Road Race. After lying fourth he retired because of brake trouble. (Guy Griffiths)

the next five years they were constantly developed and improved.

In the 158's original form as raced, power output was 195 bhp at 7,000 rpm; the adoption of two-stage superchargers in 1946 had increased this to 254 bhp and, in the final 1951 Tipo 159M form, power was 425 bhp at 9,300 rpm. By this time the cars were capable of a maximum speed of around 190 mph and with fuel, of which 98 per cent was of methanol content, consumption was around 1.6 mpg. With vast tankage, now risen to 66 gallons, but still the need for two refuelling stops in a normal Grand Prix, and with vastly impaired handling because of the weight of fuel carried, the Tipo 158/159s became vastly overdeveloped, voraciously thirsty, ill-handling beasts. Nevertheless, after that first débâcle at Paris, the Alfettas won every race entered, three in 1946, four in 1947, four in 1948, 11 in 1950 and four in 1951, before they were finally defeated in the 1951 British Grand Prix. In one race at the beginning of the 1951 season there had been a technical knock-out, because although the Alfettas had won their heats of the International Trophy at Silverstone, the final was abandoned in a torrential downpour when Reg Parnell was leading the field in Tony Vandervell's Ferrari Thin Wall Special and although there was no official classification, Parnell was awarded the prize money.

Alfa Romeo had not raced in 1949, believing that the Alfetta was outdated in the light of the opposition that was emerging, and only returning when that opposition had failed to materialize. In the main, the opposition to the Alfettas came from two Italian teams and one French. Maserati had continued to develop the Tipo 4CL four-cylinder car that had first appeared in 1949, but even in its later 4CLT/48 'San Remo' form with tubular chassis (first seen in 1947), coil springs in place of torsion bars in the front suspension, twin-stage supercharging (again first seen in 1947) and newer, much neater bodywork, the cars were absolutely no match for the Alfa Romeo opposition, although in the absence of Alfa Romeo the cars won both the 1948 and 1949 British Grands Prix. Although in 1948 Viloresi and Ascari took the first two places with cars entered by the semi-works Scuderia Ambrosiana team, Maseratis were still mainly for private owners. Indeed, the winner at

The Talbot-Lago six-cylinder engine with two high-mounted push-rod-operated camshafts and triple Zenith carburettors. (Guy Griffiths)

Silverstone in 1949 was a private entry, Emmanuel de Graffenried entered by Enrico Platé. Maseratis continued to score minor successes right through to the end of 1950, but by 1951 the Modena cars were a spent force.

Likewise the French Talbots, stalwarts of the racing scene, could never be regarded as truly competitive. Antonio (there are various other renderings of his first name, so sometimes it is easier simply to refer to him as 'Tony') Lago, born in Italy but resident in France, had formed Automobiles Talbot after the collapse of the Sunbeam-Talbot-Darracq concern, and combined the building of quality high-performance road cars in limited numbers with early sports-racing cars and, from 1939, single-seater Grand Prix cars. Powering these vastly overweight cars was a six-cylinder 4482cc ohv engine operated by high-set camshafts, push-rods and rockers and developing in early post-war form 240 bhp, rising to 280 bhp in 1950. The first single-seater had been driven by Raymond Mays in the 1939 French Grand Prix. The team was raced for the works by Ecurie France in post-war days and the cars were also run by quite a number of private owners. Talbot's greatest days came in 1949, in the absence of Alfa Romeo, when Louis Rosier drove non-stop for 3¼ hours to defeat the works Ferraris in the Belgian Grand Prix, and Louis Chiron, in the absence of works Ferraris, won the French Grand Prix. With the return of Alfa Romeo in 1950 and the growing strength of Ferrari, the great days of Talbot were short-lived, although the cars were raced through until the end of the formula and, indeed, in Formule Libre events afterwards.

The rising star of post-war years was Enzo Ferrari's Scuderia Ferrari. Much has been written over the years to criticize Ferrari's successes (or perhaps more accurately lack of them in view of the resources at his disposal) and his management style. Whatever Ferrari may or may not have achieved, and in this book much will be read of his failures

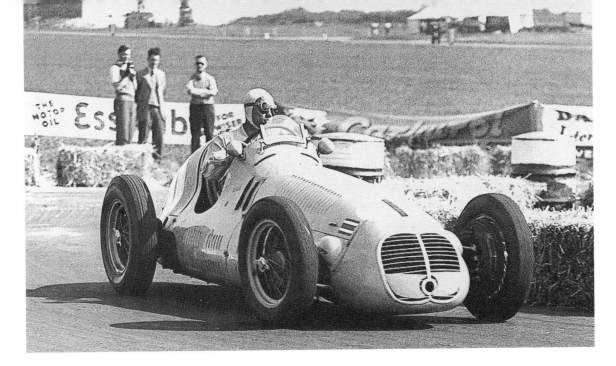

Above 'B.Bira' (Prince Birabongse of Siam) with his 4CLT/48 Maserati in the 1949 British Grand Prix. Bira set fastest lap and was leading the race when he crashed because of brake problems. (Guy Griffiths)

Right Juan Fangio with his 4CLT/48 Maserati at the 1949 Albi Grand Prix. Chief mechanic Bignami puffs unconcernedly at his cigarette as he works on the engine of his Argentine-entered car. Fangio won the race from 'B.Bira'.

rather than this successes, the Scuderia Ferrari has consistently entered Grand Prix racing since the Formula 1 cars made their race debut in the 1948 Italian Grand Prix. If Ferrari had not entered Grand Prix racing, then Grand Prix racing would probably have died. There would have been no team to battle it out with Alfa Romeo; there would have been

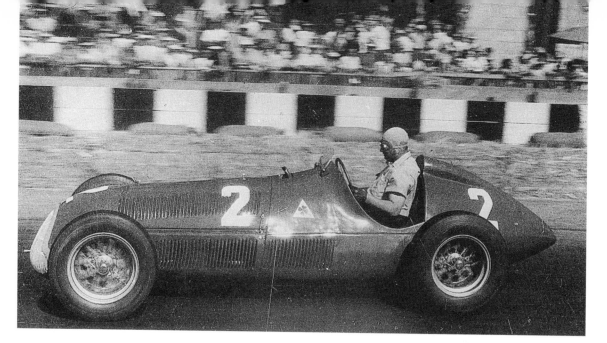

Above Juan Fangio at the wheel of his Alfa Romeo Tipo 158 in the 1950 Grand Prix des Nations held on a street circuit at Geneva. Fangio won the race from other Alfa Romeos driven by de Graffenried and Taruffi.

Right The start of the 1950 Italian Grand Prix at Monza with Farina (158) leading away from other Alfa Romeos driven by Fangio, Fagioli, Sanesi and Taruffi. Farina won with Fagioli third.

Right The eclipse of Alfa Romeo power came in the 1951 British Grand Prix. Here Fangio struggles vainly to stay with the single-plug Ferrari of Froilan Gonzalez. (T.C. March)

Above *Of limited potential only, and with insufficent finance or driver talent to exploit that potential, was the Grand Prix Alta. Here cars driven by Joe Kelly and Geoffrey Crossley are seen in the 1950 European Grand Prix at Silverstone. (T.C. March)*

Right *By 1952 the appearance of the BRM was much modified and during that year a much darker shade of green was adopted. This is Froilan Gonzalez with the V-16 in the Daily Graphic Trophy at the September Goodwood meeting. He won this 15-lap Formule Libre race from other BRMs driven by Parnell and Wharton. (Guy Griffiths)*

no team to carry on the mantle of Italian domination during 1952-53 when competitive cars, other than Ferraris, were few and far between; Maseratti would probably not have been inspired to tackle the 2500cc formula so seriously; and it is quite possible that there would have been 'no bloody red cars' for Tony Vandervell to beat.

Ferrari's first essay into Formula 1 was with the Tipo 125 single-stage supercharged V-12 car designed by Giaocchino Colombo, the former Alfa Romeo designer, who incorporated many Alfa Romeo design features into the new car. When the Tipo 125 was first raced it was far from right, and development soon followed, with shorter chassis, twin overhead camshafts and two-stage supercharging. Following the defeat of the works cars by Rosier's Talbot in the 1949 Belgian Grand Prix, Ferrari's new designer Aurelio Lampredi moved swiftly towards the development of unsupercharged 4500cc cars. In June 1950 there appeared a 3.3-litre unsupercharged car at the Belgian Grand Prix, the Tipo 330, followed a month later by a 4.1-litre version (the Tipo 340), and by the Italian Grand Prix in September, Ferrari had a full 4.5-litre version ready to race. With an immensely strong team of drivers, including Ascari, Villoresi and Gonzalez, Ferrari tackled the 1951 season with

new 24-plug cars in direct confrontation with Alfa Romeo. After a succession of second places, Froilan Gonzalez defeated Alfa Romeo in the British Grand Prix at Silverstone; further Ferrari victories with Ascari at the wheel followed in Germany and Italy, but Alfa Romeo won the last race of the season, the Spanish Grand Prix, and then finally withdrew on a high note. So the mantle of supremacy passed from Alfa Romeo to Ferrari.

At this time the development situation of the British V-16 BRM was critical. It is doubtful whether any Formula 1 project in the history of motor racing has attracted such public interest and notoriety as the BRM. Raymond Mays and Peter Berthon, key figures in the very successful pre-war ERA project, had devoted their lives in post-war years to the development of what they had hoped would be a world-beating Formula 1 car. Money for the project was raised by contributions from industry and many components were supplied by industrial companies. Unfortunately Berthon had chosen to design perhaps the most complicated car that he could conceive, with a V-16 engine of 1496cc featuring Rolls-Royce two-stage centrifugal supercharging, the banks of cylinders at 135 degrees and a hoped-for power output of around 500 bhp.

With the benefit of hindsight it is possible to say that the design was far too complex for the resources and abilities of its creators, and it would have needed a company with the financial muscle of Mercedes-Benz in its pre-war days (or later, when it had recovered from the ravages of war) to truly develop such a design, though it is also very clear that Mercedes engineers would have followed a very different design route. Development of the new car took much longer than anticipated and when it finally appeared at the International Trophy meeting at Silverstone in August 1950, its debut proved a débâcle. At the wheel was that great lion-hearted driver Raymond Sommer. When Sommer let the clutch in at the fall of the flag, the BRM jerked forward and stopped. A shaft in the rear axle had broken. Much blame was heaped not only on BRM for this disheartening race debut, but also upon Sommer, for, after all, had not a very similar happening occurred in the French Grand Prix at Lyon in 1947 when Sommer was at the wheel of another great national hope, France's own white elephant, the CTA-Arsenal? Later that year Parnell won a couple of minor races at Goodwood, and two cars retired in the Spanish Grand Prix. The following year, two cars were entered in the British Grand Prix and were driven into fifth and seventh places by Reg Parnell and Peter Walker, but apart from being hopelessly out-classed, both drivers had miserable races and finished with badly blistered feet, burnt by the exhaust system. Two cars were then entered in the Italian Grand Prix at Monza for Reg Parnell and Hans Stuck, but both cars non-started because of transmission problems.

When it became known that Alfa Romeo was withdrawing from racing, there was left only one serious force in Formula 1, the Ferrari team. The other cars, the Gordinis, the Altas, the venerable ERAs, Maseratis and OSCAs were not serious contenders. Already the Federation Inter-

*The Great Optimist:
Raymond Mays at the
wheel of a V-16 at Good-
wood in September 1952.
Roy Salvadori wrote, 'If
you listened to him long
enough, he would make
you World Champion!'
(Guy Griffiths)*

nationale de l'Automobile and the various race organizers were having
grave doubts as to whether Formula 1 in its existing form would be
viable in 1952. Already it was known that it would be for 2500cc unsupercharged cars from 1954 onwards and there was in force a very
healthy Formula 2 for 2000cc cars which had been inaugurated in 1950.
Early in 1952 it was announced that all French Grand Prix races would
be held to Formula 2 rules. Mays tried to save the situation by inform-
ing every race organizer that if they retained Formula 1 racing, a BRM
entry would be guaranteed. Mays' efforts were a total failure and it was
soon agreed that all Championship races — together with many others
— would be held to Formula 2 rules.

With a car made obsolescent by changed circumstances, BRM struggled on but in October 1952 the whole set-up was sold to the Owen
Organisation. The BRM did score wins in minor events, but in the two
international races which attracted strong opposition, the Albi Grand
Prix in 1952 and 1953, the cars failed. In 1954 BRM produced a Mk
II version of the V-16; it was shorter and lighter, and was intended as
something for the team to race and as a development test bed while
the new car for the 2500cc formula was being developed. Even so,
throughout 1954 in Formule Libre events the BRMs rarely proved a
match for Tony Vandervell's much-developed Ferrari Thin Wall Special,
perhaps the most highly developed of all Formula 1 cars from the old
formula. It was all the more ironic that Vandervell had been a great
supporter in financial and morale terms of BRM until he finally became
disenchanted and went his own way.

The decision to run races in 1952-53 to 2000cc Formula 2 rules

The twin overhead camshaft four-cylinder engine of the Tipo 500 Ferrari with two twin-choke Weber carburettors. In 1953 form it developed a claimed 180 bhp at 7,500 rpm. (Guy Griffiths)

proved immensely popular both with entrants and spectators. Not only did it give the teams a chance to develop cars in 2000cc form that could be raced with enlarged engines from 1954 onwards (a route followed by both Ferrari and Maserati), but it also opened up Grand Prix racing to many other teams that had been unable previously to compete. In 1952 the starting grids included the Cooper-Bristol, the Connaught A-Series, Frazer Nash, Alta and HWM from Great Britain, together with the French Gordinis, German AFM and Veritas, and the Italian Ferraris, Maseratis and OSCAs.

All the British cars suffered from the same problem, lack of sufficiently powerful engines, and it was the HWM team that suffered the most. John Heath and George Abecassis had been campaigning throughout Europe with their Alta-powered cars since 1950. They ran the team on the proverbial shoestring, relying on starting money to cover their costs, selling the cars at the end of the season and thus making a reasonable financial success of the venture. HWM had achieved respectability for the British Racing Green in Europe and it also helped to bring to prominence several young leading British drivers, including Stirling Moss, Peter Collins and Lance Macklin. Although during 1950-51 HWM had scored a small number of wins and a lot of good places, it was now no longer competitive. In the absence of Ferrari, the team took first and second places in the International Trophy at Silverstone, but it had lost the services of Stirling Moss who has written: 'Although I was told of their plans [HWM's] for 1952. I could see no possibility that they would break through to the point of being a winning force.' Stirling Moss signed up to drive the new Bristol-engined G Type ERA but when this was not ready early in the season, he did in fact drive HWMs on a few occasions. However, HWM slipped so swiftly from the forefront of Formula 2 that the organizers of the 1953 German Grand

Above During 1952-53
Maserati scored only one
World Championship
Grand Prix victory, at
Monza (in 1953) where
Ascari was 'encouraged'
to make a rare mistake.
Here the winner, Juan
Fangio, takes the
chequered flag with his
Maserati A6GCM.

Prix did not even invite the team to compete.

Most successful of the British cars was the Cooper-Bristol, especially when driven by young Mike Hawthorn whose performances during 1952 included a fourth place in the European Grand Prix at Spa-Francorchamps and third place in the British Grand Prix, and led to an invitation to join Ferrari for 1953.

Despite the large number of other marques competing, Ferrari totally dominated Formula 2 with the Tipo 500 four-cylinder 1980cc cars designed by Aurelio Lampredi. From their debut in the Modena Grand Prix in 1951 through to the end of the 1953 season, the works Ferraris won all but three of the races entered. The total number of wins amounted to 32, and in addition private owners won another five races. Ascari alone won 18 races and took both the 1952 and 1953 World Championships. The only times that the Ferraris failed was when Jean Behra scored what was an almost freak victory in the non-Champion-

Right Although the old
Formula 1 had come to an
end, Formule Libre races
were still part of the
British scene in 1954.
BRM produced a lighter,
shorter wheelbase Mk II
car, one of which is seen
here with Ron Flockhart at
the wheel at the Easter
Goodwood meeting in
1954. These cars were
still far from trouble-free
and Flockhart had to settle
for two fourth places in
Formule Libre 'sprint'
races, both of which were
won by his team-mate
Ken Wharton (LAT)

Throughout the years of the 1500cc blown/4500cc unblown Grand Prix formula and during 1954, Tony Vandervell entered a succession of Ferraris under the name 'Thin Wall Special'. Here Peter Collins in the much-developed, last of the line leads Moss's Maserati 250F at Aintree in 1954. Collins led until the 'Thin Wall' began to run rough and dropped back down the field before retiring.

ship Reims Grand Prix in June 1952, his Gordini showing a remarkable turn of speed and simply running away from the Ferraris; at Syracuse in 1953, when all the works Ferraris retired, three with valve spring failure, the result of a bad production batch; and in the Italian Grand Prix when the winner was Fangio with the Maserati A6GCM after Ascari had spun.

During 1952 Maserati had taken a very half-hearted approach to Formula 2, entering very few races (and in the first European race at Monza Fangio crashed so badly that he put himself out of racing for the rest of the season), selling cars to private owners (who achieved very little) and, at Monza in September, entering a new twin-plug car for Gonzalez who finished second after a refuelling stop. The following year Maserati's efforts with the six-cylinder A6GCM were much more determined. Officine Alfieri Maserati ran a full team of cars throughout the year, with Fangio and Gonzalez as leading drivers. Only two wins were scored by the works cars, in the Italian Grand Prix as already mentioned and in the following week's Modena Grand Prix which Ferrari missed. The Maserati had undoubtedly the edge in straight-line speed, but its rigid rear axle meant that the road holding failed to match the Ferraris (with de Dion rear end) and the braking was also inferior.

Despite the threat of much greater competition after the start of the 2500cc formula, both Ferrari and Maserati were complacent. Both were content to race developed versions of the 1953 cars and this was partly responsible for Italy's downfall.

1

The Italian scene

1954-55

1954

The new Formula

With effect from 1 January 1954, the new Grand Prix Formula for cars of 2500cc supercharged and 750cc supercharged came into force. The supercharged alternative was included for what, at first sight, was no good reason. However, after the V-16 BRM had, at least in Raymond Mays' view, been cut off in the prime of its development, Mays indicated to the Federation Internationale de l'Automobile that BRM was contemplating building a 750cc supercharged car based on one half of the existing V-16, and as there had been a 500cc alternative to the Formula 2 of 1950-53, the inclusion of this alternative was not entirely illogical. However, no cars were built to comply with the supercharged alternative except for a couple of minor, rather pointless efforts which are discussed in Chapter 7.

Until the end of 1957 fuel remained free, the minimum race distance of 300kms or 3 hours remained as it had since 1950, and World Championship points were awarded on the basis of 8, 6, 4, 3 and 2 points for the first five finishers, with one point for the fastest lap.

Ferrari

Although during 1953 it was not known precisely who would be competing during the new Formula, it was open knowledge that Lancia in Italy would be entering Formula 1 for the first time, that Mercedes-Benz would be making a return to racing, and that in Britain BRM, Connaught and Tony Vandervell were all developing cars. Ferrari's own plans for the new Formula dated back to 1951 at least, and there seemed no real awareness at Maranello of how serious and strong the competition was likely to prove. As has been mentioned in the previous chapter, Aurelio Lampredi had developed the Tipo 500 1980cc (90 × 78mm) four-cylinder car with two valves per cylinder, twin overhead camshafts driven by a train of gears from the nose of the crankshaft, twin plugs per cylinder, and, in 1953 form, a power output of around 180 bhp at 7,500 rpm. The four-speed gearbox was in unit with the final drive. The chassis was very much in accordance with normal Ferrari practice; a tubular ladder-type structure with cross-bracing and light tubular superstructure, front suspension by double wishbones, transverse leaf spring and Houdaille vane-type shock absorbers, and at the rear a de Dion axle located by twin parallel radius arms with, again, a transverse leaf spring and Houdaille shock absorbers. As has been mentioned, the Tipo 500 completely dominated Formula 2, but even before the first of these cars had made its race debut at Modena on 23 September 1951, Ferrari had already produced the Tipo 625 with a 2490cc engine (94 × 90mm) with, in its original form, a power output of around 200 bhp at 6,500 rpm. The first Tipo 625 car appeared at the Bari Grand Prix held on 2 September 1951 as a Formula 1 race and Piero Taruffi drove it into third place. During the next couple of years cars ran in Tipo 625 form in a number of events, including the 1952 Valentino Grand Prix at Turin at which Taruffi finished second; cars powered by 2.5-litre engines also took the first three places in the 1953 Formule Libre Buenos Aires City Grand Prix. Subsequently Farina and Hawthorn took the first two places in the Rouen Grand Prix in June 1953 and Hawthorn drove one in the Formule Libre race at the British Grand Prix at Silverstone, but retired. The Tipo 625 was to prove the mainstay of Ferrari's efforts in 1954, mainly because the Tipo 553, a much redesigned version, was unreliable and proved a dismal failure. However, as the season progressed it became evident that the Tipo 625 was becoming uncompetitive. Ferrari almost in desperation carried out a number of substantial engine modifications and the 625s then achieved a reasonable measure of success.

The Tipo 553, which became known as the *Squalo*, looked a new car, but it was essentially a development of the existing design. It first

Argentinian Froilan Gonzalez, one of the most talented drivers of the early 1950s, at the wheel of his Ferrari Tipo 553 Squalo *at the International Trophy at Silverstone in May 1954. (T.C. March)*

The front row of the starting grid for the final of the 1954 International Trophy at Silverstone with, from the camera, Froilan Gonzalez (works 625 Ferrari), Reg Parnell (private 625 Ferrari), Robert Manzon (private 625 Ferrari) and Roy Salvadori (Gilby Maserati 250F). (T.C. March)

appeared in 1988cc (93 × 73.5mm) form at the 1953 Italian Grand Prix in which there was a special prize for a new Italian design. It had a new multi-tubular chassis constructed from a small-diameter tubing, space-frame in appearance, but not a true space-frame because it was not fully stressed or triangulated. It was a more compact car than the 625, with a shorter wheelbase, narrower track and a stubby body with most of the fuel carried in side tanks, and only a small tank in the tail. At Monza in 1953 the cars were driven by Umberto Maglioli and Piero Carini. Although Ferrari's Tipo 500s, suffering a race defeat at Monza, finished second, third and fourth, the handling of the 553s was conspicuously more difficult than that of the usual cars, they appeared to be slower in a straight line and neither Maglioli nor Carini were exactly Grand Prix material. After starting from the middle of the grid, Maglioli finished eighth, whilst Carini retired.

In their 1954 form, the Tipo 553s had a capacity of 2497.5cc (100 × 79.5mm) and a *claimed* power output of 250 bhp at 7,500 rpm. The latest *Squalo* first appeared in testing at Monza in late 1953, but it was obvious that development was slow and the cars were not ready at the beginning of the season.

Ferrari had always been able to attract the very best driving talent, but the team had suffered a severe blow for the 1954 season. World Champion in 1952 and 1953, Alberto Ascari, together with his life-long mentor, Luigi Villoresi, had left Scuderia Ferrari to drive for Lancia. There is little doubt that part of the attraction of the Lancia team was greatly improved financial terms, whereas Ferrari had nothing to offer the reigning World Champion but an existing, staid design. Lancia had the services of one of the world's greatest designers, Vittorio Jano, and there were very real prospects that the new Lancia, when it appeared, would lead the field. So Ferrari persuaded Froilan Gonzalez to leave Maserati to join them, and Hawthorn stayed with the team, as did the now elderly Giuseppe Farina and Piero Taruffi. Umberto

Maglioli was available when required and, after the Argentine races in which he finished fourth in the Argentine Grand Prix and won the Buenos Aires City Grand Prix, Maurice Trintignant, formerly driving a private Rosier-entered Ferrari, was invited to take a works seat.

A small number of Formula 2 Tipo 500 cars had been sold to private owners and these were updated for the 1954 season by the installation of the 2490cc engine. Louis Rosier had two of these cars, but it seems that after the Argentine races when Trintignant had joined the works team, he disposed of one of them to fellow-Frenchman Robert Manzon. In Britain, Reg Parnell raced a private Tipo 625 during 1954 with considerable success. This was the car that had belonged to the late Bobbie Baird, who had also owned a 4.1-litre sports Ferrari. After Baird's fatal crash at Snetterton in 1953, Baird's widow was courted by a number of drivers, all anxious to clinch a deal to acquire the Ferraris and Parnell was the lucky man so far as the single-seater was concerned.

Maserati

The development of the Maserati 250F reflected the company's design policy of evolution in gradual stages. The six-cylinder engine was a direct development of that used in the 1952-53 Formula 2 cars. This in turn owed its ancestry to the Tipo A6GCS and A6G sports car engines, which in turn owed their ancestry to the pre-war Tipo 6CM *Voituertte* engine.

Maserati had pursued a very half-hearted policy during 1952, running a far from developed car for racing motorcyclist Nello Pagani in the South American races at the beginning of the year, selling a trio of cars to a South American team, and in all entering only four races. After a full racing season in 1953, when the now much improved

A fine cutaway by Vic Berris of the 1954 Maserati 250F. This drawing, based on the Gilby Engineering car, shows it in its late 1954 form with the oil tank mounted in the rear of the tail. In their earlier form, 250Fs had the oil tank alongside the engine.

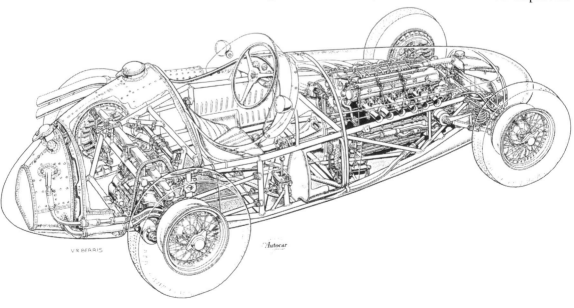

A6GCM cars showed great promise and Fangio won the last round in the World Championship at Monza, Maserati layed firmer plans for 1954.

The original A6GCM was mainly the work of designer Alberto Massimino, but the team had been joined by one of the greatest Italian designers, the rather fickle Giaocchino Colombo, for 1953. He had much improved the car for that year's races, revising the cylinder dimensions and increasing the power output, providing stiffening for the chassis, modifying the rear suspension and evolving a completely new and lower body. For 1954 engine capacity was increased to 2493cc (84 × 75mm) and the *claimed* power output was 240 bhp at 7,400 rpm, although most cars during 1954 had some 20 bhp less. There was a completely new chassis, multi-tubular and of space-frame concept, but, again, not a true space-frame. The double wishbone front suspension was much revised and at the rear there was a de Dion axle with the tube running in front of the gearbox/final drive unit and located by a central slide guide and twin forward-facing radius arms. The suspension medium was a transverse leaf spring running above the rear axle and there were Houdaille vane-type dampers front and rear. The rear suspension layout was broadly copied from that of the Ferrari Tipo 553.

Maserati first tested the 250F at Modena Autodrome in December 1953 before the cars were shipped out to race in the Argentine the following month. At this stage Maserati was not planning to run a full Formula 1 season, but Fangio, who had signed up for Mercedes-Benz in 1954, had agreed to drive for the team in the Argentine, where Maserati had strong trading connections, because it would be some while before the new German cars would be ready. Maserati's main aim was to sell the new 250F to private owners and soon it received a string of orders, including Stirling Moss (whose purchase was financed by the BP oil company), Gilby Engineering (for Roy Salvadori to drive), the Owen Organisation (who wanted a car to race until the new BRM was ready) and Siamese Prince Birabongse (whose racing career extended back to pre-war days and always entered as 'B. Bira').

Following Fangio's win in the Argentine Grand Prix, Maserati made the decision to run a full team during the year's races. They had only the services of Juan Fangio for the Belgian Grand Prix, after which he drove for Mercedes-Benz, and driver problems proved to be one of the team's shortcomings throughout the year. After the Belgian race Onofre Marimon was team leader. The young Argentinian, a protégé of Fangio and Gonzalez, was a fine driver, still developing. He was not, however, sufficient to meet the weight of the opposition, nor were the other Maserati drivers Musso and Mantovani, and the shape of the team was to change through tragedy and altered circumstances as the year progressed.

In the May 1954 issue of *Motor Racing*, Roy Pearl, the Editorial Director, reported on a visit to the Italian factories of Ferrari and Maserati. It was a fine piece of journalism, not wholly accurate but dramatic and exciting. In his account of his visit to the Maserati factory (which I have edited in the interests of accuracy) he commented:

'Soon after dawn next morning we were at Modena Autodrome watching Roy Salvadori trying out the Fl Maserati. His own car was receiving its green in the paint shop so he was driving Fangio's car. Although Roy had never driven this Fl car before he completed 15 laps in impeccable style. He was not assisted by the track's surface — on one corner this slowed him to walking pace, he said. Roy told us that he was taking things easy and was not driving the car flat out. Yet three times he equalled Ascari's 4.5-litre Ferrari lap record of 1m 4.5s. (A Maserati test mechanic has been timed by the Automobile Club at 1m 2s unofficially). Salvadori drove with the full 40-gallon tank. He was completely happy with the car and full of praise for it. He could not raise a single point of criticism and he believed he would get round the Modena circuit very much faster.

'...Our tour of the Maserati factory was prefaced by an interview with Sig Orsi, designer of the racing section of the Maserati Industrial Combine. [In fact, Alfieri Orsi was the son of Adolfo Orsi, head of the industrial company that had bought Maserati from the Maserati brothers.] We asked him why Maserati races.

'"Maserati started with racing cars 25 years ago," he said. "We hope to keep up with the tradition." As Maserati make motorcycles, lorries, machine tools, and many other components, it is obvious that they currently benefit by car-racing publicity — so long as it is not too costly.

'Sig Orsi believes that it is possible to make a profit out of motor racing and that profit and loss is relative to success in races and in selling race cars and their derivatives. We gathered that although Maserati were not making a profit yet, they are not losing very much either, despite the fact that they consider themselves independent of trade "bonus" support. This is because of their considerable sports car income. The company wishes to return to its pre-war system selling racing cars throughout the world. Ferrari will not do this.

'...Sig Orsi believes that Italy owes her racing car success to the fact that the country specializes in the production of racing cars. Every racing car part is made in Italy by racing car specialists and this, he said, is not the case in other countries, where proprietary brands invariably are used.

'Inspection of the factory showed that although Maserati racing car activity occupies much less floor area than Ferrari's, Maserati construct their own chassis and build their own bodies. It is also evident that full use of other Maserati resources, such as machine tools, forges and presses, was made.

'At the time of our visit the cars for Moss and Wharton [the Owen Organisation car] appeared set for delivery before these words appear.

'...The only British Maserati to receive works assistance will be the Greene/Salvadori machines. Both Moss and the Owen Organisation are paying the full price of about £5,000 for the F1 cars — a total of over £10,000 each including import duty and purchase tax.'

What Roy Pearl's article made clear was the seriousness of the Italian intent in motor racing, coupled with the necessary finances (which British constructors lacked), but as events were to prove what the Italians also lacked was the necessary organization to defeat a team such as Mercedes-Benz.

Lancia

The Turin company had been founded in 1906 by Vincenzo Lancia, a works team driver for FIAT, and he had built his company into a substantial manufacturer of technically interesting cars, some with distinctly sporting pretensions, but he consistently avoided motor sport. Vincenzo died in 1937, but it was not until the 1950s that his son Gianni took over control of the company. Lancia had one distinct advantage over its Italian rivals, the fact that Vittorio Jano was the company's chief engineer and designer, one of the greatest names in motor racing design and responsible for the whole range of pre-war Alfa Romeos that proved so successful. Gianni Lancia dared do what his father had avoided and embarked on a full competition programme. First the team raced competition versions of the very successful Aurelia GT car, but during 1953 the company campaigned a range of V-6 sports-racing cars, and scored a string of successes including a win in the 1953 Carrera Panamerica Road Race in Mexico.

Meanwhile, Jano had been working on the team's new Formula 1 car, the D50. Like all Lancias since post-First World War days, the D50 featured a V-layout engine; the sports cars had V-6 engines, just like the production Aurelia, but for the new Formula 1 car Jano chose a 90-degree V-8 layout, with a capacity of 2487cc (73.6 × 73.1mm) with a one-piece cylinder block and crankcase cast in Siluminum light alloy with wet cylinder liners. When the cars were first raced, power output was 260 bhp at 8,000 rpm, lower than that of the Mercedes-Benz W196, but substantially higher than that of the rest of the opposition. The five-speed gearbox was in unit with the final drive and incorporated a ZF limited slip differential. What was completely innovative about the D50 was that the engine and gearbox formed an integral part of the chassis, adding considerable stiffening, and the chassis itself was a multi-tubular structure. Front suspension was by equal-length parallel wishbones with a transverse leaf spring and tubular dampers, while at the rear there was a de Dion tube running behind the final drive, located by parallel trailing arms, with a sliding block for lateral guidance, a transverse leaf spring and, once again, tubular dampers. Between the

At the Spanish Grand Prix, the long-awaited Lancia D50 made its racing debut. This is Villoresi's car with its twin sponson fuel tanks, advanced suspension and the V-8 engine forming a structural member; it was ahead of its time but was let down by the tyre technology of the period. (LAT)

front and rear wheels were slung pontoon fuel tanks suspended on outriggers, the idea behind which was to prevent changes in fuel level during the race from affecting the handling; there was just a small additional fuel tank in the tail of the car. Compared with its rivals, the D50 was short, low and squat, and as events were to reveal, it was probably the most potent Grand Prix car then racing, its potential limited only by the comparatively unsophisticated tyre technology of the period.

To drive the new car Lancia signed up World Champion Alberto Ascari, together with Luigi Villoresi and young newcomer Eugenio Castellotti. Although the D50 was being tested as early as January 1954, and amongst those to drive it were 62-year old designer Jano and Juan Fangio, development was slow and the cars were not ready to race until the very end of the season.

The 1954 racing season

Traditionally the year's racing opened with three events in the Argentine, the Formula 1 Argentine Grand Prix, the Formule Libre Buenos Aires City Grand Prix and the Sports-Car Buenos Aires 1000km sports car race. There had been a gradual build up of importance of these races since the first Formule Libre events were held in 1947 and the 'Temporada' had now become an important fixture. The growth of importance of the races was partly due to President Péron's enthusiasm for motor racing and partly due to the strong trading links between Italy and the Argentine, there being a large Italian population in that part of South America. Most of the races were held on the Buenos Aires Autodrome, with a number of different circuit permutations, in the main park in Buenos Aires and, in the case of the sports car race, extending out on to public roads. As was so often the case in South American countries, crowd control was the biggest problem, and in the 1953 race Giuseppe Farina went off the track and mowed down a whole group of spectators who were watching the race from the edge of the road. Ten onlookers died, but the race continued.

In 1954 the winners were Fangio and Maserati. It was not, however, a clear-cut victory, for the race had been marked by a series of violent rain showers. In the wet Fangio was more than a match for the Ferrari drivers — he made a pit stop to fit a set of anchorized rain tyres which the Maserati mechanics had cut during the race and Ferrari team manager Ugolini entered a protest on the grounds that five instead of the permitted three mechanics had worked on Fangio's car. Ugolini, confident that his protest would be upheld, slowed down his cars, so that Fangio went on to take the chequered flag from the Ferraris of Farina and Gonzalez. The protest was, however, rejected, so Maserati had scored wins in two World Championship races in succession. Not that the Maseratis had been trouble-free in this race, for in practice the drivers had been unhappy with overheating and the handling (it was believed that the chassis frame was too stiff and the team resorted to the expedient of removing a couple of tubes from the cockpit section, making the chassis frame more flexible). Later, during the season, other problems were to be experienced, including frequent breakages of the de Dion tube (Moss had a specially-made stronger tube fitted to his private car), problems with the oil tank located by the engine, which was subsequently transferred to the tail immediately behind the fuel tank, and frequent breakages because components were attached too rigidly. It must be remembered that all Formula 1 cars of the period rattled, shook and vibrated appallingly compared with modern competition cars. In addition, Marimon had pranged his 250F in practice for the Argentine Grand Prix, so that only the one 250F had started the race.

The Formule Libre Buenos Aires City Grand Prix proved yet another débâcle, for both the 250Fs were eliminated. All the works Ferraris ran into problems and the unexpected race winner was Maurice Trintignant with a private 625 entered by Ecurie Rosier. This early success in fact frustrated Louis Rosier's plans to run a team of two blue-painted Ferraris in 1954, for Trintignant was immediately invited to become a works Ferrari driver. Rosier sold one of his cars to fellow Frenchman Robert Manzon and he himself raced just the one car for the rest of the year.

During this early part of the 1954 season, racing was simply between the Ferraris and Maseratis, with the French Gordinis (described in detail in Chapter 7) in the main trailing at the back of the field, but from time to time turning in an unexpected performance. Five months now elapsed before the next round in the World Championship, but in Europe there were a large number of minor Formula 1 races, mostly held on traditional road circuits with all the hazards of kerbs, traffic furniture, tram lines, trees and, of course, spectators who insisted on standing in the wrong places. These road races, never held on the British mainland, but traditional in Jersey, Northern Ireland (the Dunrod circuit) and the Isle of Man, were a familiar part of the racing scene, for both cars and motorcycles, until the tragic Le Mans disaster in 1955, which created a public awareness of the potential dangers of motor racing; street circuits gradually disappeared, until today the only survivors of this great era are Monte Carlo and Pau. Both are short circuits, both are slow and both are very carefully policed and disciplined — and both are now disfigured by miles of armco barriers.

The first of these minor Formula 1 races was the Syracuse Grand Prix held at Siracusa in Sicily. As Fangio was not now to race again for Maserati until the Belgian Grand Prix in June, and the Modena team relied on its junior drivers, there really was not much in the way of opposition for the somewhat mediocre Ferraris. However, Siracusa was the scene of yet another débâcle, caused by a Maserati. Argentine Onofre Marimon, leading initially with his 250F, and with Hawthorn and Gonzalez in hot pursuit, chopped a corner, striking a straw bale. Hawthorn, whose vision was obscured by flying straw, crashed into a wall and his 625 burst into flames. Quick-thinking Gonzalez stopped and rescued Hawthorn from the blazing Ferrari, but Gonzalez' car, the new *Squalo*, unattended, rolled forward and became engulfed in the blaze. Hawthorn suffered bad burns and did not race again until June, while Marimon retired. Farina won for Ferrari with Trintignant in second place.

Yet again, the following weekend at Pau, Scuderia Ferrari's Plans went sadly awry. Gonzalez was leading with his 625 when the engine broke its crankshaft at high speed, Farina was slowed by an engine misfire and Trintignant was not able to get to grips with Jean Behra at the wheel of the Gordini. On a slow circuit on home territory, Behra had everything going for him and he exploited the advantage to the full.

There were three more minor races before the Belgian Grand Prix and Gonzalez won them all with 625 cars, then at Bordeaux he scored another easy victory in heavy rain. However, the real significance of the race was the debut of Stirling Moss with his new Maserati 250F. He had taken delivery of the car only four days before the race, and, after a short test session at Modena, there had been a frantic rush to get the car to Bordeaux in time for the race and he drove steadily and cautiously to finish fourth. Moss's driving at Bordeaux had been deliberately restrained, while he got to grips with his new car, and the initial reaction at Scuderia Ferrari, of Maserati itself and of most enthusiasts, was to underrate the potential of this new combination. A week later, in the BRDC International Trophy at Silverstone, Moss jolted everyone back to reality; he finished third in his heat and was lying second in the final when the de Dion tube of the Maserati broke. The International Trophy was held on the basis of two qualifying heats and a final, with positions on the grid for the final decided by the speeds of the cars and not of the drivers. Gonzalez at the wheel of the 553 *Squalo* had won the first heat in the wet, at a much lower speed than Trintignant with the 625 had won the second heat in the dry. This would have given Gonzalez a place back on the third row of the grid for the final, but Ugiolini, the Ferrari team manager, announced that the engine of Gonzalez's 553 had seized between the heat and the final. Accordingly Gonzalez took over Trintignant's 625 (in pole position on the grid) and Trintignant took over Maglioli's car. Whether or not the Ferrari's engine had really seized or whether it was merely a ploy to give Gonzalez pole position we shall now never know, but Gonzalez won the race easily and, after Moss's retirement, the Gordinis of Behra and Simon took second and third places.

Gonzalez scored his fourth successive victory with a 625 in the Bari Grand Prix. Moss won the Aintree 200 race from Parnell's Ferrari and Wharton with the V-16 BRM (for this was a Formule Libre race) and the following week, while Marimon with a works Maserati was winning at Rome, Prince Birabongse, who had just taken delivery of his new 250F, won the Grand Prix des Frontières at Chimay in Belgium, a race that had always been a favourite with private entrants and virtually their exclusive bailliwick.

Spa-Francorchamps, scene of the Belgian Grand Prix, was one of the most spectacular motor racing circuits in Europe, a combination of public roads extending to 8.716 miles of sweeping curves and bends set in the delightful wooded Ardennes countryside and with excellent facilities for both teams and spectators yet taxing to the limit the skill of the finest and bravest drivers. At Spa only the very best win and happily Spa survives today, albeit in shortened, emasculated form. In practice and the race, Fangio, enjoying his last works drive for Maserati in 1954, was magnificent. Just before the end of the first day's practice, in the cool of the evening, the Argentinian turned in a lap of 4m 22.1s, unofficially breaking his own lap record which he had set with a Tipo 159 Alfa Romeo in the 1951 race. It was superb driving, beautifully precise, beautifully balanced, and very brave, and breaking the 250F's rev limit with the full consent of team manager Tavoni. After the lap the tell-tale on Fangio's tachometer stood at 8,100 rpm, 100

Ferrari again relied on the Squalos in the French Grand Prix in 1954. Mercedes-Benz routed the Italians and Hawthorn retired with engine failure. (LAT)

rpm above the permitted limit. The brakes glowed hot, oil leaked from almost every joint and the car was enveloped in a heat haze. During the final day's practice that time was not beaten and Fangio, who also set the fastest lap in the race, could then manage no better than 4m 25.5s. In the race, he made a poor start, but took the lead on lap 3 and won from Trintignant (Ferrari) and Moss with his private Maserati. In his own way Moss's performance was almost as meritorious as Fangio's, for although he was a lap in arrears, Moss had been running at a rev limit of 7,600 rpm, conserving his engine, partly because he had no spare and partly because he was hoping to get through several races without a major overhaul. At this race Ferrari had entered *Squalos* for Gonzalez and Farina, but both had retired with engine failure. In addition, the two 625s of Trintignant and Hawthorn both had the 553 engine.

Mercedes-Benz returned at Reims, and Stutgart had carefully chosen this very fast circuit used for the French Grand Prix for its debut in racing with the new streamlined W196 cars. With Fangio at the wheel of a Mercedes, Maserati was lost and leaderless. Lancia agreed to release Ascari and Villoresi to drive for them (the latter at the wheel of Moss's car loaned back to the works because the English driver was at the wheel of a works D-type Jaguar in the 12-Hours Sports Car race that preceded the Grand Prix). In 1954 Ascari, although he had won the difficult Mille Miglia 1000-mile road race in Italy with a Lancia, seemed to have lost his form, partly perhaps because he was racing insufficiently, and also perhaps because he was simply not used to driving uncompetitive machinery. To achieve a place on the front row of the grid at Reims, Ascari had taken his 250F up to 8,200 rpm and even then he was only third fastest to the Mercedes of Fangio and Kling, who took the first two places in the race, with Herrmann setting fastest lap. All three works Ferraris (two 553s and a 625 with a 553 engine) blew up their engines in vain pursuit of the Mercedes. Ascari also blew up his engine, and Marimon was eliminated by gear-selector problems. Behind the all-conquering Mercedes came the private Ferrari of Robert Manzon in third place, with 'B. Bira' fourth and Villoresi with Moss's car fifth — but these drivers were in a different race from the winners!

The Grand Prix circus then moved on to the British Grand Prix at Silverstone. Here there were only two streamlined Mercedes for Fangio and Kling. Ferrari entered three Tipo 625 cars, all powered by a new engine which combined the bottom end of the 625, reckoned to be sound and reliable, with the cylinders and head of the *Squalo*. This engine had first appeared in the non-Championship Rouen race the previous weekend, and Trintignant had driven a 625 with this engine to an easy victory in the face of weak Gordini and private Maserati opposition. At Silverstone the Maserati team was a shambles. Although they had missed Rouen, the works transporters arrived late for official practice, having gone to the wrong port for shipping across the Channel. A special practice session was laid on for them, but times recorded were unofficial and the Maseratis had to start from the back of the grid.

Once again Maserati had the services of Ascari and Villoresi and they had come to an arrangement with Stirling Moss, for whose ability they were developing an ever-increasing regard, that if he drove his car at his hardest, Maserati would foot the bill.

The race provided a complete upset of the form book. The Mercedes were never in the running on this medium-speed circuit lined with concrete-filled oil drums. Kling was simply 'all at sea' while Fangio struggling hard and had difficulty positioning his car for the corners, but by a superhuman effort near the end of the second day's practice, he managed to snatch pole position with a lap of 1m 45s, 100.35 mph, the first time that 100 mph had been exceeded at Silverstone by an unsupercharged 2500cc car. The price was battered front bodywork, bashed against the oil drums, something that repeated itself in the race in which Fangio never rose above second place and eventually finished fourth, a lap in arrears, with Kling seventh. It was Gonzalez who dominated, repeating the form he had shown in 1951 when he had won at Silverstone with the 4.5-litre Ferrari, leading throughout and with Hawthorn bringing his 625 across the line in second place.

The performance of the Maseratis was like two sides of a coin, the brilliance of Moss and Marimon, but the desperate ineffectiveness of Ascari. With his private Maserati, Moss rose to second place, having had a tussle with Hawthorn, then gradually pulled ahead, only to retire once more with a broken drive-shaft. Marimon, who had started from the back of the grid, succeeded in passing 19 cars on his first lap and drove a fine and steady race to finish third. Ascari stopped early in the race to complain about the steering of the Maserati, rejoined in a flurry of wheelspin holding on to gears much longer than any other Maserati driver, and soon retiring just past the pits because of a dropped valve. Even before Ascari had walked back to the Maserati pit, chief mechanic Bertocchi had shown Villoresi the 'come in' board and *il campianissimo* was back in the race only to retire before long with a broken

connecting rod and the tachometer tell-tale at 8,200 rpm. Apochryphal it may be, but Ascari strode back into the pits swinging his blue crash helmet to ask, 'Any more Maseratis?'

After Reims everyone believed Mercedes to be unbeatable. After Silverstone the Italian teams breathed again and realized that Mercedes *was* beatable; it was also soon appreciated that their superiority was due to Fangio's outstanding skill and that the cars themselves were only marginally superior, despite their undeniable technical complexity and sophistication. Moss was invited to join the works Maserati team and Italy had a new hero. Italian optimism, however, was short-lived. At the German Grand Prix at the Nürburgring, Mercedes produced a new version of the W196 with unstreamlined boxy bodywork and, tragically for Maserati and Italy, Onofre Marimon crashed fatally in practice. As a result the works Maseratis were withdrawn, although Moss, Mieres and Mantovani elected to run as private entrants. In this race Gonzalez's Ferrari 625 was fitted with yet another engine variation, combining the crankcase of the Tipo 735 3-litre sports car with the cylinder head of the *Squalo*. Gonzalez was devastated by the death of fellow countryman Marimon and drove a lack-lustre race. If he had been on top form, he might well have been able to challenge the Mercedes, but as it was he drove apathetically until he handed over to Hawthorn who brought the 625 across the line in second place behind Fangio, with Trintignant third.

Fangio won for Mercedes both in the Swiss Grand Prix at Bremgarten and in the Italian race at Monza. The Swiss race was the last to be held there, as motor racing in Switzerland was banned following the Le Mans disaster the following year. Bremgarten was a sad loss to the motor racing world, for this medium-speed circuit set in the woods near Bern was amongst the most difficult in Europe, its 4.52 miles consisting of a succession of curves and bends of varying speeds and with sudden changes from sunshine to shade as the drivers emerged from the woods into the open areas. Maserati had been optimistic of a good result in this race, but the cars were plagued by mechanical problems and the best Italian performance was by Gonzalez (Ferrari 625 with 553/735 engine) who finished second, splitting the Mercedes domination.

Although Fangio won in the Italian race at Monza, the real hero was Moss. Villoresi drove for Maserati, whilst Ascari appeared for the Ferrari team, and in the early laps of the race the latter duelled with Fangio for the lead and went ahead, then Villoresi took the lead but blew up his engine. Moss inched in front and was firmly in the lead when Ascari's Ferrari went out with a dropped valve. With the race three-quarters run, it was clear that not only was Moss driving the race of his life, but it seemed also that he had victory in the bag. It was not to be, however, for Moss found that the oil pressure was dropping on corners. He stopped to top up and rejoined in second place. Nine laps

Stirling Moss so nearly won the 1954 Italian Grand Prix with his private 250F, entered by the works. Unfortunately an oil pipe broke and he pushed the car across the line to be classified tenth.

Ascari with his Lancia D50 in the 1954 Spanish Grand Prix. He led briefly before retiring early in the race. (Geoffrey Goddard)

before the finish he came to a halt just before the finishing line; the suction pipe from the rear-mounted oil tank had cracked its flange with the tank, air was sucked into the system and the bearings were ruined. Almost equally unlucky was the young Italian driver Sergio Mantovani who had come through the field to duel for second place with Hawthorn, but the de Dion tube broke and he had to crawl to the finish. Fangio won by a lap from Hawthorn, with another 625 shared by Maglioli/Gonzalez third, Herrmann's Mercedes fourth and poor Moss pushing his car across the line into tenth place.

To round off the 1954 season there was one more Championship race, the Spanish Grand Prix held on the Pedralbes road circuit at Barcelona. Pedralbes was another magnificent street circuit incorporating public roads and with the very fast but bumpy long straight along the Avenida Generalissimo Franco. The race provided a remarkable contrast; the rise and fall of exhausts of the world's fastest racing cars set against a backcloth of dusty roads and buildings, the undoubted squalor of Franco's Spain that could not be concealed, and the only-too-Spanish odour of sewers. At long last the Lancias were ready to race and cars were driven by Ascari and Villoresi. Although Ascari was fastest in practice, neither of the Lancias lasted long in the race, so Schell (in a works Maserati which had started with a half-full tank) and Trintignant battled for the lead with Hawthorn playing a waiting game. On lap 27 Hawthorn took the lead, then shortly afterwards both Schell and Trintignant retired; Fangio was now in second place, but a long way behind. As the race progressed so Hawthorn extended his lead, while Fangio, whose Mercedes had sucked dust and paper into its air intake, lapped slower and slower and developed more and more of a sick, wailing exhaust note. Shortly before the finish of this long, dusty race, Luigi Musso, urged on by the Maserati pit, slipped ahead of Fangio to take second place. Hawthorn was at the wheel of a *Squalo*, now fitted with coil spring front suspension, and although his victory was a magnificent fillip for the Italian team, it must be remembered that it was also something of a lucky victory, partly because of the early retirement of the new Lancias and partly because of the unexpectedly poor performance of Fangio's Mercedes. In the Drivers' World Championship Gonzalez took second place with $26^{1}/_{7}$ points to Fangio's 42 points.

1955

This was a bad and in many respects tragic year for the Italian teams — the season was cut short by the cancellation of races following the Le Mans tragedy and every Championship race was won by Mercedes.

Ferrari

Lampredi still proved incapable of showing new initiative and the Maranello team relied on improved versions of the 1954 cars. The 625 had now been modified by the adoption of coil springs at the front, as on the 1954 Barcelona-winning *Squalo*, and with re-shaped bodywork giving the car a low nose and slightly more aerodynamic lines. In the main the cars were raced with five-speed gearboxes and 555 engines. The *Squalo* was now much modified, with a new multi-tubular chassis, larger fuel tanks, sleeker lines and lower and wider air intake, and was redesignated the Tipo 555 *SuperSqualo*.

Apart from the fact that Hawthorn had left Ferrari to drive for Vanwall, the team was largely unchanged and consisted of Gonzalez, veteran driver Farina, Trintignant and Maglioli, although quite a number of other drivers were to appear for Scuderia Ferrari during the year.

Maserati

Very few changes were made to the Maserati 250F for 1955, but a five-speed gearbox was introduced and the works cars had bodyworks without louvres, as seen on the car loaned by the works to private Spanish driver Francesco Godia-Sales at Barcelona in 1954; the team also adopted a single large-bore exhaust tail-pipe during the year. Only three new cars were completed for 1955 and there were no deliveries at all to private purchasers.

During 1954 Stirling Moss and Maserati had built up a very close working relationship and it came as a great shock to Modena when Moss signed for Mercedes the following year. If he had continued driving for Maserati, it could well have been the dominant team; to replace him they signed Jean Behra, a gutsy driver of considerable skill but not in the 'world' class, and Maserati sunk automatically to being an 'also-ran' together with Ferrari. Other members of the Maserati team in 1955 were Luigi Musso, who was to become Italy's hero, Sergio Mantovani and Argentinian Roberto Mieres.

Lancia

After its not entirely unexpected failure at Barcelona, Lancia carried out an intensive testing programme and a number of changes were made to the cars as a result. Apart from slight reductions in weight, new very wide four-shoe brake drums were adopted, the pannier fuel tanks were now suspended on struts instead of the original aerofoil-section supports and there were a number of other minor but important modifications. In addition to Ascari and Villoresi, the team would be running a third car for young Eugenio Castellotti.

The 1955 racing season

The year started with the Argentine Grand Prix, run in even hotter conditions than usual, topping 104° Farenheit and reducing what was usually a pretty shambolic event into an even greater shambles. Only two drivers, locals Juan Fangio and Roberto Mieres, were able to run through the race without relief and Mieres was delayed by fuel starvation problems. The result was the first of a succession of Mercedes victories. In second place came a Ferrari Tipo 625A shared by Gonzalez, Trintignant and Farina which had in fact lapped for much of the race at a higher speed than the winner, but had been delayed by pit stops and driver changes. As two of the three Lancias had crashed, the Turin company was rather despondent and returned home to base rather than compete in the Formule Libre Buenos Aires City Grand Prix. For this event Mercedes installed 3-litre 300SLR sports engines running on alcohol and these took first, second and fourth places on the aggregate of the two 30-lap heats. Ferrari, too, used a larger engine, the 3-litre Tipo 750 *Monza* sports engine, but its best performance was third place by Trintignant. Two similar cars with 3-litre engines had been supplied to private owners Peter Whitehead and Tony Gaze to drive in New Zealand over the winter, and in the same month's New Zealand Grand Prix, another Formule Libre event, they took second and third places behind 'B. Bira's' Maserati 250F.

In Europe, Mercedes-Benz ran only in Championship events (apart from its 'local' event, the Berlin Grand Prix), so the early European season races proved a three-sided battle between Ferrari, Lancia and Maserati. Now the true potential of the Lancias revealed itself. In the Turin Grand Prix held in Valentino Park, Ascari was the winner ahead of Mieres's Maserati, with other Lancias driven by Villoresi and Castellotti third and fourth. By the Pau Grand Prix on Easter Monday, a number of changes had been made to the Lancia including the substitution of two-leading-shoe brakes and, for some unaccountable reason, a lighter shade of red paint finish. Although Behra led with his Maserati, Ascari soon forged ahead, but when the latter made a pit stop because of a broken hydraulic brake line, the race turned into a Maserati/Behra victory, with Castellotti's Lancia in second place ahead of Mieres's Maserati and the other two Lancias of Villoresi and Ascari fourth and fifth. Maseratis were dominant in the next two races, at Bordeaux and Silverstone; in the Bordeaux road race, Behra, Musso and Mieres took the first three places with their works 250Fs, but in the International Trophy at Silverstone there were no works cars apart from the British teams. Here Peter Collins with the Owen Organisation's 250F was the winner from Salvadori (with the Gilby Engineering car) and 'B. Bira'. Lancia made no mistakes in the last of these early season European races, the Naples Grand Prix held on the picturesque Posillipo circuit in the suburbs of that town and overlooking the bay; here Ascari scored an easy victory from Musso (works Maserati 250F) with Villoresi's Lancia in third place. At this stage in the season it looked very much as though the Lancias would prove serious opposition for the Mercedes.

The First European round the World Championship was the Monaco Grand Prix, last held as a Formula 1 event in 1950, and not held since 1952 when it had been run for sports cars. It was the trickiest and most difficult of the 'round the houses' circuits, with few places for overtaking, low speeds and very much of a car-breaking circuit. All the teams were out in force, with three cars from Mercedes-Benz (including one driven by André Simon, deputizing for Hans Herrmann who was seriously injured in a practice crash), four from Lancia, including an extra entry for local veteran driver Louis Chiron, four from Ferrari, two 625As and two 555s, and four from Maserati. It was to prove quite a remarkable race. The early laps were led by the Mercedes of Fangio and Moss, with Ascari, Behra and Castellotti in hot pursuit until the latter pair dropped back because of problems. On lap 50 Fangio retired his Mercedes because of transmission problems, and Moss survived in the lead until lap 81 of this 100-lap race, when his Mercedes broke its engine. In real terms Ascari (Lancia) led the race, although he would not in fact do so until he passed Moss's stationery Mercedes and he would probably not have known that he was leading until he passed the pits and received the appropriate signal. On that lap, however, his brakes locked up on the approach to the chicane, the Lancia shot through the straw bales and sandbags and plunged into Monte Carlo harbour. Ascari was rescued, apparently unhurt apart from a broken nose. A complete outsider won the race, Trintignant with his 625A Ferrari, from Castellotti (Lancia) and Cesare Perdisa who had taken over Behra's misfiring Maserati.

The Monaco race had been held on 22 May and four days later Ascari was dead. Dropping in at Monza Autodrome during practice for the Supercortemaggiore Grand Prix for sports cars, he had asked Castellotti if he could try his Ferrari *Monza;* naturally Castellotti agreed and Ascari, dressed in a lounge suite and with Castellotti's helmet, set off round the track. His car left the course for no apparent reason on a bend that was taken almost flat-out. There has never been a satisfactory explanation for this fatal accident although tyre failure is the most likely reason.

Lancia was already in severe financial problems for various reasons; the flagging sales of its rather staid production cars, the vast costs of the competition programme, and the vast sums expended on its prestigious 16-storey office building straddling the Via Vicenzo Lancia in Turin. The Company was undecided whether or not to proceed with its entry in the Belgian Grand Prix, eventually sending a single car, ostensibly as a private entry, for Castellotti who retired when his gearbox broke. Ferraris took third and fourth places.

Tragically, Ascari's death was the excuse that both Lancia and Ferrari needed. On the latter's withdrawal from racing, the complete Lancia

Three views of the Tipo 625A Ferrari, the latest version of a model that dated back to 1951. The car is that acquired for the Donald Healey Motor Company by Peter Collins and owned in the 1960s by Ian Sievright. It was often claimed to be the 1955 Monaco winner, but was in fact the car prepared by Ferrari for de Portago for the 1955 season. (Author)

team, including cars (with the exception of just one retained by Lancia), spares, transporters and a great deal of other equipment were handed over to Ferrari who was to henceforth receive from Fiat a contribution towards his racing expenses of 50 million lire (approximately £28,500) per annum for a total of five years.

The weekend following the Belgian race saw the Le Mans 24-Hours, during which Pierre Levegh's works Mercedes-Benz 300SLR left the road opposite the pits and plunged into the spectator area, killing more than 80 spectators and injuring hundreds. Public and press reaction resulted in the cancellation of the French, German, Swiss and Spanish Grands Prix. There was never again a motor race in Switzerland and it was not until 1967 that the Spanish Grand Prix was held again. Accordingly there now only remained four Championship races in 1955.

Only a week after Le Mans the Dutch Grand Prix was held with a small entry of 16 cars, for amongst the absentees were both Vanwall and Lancia. Inevitably Mercedes-Benz took the first two places, but in this race the Maseratis had the legs of the Ferraris and the 250Fs of Musso and Mieres finished third and fourth with a very off-form Behra in sixth place. Newcomers to the Ferrari team in this race were Hawthorn, who had severed his links with Vanwall, and Castellotti, but all four Ferrari entries performed abysmally. Castellotti did well to take fifth place with his ill-handling 555, with Hawthorn trailing in seventh place.

Over a month elapsed before the British Grand Prix, another Mercedes benefit in which the Stuttgart cars took fourth place. Ferrari fielded Tipo 625s which were hopelessly outclassed and the Maseratis fared little better, with the best performance coming from Luigi Musso who took fifth place having led the fourth-place Mercedes of Taruffi for much of the race. Between the British race on 16 July and the Italian race on 11 September, there were a number of minor Formula 1 events. During the year Moss had been loaning his 250F to other drivers; it had been driven by Lance Macklin without success in the British race at Aintree, but on 30 July Mike Hawthorn drove it at the Crystal Palace,

In the 1955 International Trophy at Silverstone the results were dominated by Maserati 250Fs — despite a strong British presence. Here Roy Salvadori (Gilby 250F) leads the eventual winner Peter Collins (Owen Organisation 250F) during the early laps of the race. (T.C. March)

Undoubtedly Luigi Musso put his name on the map in Formula 1 as a member of the Maserati team. Here he is seen at the wheel of his 250F before the British race in which he finished fifth. (T.C. March)

and over this interesting but very short 1.39-mile circuit he and Harry Schell (Vanwall) put up a magnificent show in the final of the 15-lap Trophy. Mike won by less than two seconds, the first occasion on which he drove a Maserati, but Schell's performance showed that the Vanwalls were ever-improving. In August that fine by under-rated British driver Bob Gerard drove Moss's car at Carterhall in Scotland and again won, from similar cars driven by Gould and Rosier, but when Moss drove the car himself at Snetterton later in August, feeling rather unwell, he could manage no better than third place behind the Vanwalls of Schell and Wharton. This was the first-ever victory by a Vanwall and another portent for the future.

In the 1955 British Grand Prix at Aintree, Eugenio Castellotti (Ferrari Tipo 625A) leads team-mate Maurice Trintignant. Both Ferrari drivers retired. (T.C. March)

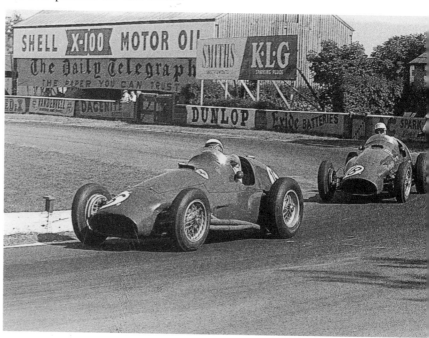

In the Italian Grand Prix Ferrari had intended to field both Lancia D50s and the latest *SuperSqualos*, now modified by Victorio Jano and fitted with five-speed gearboxes, modified suspension geometry and detailed body alterations. For the first time the race was held on the newly completed 6.214-mile Monza circuit incorporating two steeply banked concrete curves in the existing network. In practice the Lancias were almost as fast as the Mercedes, but the Belgian Englebert tyres, which Ferrari was contracted to use, were throwing treads, and it was reluctantly decided to withdraw the cars on safety grounds. Another new development in this race was the appearance of a streamlined Maserati 250F, a virtually standard car with pontoons between the front and rear wheels, and a full width nose and tail. Two of the four Mercedes retired, but Fangio and Taruffi took the first two places ahead of Castellotti (*SuperSqualo*) and Behra, whose streamlined Maserati sounded in chronic mechanical condition and crossed the line enveloped in a cloud of blue smoke. Of one thing Behra was sure — that the streamlined car had no future! Fangio and Moss had completely dominated the World Championship with 40 and 23 points respectively, and third-place Castellotti had scored a mere 12.

Although there were no more Championship races, the season was not quite over and there were two minor races, both of considerable significance. In September the Gold Cup race was held at Oulton Park in Cheshire and both Maserati and Ferrari sent works teams. For the first time Ferrari was entering the Lancia D50s and two of these cars were driven by Hawthorn and Castellotti. From Maserati came works cars for Stirling Moss and Luigi Musso. Oulton Park was the only true road circuit used for Formula 1 on the British mainland and it was

The 1955 Italian Grand Prix was held on the combined road and track banked circuit at Monza. Here Jean Behra (stream-lined Maserati 250F) leads Harry Schell (Vanwall), Horace Gould (private 250F), Jean Lucas (Gordini), Maurice Trintignant (Ferrari Super-Squalo) and da Silva Ramos (Gordini).

and still is a superb circuit from a spectator's point of view. Although Castellotti and Hawthorn led away from the start, Moss was soon in front and won the race with Hawthorn second and Titterington's Vanwall in third spot.

On 23 October came the Syracuse Grand Prix. Siracusa was an exceptionally difficult circuit, roughly triangular in shape, with two slow corners, a very tight hairpin bend and fast straights. Much of its length was lined by solid walls, giving little margin for error, and, unusually, the race was run in an anti-clockwise direction. Ferrari did not enter, but there was a strong entry of Maseratis driven by Musso, Villoresi, American Carroll Shelby, Luigi Piotti and Harry Schell at the wheel of the streamlined car. The race had all the makings of a Maserati walkover, but for the fact that the organizers had been so desperate to secure entries for what would have been a thin event, and they had offered £1,000 per car starting money to the British Connaught team who brought along two cars for young dental student Tony Brooks and Les Leston. Brooks, driving in his first Formula 1 race, proved a sensation, securing a place in the front row of the grid although practising very little, battling it out with the Maseratis and taking the lead from Musso early in the race. At the end of this 239-mile race, Brooks led by 50 seconds, with Maseratis in the next six places.

This defeat at Siracusa by a comparatively unknown car and a completely unknown driver was the final blow in a dismal year for Italy.

Both Ferrari and Maserati were now at the very nadir of their fortunes and there was only one way to go and that was up.

2

The German invasion

1954-55

In 1945 the Daimler-Benz factory at Untertürkheim near Stuttgart was a sea of ruins, completely devastated by Allied bombing. The first priority after the war was to get the Company back into production again as soon as possible with both cars and commercial vehicles, and even though racing was an essential tool in its development and marketing policies, it was something that could not be tackled for years. Indeed, Germany was not allowed to take part in International racing until 1950. By this time the Company was thinking in terms of a motor racing programme and the first tentative step was the decision to run three 1939 3-litre supercharged W163 Grand Prix cars in the Argentine 'Temporada' Formule Libre races in February 1951. None of the Mercedes ran well, and both events were won by Froilan Gonzalez with a 2-litre supercharged Ferrari. In the first race, the Péron Cup, Lang and Fangio took second and third places with their Mercedes-Benz W163 cars, with Karl Kling trailing in sixth place. In the second race, known as the Eva Péron Cup, Kling finished second with Lang third.

The Argentine was of course a country not particularly ill-disposed towards Germany, but even so there was very little adverse international comment about this return by Mercedes to motor racing and so it was decided to press on with a sports car programme in 1952. That year Mercedes-Benz fielded the new 300SL sports-racing coupés, characterized by their space-frame-style chassis, sleek coupé lines and gull-wing doors. Just as the rival Jaguar XK120C was based on production components, so the Mercedes-Benz 300SL relied on a developed version of the production 300S single overhead camshaft engine and gearbox and developed forms of its front and swing-axle rear suspension. The new Mercedes-Benz cars were, however, by no means invincible in sports car racing, being beaten in the Mille Miglia road race by Bracco's Ferrari, winning at Le Mans only after the over-tired Pierre Levegh, who was driving solo, made a mistake not long before the end of the race, and later winning the Carrera Panamericana road race. However, the whole concept of the 300SL was so satisfactory that in 1954 it was launched as a production car, and its competition heritage linked it inextricably and successfully with the new competition cars that appeared from Mercedes-Benz that year.

In July 1954 the Company that had so successfully dominated Grand Prix racing during the 1930s made a brilliant and carefully chosen return to racing in the French Grand Prix at Reims, where all the Ferraris blew up their engines in pursuit of the new German 'Silver Arrows' and Fangio and Kling took first and second places, with Hans Herrmann setting fastest lap before retiring.

What set the Mercedes W196 apart from all other cars competing was not just its performance, but the silver streamlined bodywork, perfect for the high-speed Reims circuit, but to prove a handicap elsewhere. What also set Mercedes-Benz apart from other competitors was the elaborate and well-manned organization behind the racing team. When Mercedes-Benz went racing, it was not two men and a boy, but something in the order of 200 technicians behind the programme, together with 300 toolmakers to machine the parts for the competition cars.

Powering the W196 was an in-line eight-cylinder engine of 2496cc (76 × 68.8mm), known as the M196 and developing 257 bhp at 8,250 rpm when it was first raced. In accordance with pre-war Mercedes-Benz practice, the engine was based on individual cylinders surrounded by a sheet metal welded cowling to form the water jacket, with a non-detachable cylinder head. The twin overhead camshafts per bank of cylinders were driven by gears from the centre of the crankshaft and from this point also the drive was taken to the prop-shaft. Other features of this very sophisticated engine were the desmodromic valves — that is, opening and closing by cams and rockers without springs — Bosch high-pressure fuel injection into the cylinders and roller bearing main and big-ends. The 300SLR 3-litre sports-racing car was developed in parallel with the Grand Prix car and in fact there were very few differences between them mechanically other than the fact that the sports-racing cars featured aluminium cast cylinder blocks. In the W196 the engine was laid almost horizontally, at an angle of 37° to the right to achieve a very low bonnet line, but this caused maintenance difficulties in that it was necessary to remove the off-side front wheel and a panel before a sparking plug could be changed. The transmission incorporated a ZF limited slip differential and five-speed and reverse gearbox.

Daimler-Benz, wisely, chose the 1954 French Grand Prix on the high-speed Reims circuit for the debut of the W196 cars. Fangio and Kling finished in the order seen here, first and second, and, in addition, Hans Herrmann set a new lap record.

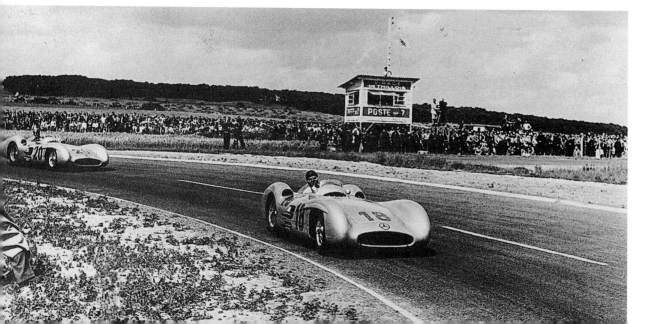

The W196 streamlined cars of Karl Kling and Juan Fangio in the paddock at Silverstone for the 1954 British Grand Prix. (T.C. March)

The chassis had been inspired by the multi-tubular structure used in the 300SL and was a space-frame constructed from small-diameter steel tubing. At the front there was independent suspension by double wishbones, with longitudinal torsion bars and telescopic shock absorbers. For the rear suspension, Mercedes-Benz chose an independent system by low-pivot swing-axles, with the central pivots below the differential housing, the hubs located fore and aft by a Watts linkage and, again, with telescopic shock absorbers and longitudinal torsion bars. It came as a surprise to many that the team had elected to use an independent swing-axle rear suspension system with all its inherent defects, rather than the de Dion system which Mercedes-Benz had resurrected in 1937. One of the reasons was that the Mercedes engineers did not think that they had time to develop a suitable de Dion rear end for the new car; also, of course, this swing-axle layout retained a family relationship with the production Mercedes cars that used a less sophisticated form of this layout. On the W196, Mercedes chose to use massive inboard drum brakes front and rear, eschewing the disc brakes developed in Britain and used on the 1953 Le Mans-winning Jaguar. It seems that one of the reasons for not adopting discs was that Mercedes could not feel confident that they would have the fullest co-operation of British disc brake manufacturers, rather than it being a case of not wanting to use a foreign concept. As first raced, the W196 had a wheelbase of 92.5 in, with a front track of 52.4 in and a rear track of 53.0 in. The streamlined body, the result of extensive wind tunnel tests with a one-fifth scale model, was constructed from magnesium sheeting.

When the Mercedes team appeared at the French Grand Prix in 1954, it was almost as though the clock had been turned back, for although the cars had changed, as had the drivers, the complete Mercedes entourage of pre-war days was little different, with Rudolf Uhlenhaut in charge of the engineering side and Alfred Neubauer responsible once again for team management. The choice of drivers for the new cars

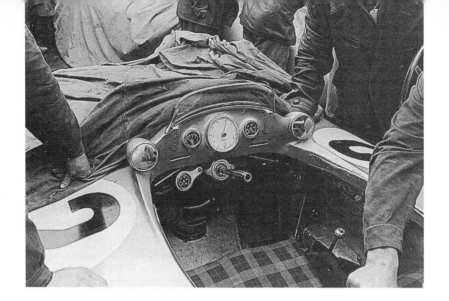

Two views of the very simple cockpit of Kling's car at Silverstone — without the steering wheel, and with the steering wheel being put in place. The tartan upholstery was also being featured on the production 300SL coupés, the majority of which were painted silver like the competition cars. (T.C. March)

was something of a problem for Mercedes-Benz. It was very anxious to use German drivers, but there was no German driver of truly star calibre and accordingly Argentinian Juan Fangio was signed up to lead the team, backed up by German drivers Karl Kling and Hans Herrmann, both of whom were very talented, but not really Grand Prix-winning material. So although throughout 1954 the Mercedes team had a substantial advantage over the opposition in that it was far better organized and that its cars were faster, better prepared and generally more reliable, an immense burden was thrown on Fangio for he alone was capable of winning races.

After the German success at Reims, the Italian teams were left in a state of complete despondency and despair, believing that the rest of the season would prove a complete walk-over for Mercedes-Benz. The next race was the British Grand Prix at Silverstone, and here Mercedes entered just two W196 cars for Fangio and Kling, both still with stream-

Above This Daimler-Benz photograph formed part of the pack given to journalists at Reims in 1954 and makes an interesting contrast with the cars as actually raced. On this car there are no cooling inlets in the rear wings for the brakes. At Reims the cars ran with completely uncluttered radiator intakes (because of the high temperatures expected), whereas at Silverstone the three-pointed star was linked to cross-bars running to either side of the intake. In addition, this car lacks any aero-screen.

Above right The mechanics push Fangio's car out to the circuit during practice for the British Grand Prix in 1954. (T.C. March)

Right Service! A mechanic puts a jacket round Fangio's shoulders while he waits to go out for practice at Silverstone. (T.C. March)

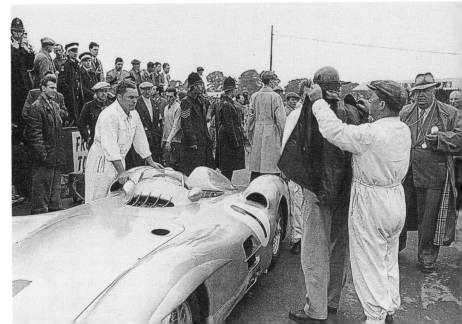

Above and right *The great Alfred Neubauer, with legendary stop watches, supervises the W196 cars in practice at Silverstone while in the pits Geier, former driver and Neubauer's assistant, keeps his own time-keeping records which he later cross-checks with Neubauer. (T.C. March)*

Right *The straight-eight engine as installed in one of the streamlined Mercedes at Silverstone in 1954. (T.C. March)*

lined bodywork. As we have seen in the previous chapter, the expense of bodywork battered on the oil drums and by very hard work, Fangio succeeded in taking pole position with a lap in at 100.35 mph. Gonzalez took the lead at the start of the race with his Ferrari, steadily pulling away from his fellow-Argentinian with the Mercedes. Moss moved up into second place and Hawthorn also passed Fangio with his Ferrari. Moss retired, then Marimon with his Maserati passed Fangio, whose Mercedes, battered by contact with the oil drums, now had failing brakes, jumping gears and an oil leak. Kling took seventh position, never really being in contention throughout the race.

The Silverstone race had posed questions that remained unanswered but had answered one other major question, which was whether or not the Mercedes W196 cars were invincible — and they clearly were not. Certainly the Mercedes streamlined bodywork was unsuitable for this circuit, but what was not known was how far advanced Mercedes-Benz were with the development of unstreamlined conventional bodywork. The cars had evidently been designed for such bodywork, for there were no mechanical components within the space between the front and rear wheels. Another question was to what extent the battered bodywork on Fangio's car was due to genuine difficulties in lining the car up for the badly marked corners as opposed to Fangio's inability to cope with a car with full-width bodywork. It has to be said that whilst Stirling Moss was supreme with both single-seaters and sports cars, the same was not really true of Fangio who always seemed less happy in a sports car. On one occasion at the Nürburgring, when Spanish privateer Francesco Godia-Sales was expected to take over a Maserati which had been battered almost beyond recognition by Fangio, he commented, 'You don't have to be Fangio to do that!'

At the European Grand Prix at the Nürburgring, Mercedes revealed the conventional unstreamlined bodywork, very chunky in shape and

At the end of the race Kling's car was unbattered, but he had driven a poor race and finished seventh. (T.C. March)

appearance and looking as though it was something of a last-minute lash-up. Nothing could have been further from the truth, for the unstreamlined bodywork had been planned all along, but had simply not been ready for Silverstone. In Germany the team entered four cars for Fangio, Kling, Herrmann and pre-war Mercedes Grand Prix driver Hermann Lang. Herrmann alone drove one of the familiar *Stromlinienwagen*. Fangio did all that was expected of him, leading for most of the race and taking an important victory for the team on home territory, whilst Kling lost second place as a result of a refuelling stop, not up to Mercedes' usual standards of efficiency and done from churns. He eventually finished fourth behind the Ferraris of Hawthorn and Trintignant. The other two Mercedes retired.

Mercedes-Benz was to win three races in succession, for Fangio scored another victory in the Swiss Grand Prix held on the medium-speed Bremgarten circuit, a real driver's circuit with difficult bends and turns; as we have seen, following the ban on motor racing in Switzerland after the 1955 Le Mans disaster, this was the last time the circuit was to be used. Here all three drivers had cars with exposed wheels. Herrmann took third place, but Kling retired with a broken injector pump drive. At the Italian Grand Prix at Monza, the Italian teams made a major onslaught to prevent a Mercedes victory, and Fangio at the wheel of a streamlined car had to fight every inch of the way. Victory should have gone to Stirling Moss; he had overtaken Fangio and was holding the Argentinian at bay with victory in sight when his Maserati broke an oil pipe. Fangio with the streamlined car went on to take his sixth Grand Prix victory of the season, with Herrmann in an unstreamlined

The Italian Grand Prix 1954. Fangio, the eventual winner, corners inside Gonzalez' Ferrari Squalo. *(LAT)*

car in fourth place. Poor Kling had again been the victim of misfortune. On lap 37 he removed his goggles which were smeared with oil, and an oil pipe broke and squirted hot oil in his eye; temporarily blinded he went off the road, the W196 went through a hedge and felled several trees before coming to rest; fortunately the driver was unhurt.

Later in September Mercedes-Benz ran in the Berlin Grand Prix held on the Avus circuit. Originally this circuit had had two steeply banked turns linked by the autobahn, but the south turn was now in East Berlin so the circuit length was reduced to 5.15 miles with the southern end consisting of a simple loop. It remained an exceptionally fast circuit and Kling won the race at an average of 132.6 mph, with Fangio and Herrmann in second and third places. Fangio had clearly been instructed to let Kling win on home territory, but he politely commented after the race that 'Kling was unbeatable that day'.

The final round of the 1954 World Championship was the Spanish Grand Prix on the Pedralbes street circuit at Barcelona. The Mercedes engineers were unable to work out whether streamlined or unstreamlined cars would be better and in fact took three of each to the race; the open-wheel cars were eventually used. The race was marked by the debut of the Lancia D50s, and Ascari with the new Italian V-8 was faster in practice than Fangio. The race proved a débâcle for Mercedes for, although Ascari retired very early with his brand-new car, Fangio was never in contention for the lead. As the race progressed, newspapers, sandwich wrappings and cigarette cartons scattered on the course by spectators were blown by the wind and sucked into the air intake of the Mercedes, the W196 began to run hotter and rougher and started to lay an ominous smoke trail, whilst the engine developed a painful grinding note. The winner was Mike Hawthorn with the *Squalo* Ferrari, with Musso (Maserati) in second place, Fangio third, a lap in arrears, and Kling fifth. Herrmann retired with fuel injector pump trouble. As a result of the litter problem, Uhlenhaut tried the W196 with a grille consisting of vertical bars and also evolved an opening grille for the nose operated by a control wire so that the grille opening was cleaned by air pressure and then closed by a return spring. In fact, neither of these features was used on the cars in 1955.

The main changes made for 1955 resulted from an effort to make the cars lighter and handle better. The 1954 car with its wheelbase of 92.5 in became retrospectively known as the 'long wheelbase' car, whilst there were two new chassis lengths for 1955; a new medium-wheelbase car of 87.0 in and, for the Monaco race, a 'short-wheelbase' car at 84.6 in. The latter also featured outboard front brakes, which the drivers preferred as they considered them to be smoother. A significant change was the invitation from Mercedes for Stirling Moss to join the team, a clear recognition of the fact that Fangio did need a top-line back-up driver. With the exception of one race, and in accordance with team discipline, Moss had to play second fiddle to Fangio throughout the year.

The first race of the 1955 season was the Argentine Grand Prix, and Fangio was one of only two drivers able to run throughout the unusually hot race without relief. He won by 1½ minutes from the Ferrari shared by Gonzalez, Farina and Trintignant, whilst Moss and Kling shared the fourth-place car. In the Formule Libre Buenos Aires City Grand Prix, Mercedes-Benz used the 3-litre engines as designed for the 300SLR sports-racing cars. In this race Fangio and Kling took first and second places.

Mercedes-Benz did not race again until the Monaco Grand Prix in May and here three cars were entered, two of the new short-wheelbase models with outboard front brakes for Fangio and Moss and a medium-wheelbase car for Herrmann, all of course with unstreamlined body-work. Unfortunately Herrmann crashed badly in practice, putting himself out of racing for some while, and his place was taken by French driver André Simon. As has already been described in the previous chapter, it was to prove a remarkable race, with a remarkable result. In the early laps there was a four-sided battle between Fangio and Moss and the Lancias of Ascari and Castellotti, but the two Mercedes steadily drew away and looked to have the race under complete control. On lap 50 Fangio retired because of a broken gearbox and 30 laps later Moss was eliminated by engine problems. This meant that Ascari had a lead with his Lancia, although of course he would not strictly be leading the race

Fangio in early morning practice for the 1955 Monaco Grand Prix with the short wheelbase, unstreamlined W196. Fangio was eliminated in the race by engine problems. (LAT)

until he passed the stricken Mercedes of Moss on the road. He never completed the lap, however, for at the exit from the tunnel the Lancia's brakes locked, Ascari swerved into the straw bales and plunged into the harbour after bouncing off a stone bollard. Simon's Mercedes retired because of a broken oil union, and Moss pushed his car across the line, something he did many times during his career, to take ninth place. After all these incidents, the race was won by Trintignant's Ferrari, an unexpected result.

During the rest of the season the Mercedes-Benz team made absolutely no mistakes and in the face of weak Italian opposition completely dominated the remaining races, although of course the calendar was somewhat limited following the cancellation of races as a result of the Le Mans disaster. At the Belgian Grand Prix the Mercedes team produced a new car designed especially for the fast curves of Spa-Francorchamps, with a medium-length chassis but outboard front brakes. It was tried by all the drivers, but Fangio eventually chose a long-chassis car for the race. Although the Mercedes was challenged by Castellotti's Lancia in the early stages of the race, Fangio and Moss ran away from the rest of the field to take first and second places, whilst Kling retired because of a broken oil unit.

After the Le Mans disaster, there was initially a very real question mark as to whether Mercedes would continue racing for the remainder of the season, but it decided to carry on until the end of 1955, stating that it wished to be satisfied as to the safety of circuits before taking part. This caused something of a furore, but in the event the Mercedes team fulfilled all its commitments that year regardless of what it really thought of the circuits. The Dutch Grand Prix was held only a week after Le Mans and was an event very much overshadowed by the earlier tragedy. Again Moss and Fangio took the first two places, with Fangio at the wheel of a short-chassis car and Moss with a medium-length chassis. Alongside them on the grid was Kling with the special car built for Spa, but he spun off during the race and was unable to restart.

Next came the British Grand Prix at Aintree where Mercedes-Benz entered a total of four cars, all with outboard front brakes; Fangio and Moss were at the wheels of short-chassis models, whilst Kling and veteran Italian driver Piero Taruffi, deputizing for Herrmann, drove medium-length chassis. In the face of the demoralized Italian opposition, the Mercedes-Benz W196 cars took the first four places, with Moss winning from Fangio, Kling and Taruffi. Whether Fangio allowed Moss to win or whether Moss actually beat the great Argentinian remains an unanswered question. Because of the cancellation of the German and Swiss Grands Prix, there remained only the Italian Grand Prix at Monza, a circuit combining the new banking with the existing road course. As a result of tests at the circuit, Mercedes-Benz decided that the ideal cars would be medium-length chassis with outboard brakes and the aerodynamic body. However, when the team arrived at the circuit it found that many of the bumps on the banking had been smoothed out, and it was then realized that the ideal cars would be the long-

67185

Above The Mercedes-Benz transporter based on production 300SL components.

Below At the British Grand Prix at Aintree in 1955, the winner was Stirling Moss, with the medium-wheelbase W196. The Mercedes dominated the race and who won was really a matter of team tactics. (T.C. March)

wheelbase *Stromlinienwagen*. The team had one of these cars with them and this was driven by Fangio; another was rapidly built up at the factory for Moss and transported to the circuit on one of the amazing transporters powered by the 300SL engine, capable of carrying a single car at over 100 mph and distinguished by the proud wording on the cab doors, *Mercedes-Benz Rennabteilung* ('racing department'). Fangio and Taruffi took the first two places, whilst both Moss and Kling retired. Fangio thus took the Drivers' World Championship with 40 points to the 23 of Stirling Moss, with third-place Castellotti trailing with only 12 points.

The decision to withdraw from racing had been made not long after

The final race outing for the W196s was in the 1955 Italian Grand Prix where Juan Fangio won — and clinched his third World Championship — with this streamlined car.

Le Mans, and Mercedes left on a high note, for in addition to the Grand Prix successes, the 300SLR sports-racing cars had taken first and second places in the Mille Miglia, the first three places in the Tourist Trophy on the Dundrod circuit and first, second and fourth places in Sicily, convincingly winning the Sports Car World Championship. In addition, the team had withdrawn from Le Mans whilst leading the race and had scored minor successes in both the Eiffelrennen at the Nürburgring and in the Swedish Grand Prix.

When Mercedes-Benz withdrew from racing it was thought that it would seen return perhaps with much-modified versions of the W196 cars in 1958, but in fact 24 years have now elapsed without Mercedes-Benz making a direct return to racing, although they now openly support and sponsor the Mercedes-powered Sauber team in Group C racing. The impact of Mercedes-Benz on Grand Prix racing was such that the team still reaps publicity value from those two golden years, aided by the fact that, whilst they were truly dominant, the margin of their superiority is frequently exaggerated. Mercedes' two years in Grand Prix racing was but a brief interlude, for no sooner had they gone than the Italian teams restored the status quo and racing settled down again to a lower level of efficiency and engineering sophistication.

3

Return to the status quo

1956-57

The withdrawal from racing of Mercedes-Benz at the end of 1955 was not entirely unexpected. Originally the Company had planned to stay in racing much longer, and apart from the bad publicity that motor racing generally had suffered as a result of the Le Mans disaster it had proved a magnificent publicity medium for the team. In 1955 Mercedes-Benz had won every Formula 1 race and had also won the Sports Car World Championship with the 300SLR, losing but one race, Le Mans from which the team had withdrawn following the tragedy. The result of this withdrawal was that racing reverted to its former status, a duel between Ferrari and Maserati, but the rise in strength of the British teams could not be overlooked.

1956

Ferrari

At Maranello there was a vast collection of cars of different configurations, Tipo 555 *Supersqualos*, Tipo 625s and the Lancias taken over from the Turin company. In the Argentine at the beginning of 1956 Ferrari entered both the standard *Supersqualo* and also a *Supersqualo* powered by the Lancia V-8 engine. These cars were run, however, purely for reasons of comparison and the team had already decided to run modified versions of the Lancias.

At Buenos Aires Ferrari produced what became known as the 'Argentina'-type. This differed from the original D50 specification by having a single main fuel tank in the tail and small reserve fuel tanks in the front end of the side panniers only. There was a new exhaust system running through the pannier tanks, the transverse leaf spring at the rear was now mounted above the final drive, and, as Ferrari was unhappy that the engine should act as a main frame-member, bracing struts ran between the front cross members and the bulkhead.

A further version of the D50 appeared at the Syracuse Grand Prix and this became known as the 'Siracusa'. Now the panniers contained no fuel tanks at all, for the reserve tanks had been transferred to positions on either side of the chassis frame just behind the bulkhead, and the space between the panniers and the body had been filled in by sheet metal, giving the car the appearance of a full-width body. In addition, the team was still racing standard D50s.

The offset V-8 engine with four twin-choke Solex carburettors as installed in the 1956 Lancia-Ferrari. (LAT)

With Mercedes out of racing, the two greatest drivers of the era, Juan Fangio and Stirling Moss, were on the market looking for drives. Fangio, for the only time in his career, signed to drive for Ferrari, and although he won his fourth World Championship, he suffered a thoroughly miserable season. Used to being team leader, with all the preferential treatment that goes with that title, Fangio found that he was just a member of the Scuderia with no special privileges, although his manager Giambertone fought for them on Fangio's behalf all season. Eugenio Castellotti remained with Ferrari and was joined by former Maserati driver Luigi Musso, Peter Collins, the Marquis de Portago and Belgian driver Olivier Gendebien. Peter Collins had been given a works drive by Maserati at the 1955 Italian Grand Prix and had been strongly tempted to join that team. However, Ferrari offered him better inducements, in particular allowing him to go on driving for Aston Martin in sports car races. Although Gendebien drove Formula 1 cars in the Argentine, Ferrari soon decided that the young Belgian was not really Formula 1 material and during the remainder of the year he concentrated on sports car racing, his only other Formula 1 appearance being at the French Grand Prix at Reims.

Maserati

Maserati made few changes to the 250F at the beginning of the 1956 season, although wider brake drums were adopted. Many changes to the cars were, however, to be seen during the year. The Company wooed Stirling Moss hard to drive for them as team leader in 1956. Moss had always been anxious to drive a British car and before he decided to return to Maserati he tried all three British contenders, BRM, Connaught and Vanwall at Silverstone. With the Vanwall, Moss lapped Silverstone in 1m 46.9s, slightly faster than the lap record set by Salvadori with a 250F in the 1955 International Trophy race. However, he was still not convinced and believed that he could lap faster with a Maserati. He solved the dilemma in an unusual way. Together with his father, Alfred Moss, and manager Ken Gregory, he entertained 17 journalists at the Royal Automobile Club for dinner. After the meal he addressed the journalists, saying that he thought that Maserati had the best chance of winning the World Championship in 1956 and that he could if he wished return to the Italian company as team leader. He described the tests at Silverstone and the various times he had recorded, but did add that he thought he could lap faster with the Maserati. The journalists were then asked their views as to the team that he should join. Nine voted in favour of Maserati, and shortly afterwards Moss signed up with that team.

Jean Behra, who had led Maserati in 1955, remained with the team, but was always slightly miffed that his place as leader had been taken by Moss, a driver to whom he reckoned, mistakenly and egotistically, he was superior. The team was completed by young Cesare Perdisa.

Maserati's biggest shortcoming through 1956 was sheer lack of organization, a constant confusion caused by running sports cars as well as Formula 1 cars, and in addition the preparation of the private Formula 1 and sports car entries of many owners who brought their cars to the factory. In reality, throughout 1956, Maserati's main business was dealing with private owners rather than running a works team, and the results achieved by Moss and Behra suffered accordingly.

The 1956 season

At the Argentine Grand Prix, Maserati entered four cars for Moss and Behra, and Argentinian drivers Carlos Menditeguy and Froilan Gonzalez (who was racing for the first time since the 1955 Argentine Grand Prix). Ferrari fielded a mixed bag of cars for Fangio, Musso, Castellotti, Gendebien and Collins. Fangio took pole position in practice, but his car was running roughly in the race and he took over from Castellotti. While Maseratis briefly led the race, including Moss (who was in considerable pain because his foot had been run over by his own 250F as it was pushed out to the grid), Fangio came through to take the lead and win from Behra with Mike Hawthorn in third place with the privately entered Owen Organisation 250F. Another win for Fangio followed in the Buenos Aires City Grand Prix, held on the 2.6-mile Mendoza Autodrome, all of 650 miles to the west of Buenos Aires, with the Maseratis of Moss, Behra and Menditeguy in second, third and fourth places. This circuit, at a height of 2,200 feet above sea level, caused carburation problems, especially for the Maseratis which were never able to challenge for the lead.

The European season opened with the traditional Easter Monday meeting at Goodwood, and here Moss drove a new works 250F, fitted experimentally with fuel injection. This OM/Bosch system offered only marginal power advantage over the standard set-up with Weber carburettors, the torque range was more limited and Moss was thoroughly unhappy with the car. Only after Archie Scott-Brown's Connaught retired because of a broken crankshaft did Moss take the lead to win the Richmond Trophy race. Shortly afterwards Lancia-Ferraris took the first three places in the Syracuse Grand Prix and the only Maserati entered, for Behra, retired very early because of a broken oil pipe. The next two Formula 1 races, both of a comparatively unimportant nature, were won by Stirling Moss. In the Aintree 200 race, he drove his now ageing private 250F to victory and in the International Trophy at Silverstone Maserati again did not enter, so Stirling Moss was free to drive for Vanwall. Although there were two Lancia-Ferraris present, driven by Fangio and Collins, both retired and Moss scored an encouraging victory from Scott-Brown with the Connaught. Again, Ferrari's nose was rubbed in the dirt the following day at Naples where the Lancia-Ferraris of Musso and Castellotti retired and Robert Manzon scored a totally unexpected victory with his six-cylinder Gordini.

Ferrari's humiliation continued in the first European round of the World Championship at Monaco where Moss was first away, shut the door on Castellotti's Lancia-Ferrari at the hairpin and drove a fast, relaxed and error-free race to score a resounding victory for Maserati. In contrast, the Ferrari team was in disarray. For some reason Fangio seemed at sea with his Lancia-Ferrari, spinning wildly on lap 3, and later crumpling his car's nose against the straw bales and buckling a rear wheel. He eventually took over Peter Collins's car to finish second, with Jean Behra's Maserati in third place.

In the Belgian Grand Prix held at Spa-Francorchamps, Ferrari managed to scramble back on top again, but the margin was not clear cut, mainly due to the lack of sheer speed on the part of the Maseratis on this high-speed circuit. Moss led initially, but then Fangio with the Lancia-Ferrari went into the lead, after a nasty moment for Moss when the left-hand rear wheel complete with hub and brake detached. He rejoined the race driving Perdisa's car. Then Fangio retired with transmission

In the International Trophy race at Silverstone in May 1956 the works Ferraris were surprisingly beaten by Stirling Moss with the Vanwall. Here, Fangio temporarily leads Moss. (T.C. March)

failure and the winner was young Peter Collins, scoring his first World Championship race victory, with the similar car of Paul Frère in second place, and behind them the Maseratis of Behra and Moss. One of the most significant performers in the race had been Harry Schell with the British Vanwall, a true portent for the future and one to be discussed in greater detail in Chapter 4.

It was much the same story in the French Grand Prix at Reims where the Maseratis were completely outpaced by both the Lancia-Ferraris and Harry Schell's Vanwall. While the 250Fs were never in the picture, Schell took over Hawthorn's Vanwall to fight his way right through the field and battle with the Lancia-Ferraris until the fuel-injection linkage fell apart. Fangio was forced to stop in the closing laps of the race for a split fuel line to be repaired, so Collins and Castellotti took the first two places ahead of Jean Behra's Maserati, with Fangio rejoining to finish fourth.

Both Ferrari and Maserati produced streamlined cars at Reims. In Ferrari's case it was a more or less standard 'Syracuse'-type Lancia-Ferrari with streamlined nose and tail sections, whilst Maserati had taken the dust covers off the streamlined car that had run at Monza in 1955. The streamlined Lancia-Ferrari proved no faster than the standard version and was quickly abandoned. To the streamlined 250F, Maserati had fitted a fuel injection engine and Dunlop disc brakes — but without servo, as this could not be used with the five-speed gearbox needed for Reims. As a result the pedal pressure was far higher than any of the drivers could have sustained during a race of this length, so this car too appeared in practice only; it was later destroyed in a fire in the Maserati works. Incidentally, at Reims the Ferrari drivers wore black armbands as a tribute to Enzo Ferrari's son, Alfredino, who had just died.

Although the results of the British Grand Prix at Silverstone indicate Lancia-Ferrari domination, in fact both cars and drivers put in a poor showing. The race was initially led by the BRMs of Hawthorn and Brooks,

Juan Fangio with his Lancia-Ferrari at Reims in 1956. The Argentinian finished fourth in this race, which was won by young Peter Collins. Although it is not visible in this photograph, all the Ferrari drivers in the French race wore black armbands as a tribute to Dino Ferrari who had just died.

Right The starting grid of the 1956 British Grand Prix at Silverstone. (T.C. March)

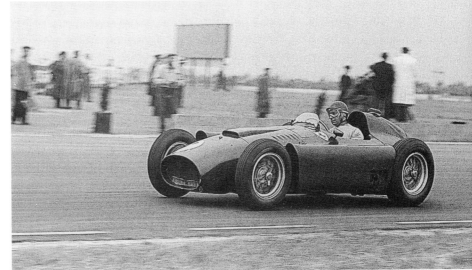

Right Fangio won the Silverstone race in his Lancia-Ferrari. (T.C. March)

Below Moss's race came to an end when the final drive broke at Stowe corner. The back end was one of the weaker aspects of Maserati design. (T.C. March)

but Moss and Salvadori came through with their Maseratis to hold the first two places. In contrast, Fangio was fighting his way back from sixth place after a spin and the great Argentinian never seemed at home in the Lancia-Ferrari, the handling of which was critically sensitive at the limits of adhesion. Whilst Fangio drove with what might best be described as an untidy determination, the failure of, first, Salvadori's Maserati and then the Moss car allowed him to come back through into the lead; in second place came Collins who had taken over de Portago's Lancia-Ferrari. The truly outstanding driver at Silverstone was Roy Salvadori who for so many laps had held second place with this three-year-old 250F, a private entry, until it ran into fuel-feed problems. No one deserved a works drive more than Salvadori, but in 1957 it was to be with BRM and this was to prove a complete disaster.

In the mid-1950s Juan Fangio was the complete maestro at the Nürburgring and he completely dominated the German Grand Prix. He and Collins were easily fastest in practice and he led throughout the race, during which the lap record that had stood since 1939 with Hermann Lang in a Mercedes-Benz W163 was shattered again and again and finally stood to Fangio with a lap in 9m 45.5s (compared with the original record of 9m 52.2s). Collins, in second place, was overcome by fumes from a split fuel tank; he came into the pits and, after recovering, took over de Portago's car, thus allowing Moss to move up into second place where he finished ahead of team-mate Behra. Fangio's was the sole Lancia-Ferrari to finish out of five starters and in fact there were only five classified finishers.

There was now an interval of over a month to the next round in the World Championship, the European Grand Prix at Monza, again held on the combined banked and road circuit. Here Maserati, which had been running a permutation of cars all season, produced two new models of substantially revised design for Stirling Moss and Jean Behra in the hope, apart from anything else, of winning the worthwhile financial prize offered by the organizers to any Italian manufacturer racing a new design. What Maserati could not find overnight was speed, and in that respect they still could not match the Lancia-Ferraris, but the latest 250Fs were a vast improvement on the previous cars. A lower centre of gravity and reduced frontal area was achieved by using a tubular steel frame that followed the same general layout as that of the earlier cars, but with the engine angled so that the nose of the crankshaft pointed towards the right-hand front corner and the line of the transmission ran across the car at an angle. This meant the driver's seat could be mounted on the undertray alongside the prop-shaft, lowering him by around 8 inches. The low bodywork featured a long tapering nose which had to be removed so that the cars would fit into the team's transporter. It had been a rush job to finish them in time for the race and when they appeared in practice they were still in unpainted aluminium.

In some ways the race proved a repetition of 1955, because the Englebert tyres used by Ferrari were throwing treads, but the cars were still

Above The start of the 1956 Italian Grand Prix at Monza, with the Lancia-Ferraris of Musso, Castellotti and Fangio leading away from the Maserati of Moss and the Lancia-Ferrari of Collins.

Below On the banking at Monza in 1956, Jean Behra (Maserati) leads de Portago (Lancia-Ferrari).

faster than the Maserati opposition. It seemed that if the Ferraris were plagued by tyre trouble, as was expected, provided that the Maseratis could last the distance, then the race would be Modena's. Initially the Lancia-Ferraris held the first three places, hotly pursued by Schell's Vanwall, but this order was soon to change. Race-leaders Musso and Castellotti made stops for new tyres very early in the race, the Vanwall held the lead briefly, then Moss went ahead with his 250F. Schell had started the race with a half-full tank and after refuelling he survived only another four laps before retiring with transmission trouble. Behra had retired his 250F with magneto trouble and a split fuel tank. Once again, Moss seemed all set for victory, but the engine of his 250F cut

Castellotti's Lancia-Ferrari after a rear tyre had blown.

out at the Lesmo curves and he started to coast towards the pits. When Luigi Piotti arrived on the scene, he rapidly summed up the situation, gently nosed behind Moss's 250F and pushed him hard enough so that he continued to roll on back to the pits. The 250F — totally unexpectedly — had run out of fuel due to a split in the tank. The tank was quickly filled and Moss was back in the race, but now in second place behind Musso's Lancia-Ferrari. Three laps from the finish the left-hand steering arm on Musso's car broke, the car slithered across the track out of control and came to rest just short of the pit counter. Moss went on to win, a reversal of the fortunes that he had enjoyed in the 1954 race, by just under 6 seconds from the Lancia-Ferrari of Collins and Fangio. Fangio had retired his own Lancia-Ferrari with a broken steering arm which, when repaired, was taken over by Castellotti. When Peter Collins had come into the pits at half-distance for the tyres to be checked, he had voluntarily handed over his car — and his chance of winning the World Championship — to Fangio. The result was that Fangio took the World Championship for the fourth time with 30 points with Moss in second place with 27 and Peter Collins third with 25 points.

Certainly Lancia-Ferrari had dominated the season, but it had not been the happiest of years for the team. Juan Fangio had been thoroughly disenchanted and was very glad to leave Scuderia Ferrari at the earliest possible opportunity. Despite on occasion fielding five cars, the

Lancia-Ferraris had not always shown the reliability expected of them and with a little more speed Maserati would have swept all before them.

1957

Ferrari

Whatever Ferrari did to the Lancia-Ferraris for the 1957 season proved unsuccessful, and throughout the year the cars seemed down on power compared with both the Maseratis and the Vanwalls. A number of engine experiments were carried out, including a markedly over-square engine of 80 × 62mm that was tried at the French race, and the fitting of Weber carburettors, but ultimately the cars remained in what was basically their original engine form. However, early in the year at Siracusa, Ferrari produced the much modified Tipo 801 car with a chassis based on larger-diameter tubing, a narrower frame and a body fitting closely round the chassis so that the original side panniers completely disappeared.

Fangio had left to drive for Maserati, so the team had no natural leader (not that Ferrari would have recognized one anyway). Mike Hawthorn had returned to the team after a very unhappy year with BRM and worked in perfect harmony, friendship and partnership with Peter Collins, who now drove exclusively for Ferrari. In contrast there was the relationship of Italians Eugenio Castellotti and Luigi Musso, locked in bitter rivalry that ended early in the year when Castellotti was sadly killed in February in a testing accident. Also in the team were Wolfgang von Trips, Alfonso de Portago and Cesare Perdisa. Perdisa left the team for what was described as 'family reasons', but the truth of the matter was that he had never really fully recovered his confidence and form following a bad crash in a sports car race at the Nürburgring the previous year. Following Castellotti's death, veteran French driver Maurice Trintignant joined the team.

It was to prove a thoroughly unhappy year for Ferrari, now in its last season with the Lancia-based cars, but there were new and exciting developments under way.

Maserati

The main change at Modena was that chief engineer Giulio Alfieri had realized the error of his ways. Instead of constantly playing around with different permutations of the car, as he had in 1956 when there was no fixed specification, three new cars were built; they followed the layout of the offset cars that had appeared in Monza in 1956, but without the angled engine and offset transmission, and with a new multi-tubular chassis constructed from smaller-diameter tubing and with tubular struts reinforcing the corners between the main tubes. The new chassis was both lighter and stronger than its predecessors. This low, sleek and purposeful-looking car with distinctively tapering nose, bulbous, rivetted-alloy rear tank forming a headrest and scuttle-top air intakes

A mechanic works on the engine of Jean Behra's 250F at Aintree in 1957. (T.C. March)

is usually known as the 'lightweight' car although this has no real meaning.

Maserati's hopes for the future were very dependent on the latest project, the *Dodici*, a new V-12 engine of 2490cc (68.7 × 56mm) with twin overhead camshafts per bank of cylinders driven by a train of gears from the nose of the crankshaft and three specially made Weber twin-choke carburettors mounted in the vee of the engine. For much of the year the V-12 engine was tested in 250F chassis, but a lightweight version of the V-12 car appeared in practice for the 1957 French Grand Prix. At the Italian Grand Prix at Monza, the only Championship event in which the V-12 Formula 1 car actually raced, there was another new lightweight chassis with offset transmission. The V-12 would have formed the backbone of the team in 1958 if Maserati had remained in racing, but instead the majority of its appearances were in sports car events. Hans Herrmann drove a 300S sports car with a 3.5-litre version of the V-12 engine in the 1957 Mille Miglia, Stirling Moss tested a car with the V-12 engine in 3-litre form in 1958, and it was used to power subsequent versions of the 'Birdcage' sports cars in the early 1960s. In addition, this engine formed the basis of the V-12 used in the Cooper Grand Prix cars of 1966-67.

Juan Fangio and the Maserati 250F were the dominant combination in the early part of 1957 and the Argentinian was at the peak of his form at the wheel of a car with superb controllability and good all-round handling and performance. Stirling Moss had decided to drive for Vanwall, so Jean Behra remained number two and the third car was usually driven by Harry Schell. In the early part of the year another car was usually entered for Argentinian Carlos Menditeguy but, later, his place was taken by Italian Giorgio Scarlatti. Three years after the Formula had started, private owners with 250Fs still filled the places at the back of the grids.

The 1957 racing season

As usual the year started with the Argentine races and these were dominated by Fangio and Maserati, a combination which won both the Argentine Grand Prix itself and the Buenos Aires City Grand Prix, this year back on the Buenos Aires Autodrome and for the first and only time held as a Formula 1 as opposed to a Formule Libre race. Because Vanwall had not entered the Argentine races, Moss drove for Maserati in the Argentine Grand Prix. He was fastest in practice, but only a matter of a few hundred yards from the start his accelerator broke and many laps were lost while this was repaired. He eventually rejoined the race to finish eighth, seven laps in arrears, but having set the fastest lap. Ignoring the time wasted by the repairs, Moss's race time was in fact quicker than Fangio's.

There were the usual early season Formula 1 races in Europe, but in 1957 the International Trophy at Silverstone was postponed until September because of the preceding year's Suez crisis and the petrol rationing that resulted. The first of the European races was the Syracuse Grand Prix; this was so nearly won by Moss with the Vanwall, but after he ran into trouble, Collins and Musso took the first two places for Ferrari. Next came the Naples Grand Prix where Ferrari entered three cars, and was unopposed apart from Stuart Lewis-Evans with a

Juan Fangio, the eventual winner of the 1957 Argentine Grand Prix, leads Stirling Moss who dropped back because of problems. Fangio is holding his car in a superb four-wheel drift.

Connaught. The sensation of the race was not that Collins and Hawthorn took the first two places with the familiar Tipo 801 cars, but the Ferrari that finished third. This was the Scuderia's new Formula 2 car, the Tipo 156, with a 1490cc (70 × 64.5mm) V-6 engine, which was to prove the pointer for Ferrari development in the future. Designed under the supervision of Vittorio Jano, the new 'baby' Ferrari was a jewel of a car, beautifully compact and engineered, and clearly with immense development potential. Ferrari had not entered the Pau Grand Prix on Easter Monday, a race which in 1956 had been cancelled following the Le Mans disaster, so Jean Behra, faced by works Gordinis and Connaughts together with private Maseratis, was able to cruise to victory.

At Monaco, however, the first European Championship race, the competition was intense, not just between Ferrari with four entries and Maserati with five, but also because it was only too obvious that the Vanwall team was finding its form. Moss took the lead at the start of the race, heading Fangio and Collins, with Collins moving up into second place on the first lap with his Lancia-Ferrari. On the fourth lap this race of immense promise was completely ruined when Moss went straight into the barricades at the chicane because of brake failure. The barricade was constructed from telegraph poles which shot all over the track. Collins, in trying to avoid the Vanwall, hit the barricade on the other side of the track, whilst both Fangio (Maserati) and Brooks with the second Vanwall, reducing their speed to a crawl, managed to wend their way through the wreckage. Next on the scene was Hawthorn who hit a rear wheel of Brookes's almost stationary Vanwall, tearing off the left-hand front wheel of his Lancia-Ferrari which slid up the tail of Collins's car. Fangio had the race in the bag and Brooks wisely settled for second place. Already Fangio had a commanding lead in the World Championship.

Financial problems resulted in the cancellation of the Belgian and Dutch Grands Prix so the next race was the French event, held on the superb 4.06-mile Circuit des Essarts close to the city of Rouen and with a magnificent combination of tight hairpin bends, steep uphill sections and superb 100-120 mph downhill curves and near flat-out 150 mph bends. Before the race the form was clear. Vanwall were without their regular drivers (Moss was ill and Brooks had crashed his Aston Martin and would be out of racing for several weeks) so really could not be regarded as serious contenders. The Maseratis were likely to prove dominant, but it was also likely the the Lancia-Ferraris would finish well up behind the leading 250Fs. Fangio drove one of the two finest races of his career (the other was to come later in the year) and put on a magnificent display of speed, car control and judgement, aided by the Maserati pit who misled the Ferrari team in to believing that Fangio's driving style was causing excessive tyre wear and that he would need a stop for the back wheels to be changed. Luigi Musso tried everything he knew to catch the leading Maserati, but at the finish he was still over 50 seconds behind, with other Lancia-Ferraris driven by Collins

A famous photograph — Juan Fangio with his Maserati 205F on his way to a win in the 1957 French Grand Prix at Rouen. How he damaged the nose of the car is far from clear. (LAT).

and Hawthorn in third and fourth places.

On the two occasions in the 1950s that the French Grand Prix was held at Rouen, 1952 and 1957, there was also a full-length Grand Prix held at Reims, the usual venue for the French race, and this attracted a full Championship field. Somewhat understandably, Maserati did not take the race as seriously as the Grand Prix itself and while two of the usual team cars were returned to the factory for preparation for the British Grand Prix, Fangio drove a modified version of one of the 1956 Monza cars, Harry Schell had Fangio's very tired Rouen-winning 'lightweight' car, and Behra drove a 1956 car. Vanwall still had driver problems and this was the one race that Lancia-Ferrari could and did win. Also, Lewis-Evans, who with Salvadori was deputizing for the usual Vanwall drivers, showed exceptional form, pulling away into the lead at the start from Musso's Lancia-Ferrari with Fangio in third place. As the race progressed, so an oil leak from the Vanwall's engine seeped into the cockpit, blew over Lewis-Evans's goggles and gloves and forced him to ease up to allow the Lancia-Ferrari to take the lead. Fangio and Behra moved up into second and third places ahead of Lewis-Evans, but then Fangio made a rare error, locked his brakes at the Thillois hairpin and thumped the 250F into an earth bank. At the chequered flag Musso led by 25 seconds from Behra and Lewis-Evans. In this race Menditeguy drove the original V-12 Maserati, which shortly before had been fitted with a 3.5-litre V-12 engine for the Monza 500 miles race, an event intended to provide a match between the best and fastest of the Indianapolis cars and their European counterparts. During the two years in which this event was run it proved, because it was held on the banked circuit at Monza only, a complete and pointless American whitewash. At Rouen the V-12 Maserati retired with a burnt piston, but at least it had made the start of the race.

As the season progressed, so the principal battling teams ceased to be Maserati and Ferrari, but instead Maserati and the British Vanwall, and again, as the season progressed, so the Maserati team lost its dominant edge as the Vanwalls found the reliability to match their speed. At the European Grand Prix at Aintree, Maserati entered the usual three 'lightweight' cars for Fangio, Behra and Schell. From Scuderia Ferrari there came four Tipo 801 cars for Collins, Hawthorn, Musso and Trintignant, while Vanwall now had Moss and Brooks back in the team and a third car was entered for Lewis-Evans. Aintree proved a race of remarkable attrition. Moss took the lead from Behra and Hawthorn, half-way round the first lap, followed by Collins and Fangio, neither of whom were happy with their cars. On lap 21, as Moss accelerated past the pits, the Vanwall's engine was clearly misfiring and soon he was in the pits where a loose plug lead was suspected. He returned to the pits not long afterwards and Brooks, well down the field because he had still not fully recovered from his bad crash at Le Mans with an Aston Martin, was called in for Moss to take over.

Moss rejoined the race in ninth place while out in front Behra led Hawthorn, Collins and Lewis-Evans. By just over half-distance, Moss had pulled back to fourth place, Collins and Fangio had both retired, and in front were Behra (Maserati), Hawthorn (Lancia-Ferrari) and Lewis-Evans with the third Vanwall. Moss took his team-mate for third place on lap 69 and suddenly the whole face of the race changed. The clutch of Behra's Maserati exploded, scattering pieces of metal across the track, and Hawthorn punctured a tyre on one of the fragments, Now Moss and Lewis-Evans were in first and second places, with Luigi Musso (Lancia-Ferrari) third. After only two more laps Lewis-Evans stopped out on the circuit because of a familiar Vanwall problem, a faulty throttle control, so Musso moved up into second place, although over a minute behind Moss. In the closing laps of the race Moss made a precautionary pit stop and at the chequered flag was nearly a minute and a half

Fangio in practice for the 1957 European Grand Prix at Aintree with Harry Schell's Maserati 250F. (T.C. March)

ahead of the Lancia-Ferrari. It had been a remarkable race, and not only just because the might of Italy had been defeated by the Vanwalls. Fangio's driving had been mediocre and the true hero of the day had been Behra, so very unlucky not to win his first Championship race. This was the first victory by a British car in a Grande Epreuve since Segrave's win with the Sunbeam at Tours in 1923.

The German Grand Prix at the Nürburgring became a straight duel between Lancia-Ferrari and Maserati. The Vanwall team had never raced at the German circuit before and was all at sea with suspension settings, so apart from the fact that the cars were uncompetitive, the drivers had a thoroughly miserable time. From Scuderia Ferrari came three of the Tipo 801 Lancia-Ferraris and there were also the three 'lightweight' cars from Maserati for Fangio, Behra and Schell, whilst Giorgio Scarlatti had now replaced Menditeguy who had been dissatisfied with the preparation of his cars. Since 1956 the Nürburgring had been completely resurfaced, so it was expected that not only would the race be

The Lancia-Ferraris of Hawthorn and Collins, soundly trounced in the 1957 German Grand Prix by Fangio.

much faster than in 1956 but also that Fangio's lap record would be substantially lowered. The race proved a complete Fangio/Maserati benefit. Maserati pursued tactics that it had followed previously, starting cars with half-full tanks. The Company had done this out of necessity in 1952 when Gonzalez finished second in the Italian Grand Prix and had repeated it with Schell's 250F in the 1954 Spanish Grand Prix. The benefits were marginal, for whilst a driver could pull out a very satisfactory lead prior to his refuelling stop, he simply had to drive that much harder afterwards because the time lost in the pits almost certainly exceeded any gain on the road during the first part of the race. But for Fangio's sheer brilliance and the fact that he was at the peak of his form, the plan would have come thoroughly unstuck. Fangio built up a good lead during the opening laps of the race, then stopped at the end of lap 12 with a lead of 28 seconds. By the time the car had been refuelled and the rear wheels had been changed, 52 seconds had been lost without allowing for the slowing off for the stop and the time spent in rejoining the race. All in all the total time lost was well over 1m 15s. By now the Lancia-Ferraris of Peter Collins and Mike Hawthorn were way in front, swapping the lead at will, and Fangio's chances looked slim indeed. For the first three laps after his pit stop he made little gain in ground, but then he speeded up, progressively lowering the lap record which he had already broken before his pit stop. He closed right up on Collins, then passed both Ferrari drivers on the next lap and carried on in the finest drive of his career to win the race from the Lancia-Ferraris of Mike Hawthorn, Peter Collins and Luigi Musso. Fangio and Maserati may have been dominant, but the Lancia-Ferraris had turned in a remarkable display of reliability and consistency.

Because of the cancellation of the Dutch and Belgian Grands Prix,

Italy was allowed two rounds in the World Championship with the inclusion of the Pescara Grand Prix, a race first held in 1924 and run without breaks — except for the Second World War — until 1954. In 1955 there had been no race and the following year it was held as a 2-litre sports car event. Now for the first and only time it was a round in the World Championship. The Pescara circuit was an arduous 15.9-mile course on the Adriatic coast, incorporating mountainous twists and turns, uphill and downhill swoops, and the long and very fast Montesilvano straight; the whole circuit was made up from normal roads and with all the usual roadside hazards.

In the 1957 Mille Miglia road race, the last to be held, de Portago's Ferrari had crashed with fatal results for both de Portago, his co-driver Eddie Nelson and ten spectators. One result of the accident was the end of this famous road race that had first been held in 1927, but another was an enquiry into the accident and a considerable controversy over the tyres used by Ferrari. Already these Belgian-made Engleberts had been criticized following failures on the banked circuit at Monza in 1955 and 1956, and at this time motor racing was not a popular sport. So high had the temperature become that Ferrari decided as a protest to refrain from entering the Pescara Grand Prix, but Luigi Musso eventually persuaded him to send a single car. Facing this sole entry was a full team of Maseratis and Vanwalls. Initially Musso led the race, but on lap 10 his car, which had been leaking oil, seized out in the mountains. Moss won for Vanwall — and I shall have more to say about this in a later chapter — and Fangio had to settle for second place with Schell's Maserati third. Gregory, with the privately entered 250F of Scuderia Centro-Sud, was fourth.

Next came the second Italian round in the Championship, the Italian Grand Prix at Monza, held on the road circuit only. Now the duel was between Maserati and Vanwall, with the Lancia-Ferraris also-rans. Moss won by a margin of over 40 seconds from Fangio, who had been forced to make a pit stop for new tyres; Behra made a magnificent, gallant effort with the V-12 Maserati, but, after two stops to take on more water, was forced to retire with internal engine damage. In third place came the Lanci-Ferrari of von Trips with the other survivor of a team of four cars, that of Musso, back in eighth place. This was to be the last race outing of the Lancia-Ferrari, a car which had gradually evolved through retrogressive development and was no faster at the end of 1957 than it had been two seasons previously.

Monza clinched Juan Fangio's fifth World Championship, but the season was not yet over. In September, Ferrari entered two of the Dino Formula 2 cars with engines bored out to 1860cc for Peter Collins and Luigi Musso in the Modena Grand Prix. Vanwall did not enter this race and although Behra scored an easy win with his 'lightweight' Maserati, Musso and Collins finished second and fourth in both heats. The season was rounded off by the Moroccan Grand Prix held on the Ain-Diab circuit near Casablanca. The whole idea was that the race, if it proved successful, would be the forerunner of a World Championship event

Above In the early stages of the 1957 Italian Grand Prix Fangio (Maserati 250F) leads Moss (Vanwall), Brooks (Vanwall), Behra (Maserati V-12) and Lewis-Evans (Vanwall). The race was won by Moss with Fangio second.

Below Meanwhile, what it was all about at the lower end of the scale — the 250F Maseratis of Horace Gould (No 14), Francesco Godia-Sales (No 10) and Bruce Halford (No 16) scrap for the lower places.

to be held in 1958 and all the serious teams appeared. Again Ferrari ran the Dino Formula 2 based cars with an interim 2195cc version (81 × 71mm) driven by Hawthorn and a 2417cc (85 × 71mm) version driven by Collins. Several drivers were suffering badly from influenza and Stirling Moss was too unwell to drive his Vanwall. Both of the new Ferraris retired, so the winner was Jean Behra with his Maserati 250F from the Vanwall of Stuart Lewis-Evans. Incidentally, Fangio appeared in neither of these races because his contract with Maserati was for World Championship events only.

The year 1957 was a watershed in Grand Prix racing as it witnessed the balance switch from Italian supremacy to British domination in three of the last four World Championship events of the year. It was a pattern of performance that was not to be reversed until 1961, and overall there was to develop a British domination of Grand Prix racing that was never to waiver.

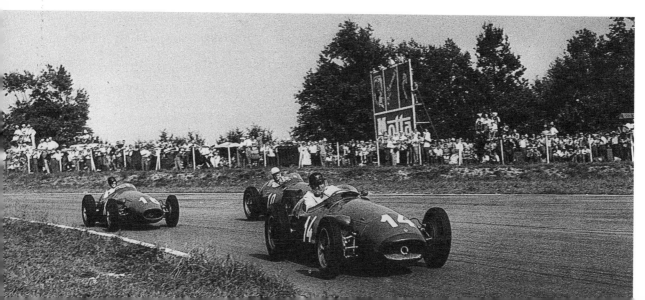

4

The rise of the British Racing Green

1954-58

Traditionally Britain had not been a strong force in motor racing, although Napier had performed with distinction in the early years of the century and Sunbeam, as a member of the Sunbeam-Talbot-Darracq Group, had achieved two Grand Prix wins, both by Sir Henry Segrave, in the 1923 French Grand Prix at Tours and the 1924 San Sebastian Grand Prix. ERA had achieved distinction in *Voiturette* racing in the 1930s and that, coupled with Bentley's successes at Le Mans in the 1920s, almost sums up British international motor racing successes before the Second World War.

Motor racing was part of the life-blood of the European mainland, especially in France and Italy, and it soon started again after the Second World War. There was, however, a growing interest in motor racing in Great Britain, not just the puny but enthusiastic and successful efforts of HWM and the pathetic and expensive failure of the BRM V-16. The new surge of motor racing enthusiasm was partly stimulated by what might be described as the 'fighter pilot instinct', and it is surprising just how many former flying members of the Royal Air Force became involved in motor racing either as drivers or constructors. Thus motor racing in Great Britain blossomed, with the popularity of the 500cc Formula 3 and the 2000cc Formula 2 encouraging many would-be drivers and entrants to move into a bigger league. When the 2500cc Grand Prix Formula for 1954 onwards was announced, there was a great deal of interest and potential support for it. The problem remained the same as it had been during the preceding Formula 2, however — the lack of a suitable engine.

A number of constructors had made approaches to Coventry Climax to see whether that Company, which had a reputation as a builder of proprietary engines, could be persuaded to produce a suitable Formula 1 engine. Eventually the Company decided that it would give the project a go, and produced, under the design control of Walter Hassan, the so-called 'Godiva' V-8 engine of 2477cc, with twin-choke, down-draught Solex carburettors developing in 1954 approximately 264 bhp at 7,900 rpm on a fuel mixture of 65 per cent alcohol, and with a compression ratio of 12.32:1. It has often been written that Coventry Climax abandoned production of the engine because it had listened to the rumours of claimed power outputs by Ferrari and Maserati and believed that the new engine would be uncompetitive. This simply does not add up. The production of a single running engine is but a mere fraction of the cost of laying down such engines in series. Apart from any other question mark, the financial calibre of the potential purchasers of this engine, Connaught, Cooper, HWM and Kieft, would not give anyone real confidence in investing the sums of money needed to put the engine into production. It seems likely that Coventry Climax was prepared to expend the necessary monies on the production of a prototype engine, but was hoping that a concern with real financial muscle would step into the Formula 1 arena and give it the financial security that it would need.

As it was, all the would-be constructors of Formula 1 cars in Great Britain had their initial prospects of entering the Grand Prix arena destroyed by Coventry Climax's decision. Fortunately, not only was Tony Vandervell pursuing his own course of engine and chassis development which would result in the car that made a real breakthrough in Grand Prix racing, but Coventry Climax itself embarked on a less expensive course of engine design and development that would during the years of the 2500cc Formula produce an engine powering the World Manufacturers' Championship winning cars; those that proved truly successful were Vanwall and Cooper (the latter described in greater detail in Chapter 6), but it is first necessary to consider the existing contenders who had Formula 1 hopes.

HWM

The small team based at Walton-on-Thames run by John Heath and George Abecassis had enjoyed immense success in Formula 2. Abecassis had raced a 1500cc supercharged Alta in pre-war days and he was the first owner to take delivery of the new Grand Prix Alta in 1948. Heath also raced an Alta, but a sports car with a supercharged 2000cc engine, together with the first 1934 ERA, R1A; during 1948 he ran his Alta with a very streamlined body but achieved little success. Heath had already learned, however, that the way ahead was to compete in Continental races, where there was good starting money and, if the car lasted the distance, good prize money too. For 1949 he built a new car, known as the HW-Alta, with a new tubular chassis, simple bodywork with cycle wings and the Alta engine in unsupercharged form. The new car achieved a good measure of success and for 1950 Heath and Abecassis decided to run a full team of cars under the name HWM. Whilst the BRM V-16 project was absorbing vast sums of money which were to produce little in the way of results, the HWM team, with its very basic and very simple cars built with two-seater bodywork, ran in a total of 26 events during the year and scored a whole string of good places, with the occasional win in very minor events. Already Stirling Moss was in the team, Lance Macklin joined in 1951 and the following year Peter Collins joined to replace Stirling Moss who had lost faith in the team's prospects and had left to drive the G-type ERA. From 1951 onwards the cars were single-seaters and during 1951 and 1952 their run of successes continued. However, as Formula 2 increased in strength and competition, so the successes of the HWMs slowly slipped away and by 1953 they were nothing more than 'also-rans'. The cars were raced almost every weekend with no time for development work or proper testing, the team was dependent on starting and prize money from constant racing to keep the project going and the Alta engine was sadly deficient in power output compared with many of its rivals.

In June 1953 in the Shelsley Walsh Hill Climb, George Abecassis drove a new HWM, a sports car that incorporated the existing Formula 2 chassis with a Jaguar C-type engine and gearbox. A second HWM-Jaguar was built for 1954 for Tony Gaze, and this and the works car were raced throughout the year. However, John Heath very much wanted to continue racing in Formula 1 in 1954 and was planning a car powered by the Coventry Climax 'Godiva' engine. If that engine had become available, the 1954 HWM, even if it still used the existing heavy and unsophisticated tubular chassis, would have been far from uncompetitive against the Ferrari and Maserati opposition, except that it is likely that HWM would never have found a really suitable driver. Unable to obtain the latest Alta engines which were to be pledged to Connaught, Heath decided to enlarge the existing Alta engine from 1960cc (83 × 90mm) to 2464cc (86 × 106mm) and in this form power output was probably only around 180 bhp. One of these cars was retained by the works and the other was sold to Ted Whiteaway.

In its few outings, the 1954 Formula 1 HWM was driven by Lance Macklin. At the Easter Goodwood meeting it ran in three races and took fourth, fifth and sixth places. Macklin drove it in the French Grand Prix at Reims in July where the new Mercedes-Benz W196 cars made their début. Whilst Fangio with the Mercedes dominated the race, lapping it close to 120 mph, Macklin trailed round in last place, averaging 107 mph, and retired after 11 laps with engine trouble. The works car was then fitted with a Jaguar engine for Formule Libre racing and

Lance Macklin in the 1954 French Grand Prix with the works HWM, one of the 1953 cars with engine enlarged to 2464cc and hopelessly outclassed. Macklin retired on lap 10 because of engine problems and this was his last Formula 1 race until he drove Stirling Moss's private Maserati in 1955. (LAT)

it was eventually crashed by Tony Gaze at the autumn Goodwood meeting.

Ted Whiteaway persevered with his private car but achieved nothing. Apart from the fact that the HWM had little potential, Whiteaway was far too inexperienced to exploit what potential there was. I met him at the September race meeting at the Crystal Palace in September 1954. He was a thoroughly pleasant and enthusiastic character, somewhat out of his depth in single-seater racing, even at this rather parochial level, and not really quite understanding why his car went so badly. In later years he raced an AC Ace-Bristol with considerable success as a member of the Ken Rudd team, a lower level of racing, at which he could achieve success.

HWM continued to field works Jaguar-powered sports cars until the end of the 1956 season, and although they were very often successful in obtaining good places, they rarely scored an outright win. Poor John Heath was killed driving one of his cars in the 1956 Mille Miglia.

Cooper

In early post-war years Cooper had made a tremendous reputation as a manufacturer of 500cc cars, the motorcycle-powered single-seaters that became internationally recognized as Formula 3 in 1950. All Cooper 500cc cars were rear-engined and this of course was to be the layout that made Cooper famous. However, from 1949 onwards the Coopers, father Charles and son John, had built a small number of front-engined sports cars and these were followed in 1952 by a new Bristol-powered Formula 2 car. The Cooper-Bristol featured a simple drilled box-section chassis, the familiar Cooper suspension of a high-set transverse leaf spring together with wishbones and telescopic dampers, and a four-speed Bristol gearbox. The most famous and successful Cooper-Bristol was the car entered in 1952 by Bob Chase for young Mike Hawthorn who raced the car with tremendous success, taking a fourth place in the Belgian Grand Prix, a third in the British Grand Prix, second to Villoresi's 4.5-litre works Ferrari at Boreham in August and a third again in the Dutch Grand Prix at Zandvoort.

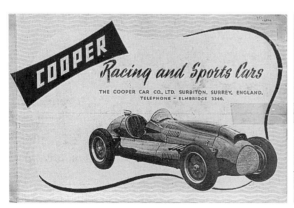

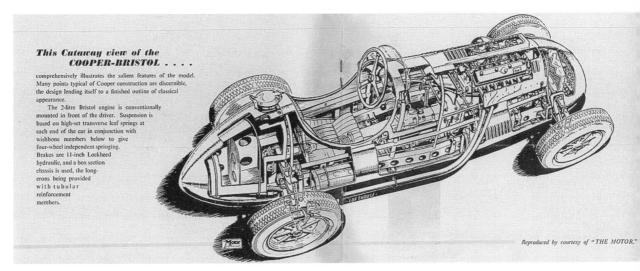

This Cutaway view of the COOPER-BRISTOL . . . .

comprehensively illustrates the salient features of the model. Many points typical of Cooper construction are discernible, the design lending itself to a finished outline of classical appearance.

The 2-litre Bristol engine is conventionally mounted in front of the driver. Suspension is based on high-set transverse leaf springs at each end of the car in conjunction with wishbone members below to give four-wheel independent springing. Brakes are 11-inch Lockheed hydraulic, and a box section chassis is used, the long-erons being provided with tubular reinforcement members.

Reproduced by courtesy of "THE MOTOR."

This page and opposite bottom Cooper's catalogue produced at the end of 1952 season showing the Formula 2 car.

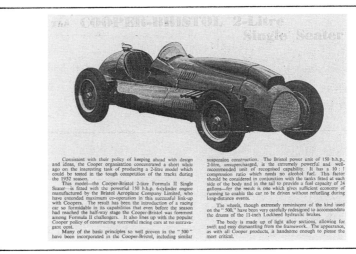

Consistent with their policy of keeping ahead with design and ideas, the Cooper organisation concentrated a short while ago on the interesting task of producing a 2-litre model which could be tested in the tough competition of the tracks during the 1952 season.

This model—the Cooper-Bristol 2-litre Formula II Single Seater—is fitted with the powerful 150 b.h.p. 6-cylinder engine manufactured by the Bristol Aeroplane Company Limited, who have extended maximum co-operation in this successful link-up with Coopers. The result has been the introduction of a racing car so formidable in its capabilities that even before the season had reached the half-way stage the Cooper-Bristol was foremost among Formula II challengers. It also lines up with the popular Cooper policy of constructing successful racing cars at no extravagant cost.

Many of the basic principles so well proven in the "500" have been incorporated in the Cooper-Bristol, including similar suspension construction. The Bristol power unit of 150 b.h.p., 2-litre, unsupercharged, is the extremely powerful and well-recommended unit of recognised capability. It has a 10 : 1 compression ratio which needs no alcohol fuel. This factor should be considered in conjunction with the tanks fitted at each side of the body and in the tail to provide a fuel capacity of 24 gallons—for the result is one which gives sufficient economy of running to enable the car to be driven without refuelling during long-distance events.

The wheels, though extremely reminiscent of the kind used on the "500," have been very carefully redesigned to accommodate the drums of the 11-inch Lockheed hydraulic brakes.

The body is made up of light alloy sections, allowing for swift and easy dismantling from the framework. The appearance, as with all Cooper products, is handsome enough to please the most critical.

Specification of the COOPER-BRISTOL 2-Litre Formula II Single Seater

ENGINE DIMENSIONS :
Cylinders : 6. Bore : 66 mm. Stroke : 96 mm. Cubic Capacity : 1,971 c.c. Piston Area : 31.8 sq. in. Valves : Inclined pushrod o.h.v. in hemispherical heads. Compression ratio : 10 : 1.

ENGINE PERFORMANCE :
Max. b.h.p. : 150 at 5,800 r.p.m. Max. b.m.e.p. : 152½ lb./sq. in. at 3,500 r.p.m. B.H.P. per sq. in. piston area : 3.78. Peak piston speed ft. per min. : 3,460.

Guy Griffiths

ENGINE DETAILS :
Carburetter : 3 Solex 32BI down-draught. Ignition : Coil or vertical magneto. Plugs—make and type : K.L.G. P.Ten.L.80, 10 mm. Fuel Pump : A/C mechanical. Fuel Capacity : 24 galls. Oil Filter : Vokes full-flow. Oil Capacity (including filter): 10 pints. Cooling System : Pump assisted.

TRANSMISSION :
Clutch : Borg and Beck. BB8/62A, s.d.p. Gear Ratios : (Top) 3.46 ; (3rd) 4.47 ; (2nd) 6.31 ; (1st) 10.1 ; (Rev.) 10.0. Prop. shaft : Open. Final Drive : Bevel gear on frame.

CHASSIS DETAILS :
Brakes : Lockheed hydraulic, 2 l.s. front and rear. Brake drum diameter : 10 ins. Friction lining area : 134.4 sq. ins. Suspension : (Front) Transverse leaf and wishbone I.F.S.; (Rear) Transverse leaf and wishbone I.R.S. Shock absorbers : Telescopic hydraulic. Wheel type : Cast alloy, incorporating brake drum. Tyre Size : (Front) 500 x 15 ; (Rear) 5.50-15. Steering gear : Rack and pinion. Steering wheel : Light alloy.

DIMENSIONS :
Wheelbase : 7 ft 6 ins. Track (Front and Rear) : 4 ft. 2 ins. Overall length : 11 ft. Overall height : 3 ft. 2 ins. Ground clearance : 5 ins. Dry weight : 9 cwt. 3 qr. 12 lbs.

MAXIMUM SPEED : 145 m.p.h.

BODY :
18 gauge alloy fitted with DZUS fasteners. All panels removable by two men in 3 minutes.

FUEL :
80%, 80 octane petrol ; 10% Benzol ; 10% Methnol. Fuel consumption between 12 and 15 m.p.g.

PERFORMANCE DATA (Based on approx. dry weight) :
Piston area, sq. in. per ton : 73.6 Brake lining area, sq. in. per ton : 269. Top gear m.p.h. per 1,000 r.p.m.: 21.5. Top gear m.p.h. at 2,500 ft./min. piston speed : 85.5. Top gear m.p.h. at 5,500 r.p.m. : 118. Litres per ton-mile, dry 5,500.

For 1953 Hawthorn joined Ferrari and in real terms that was the end of Cooper successes in Formula 2. Cooper produced an improved car for 1953 with a tubular chassis, known as the Mk II. The most successful driver in 1953 was Ken Wharton who drove a semi-works car with pre-selector gearbox. Although he did well in minor British events, no impact was made on the international scene. Other Coopers were fitted with Alta engines and Stirling Moss had built for him a very special Cooper-Alta designed by Ray Martin, who, with John Cooper, Technical Editor of *The Autocar*, had been responsible for the 500cc Kieft. This incorporated a small number of Cooper of Surbiton components including certain frame tubes, body panel and wheels, but it featured coil spring front suspension and a de Dion rear axle, disc front brakes and inboard-mounted rear brakes. It proved a complete failure and hastily, in mid-season, Moss transferred the Alta engine and gearbox to a standard Mk II chassis. With the engine running on SU fuel injection and with nitromethane fuel additive, it was reckoned that power output was boosted from 150 bhp to 200 bhp. In this form Moss raced the car in the 1953 Italian Grand Prix and although at one stage he rose as high as fifth place, the extra power revealed the deficiencies of the Cooper chassis and the inability of the tyres to withstand such high speeds.

After the start of the 2500cc Formula, Cooper-Bristols were still seen in Formula 1 events in Great Britain and, together with Connaught A-Series cars, they made up most of the places at the back of the grids. They still continued to enjoy some success in minor British events, especially when driven by Horace Gould, a stalwart Formula 1 privateer during the 2500cc years who later graduated to Maserati 250F cars, and Bob Gerard, who had enjoyed so much success in early post-war years with ERAs. Gerard continued to race his car until 1956 by which time it was fitted with an enlarged 2246cc engine. Subsequently he transferred this engine to a rear-engined Cooper chassis which was

One of the amateur stalwarts of Formula 1, Horace Gould, often called 'The Gonzalez of the West Country', is seen with his Cooper-Bristol, about to lap Leslie Marr's Connaught, in the 1954 British Grand Prix at Silverstone. (T.C. March)

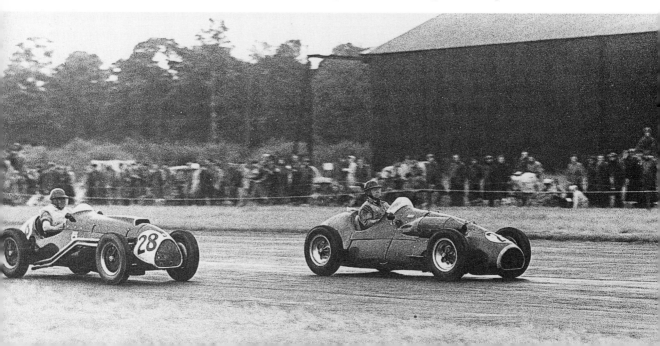

entered as the Cooper-BG-Bristol, but sadly this brave amateur venture proved a complete failure.

Like the other British constructors, Cooper had planned to use the Coventry Climax 'Godiva' engine, but once it became known that this would not be available the Surbiton firm abandoned its Formula 1 plans. In all probability any such 'Godiva'-engined Cooper would have been little more than a Cooper-Bristol with a lower bonnet line (the Bristol engine was very deep, partly because of the wet sump, and necessitated the high bonnet line of the Formula 2 cars).

In 1955 Cooper introduced a rear-engined sports car, the T39, often called the 'Manx' tail or 'Bobtail' Cooper. This was usually powered by the 1100cc Coventry Climax FWA and was intended to meet Lotus head-on in sports car racing. By 1956 these cars were being raced with 1460cc Coventry Climax FWB single-cam engines. However, in early 1955 Jack Brabham arrived from Australia and bought Peter Whitehead's Cooper-Alta which had an enlarged 2464cc engine. This engine proved pretty useless and Brabham had soon substituted a Bristol unit. Within a very short time of his arrival in England Brabham had virtually moved in with the Coopers and was working for them and with them. He decided to build up a 'Bobtail' Formula 1 to be powered by a Bristol engine. This was initially entered at the British Grand Prix at Aintree, with the entry form claiming that the engine was of 2.2 litres. This was one race that the organizers did not want cluttered up with old Formula 2 cars, and if Brabham had been honest and said that the car had a 1971cc engine (which it really had and which the organizers knew it had) then they would have had little alternative but to reject the entry. The car showed no fireworks in practice and the clutch failed before the start. Not surprisingly Brabham retired, but very shortly afterwards he finished fourth behind two Vanwalls and a rather off-colour Stirling Moss (private Maserati 250F) in a Formula 1 race at Snetterton. That winter Brabham took the Cooper-Bristol back to Australia

Jack Brabham on his arrival in England in 1955 bought Peter Whitehead's 2.5 litre Mk II Cooper-Alta. He was far from happy with the engine and soon substituted a Bristol to power what was entered as the 'RedEx Special'. Here he is seen with the Cooper-Alta in the International Trophy at Silverstone, about to be lapped by Rosier's Maserati 250F. (T.C. March)

Mike Hawthorn (Ferrari) about to lap Jack Brabham's rear-engined Cooper-Bristol in the 1955 British Grand Prix at Aintree. The Cooper was very much a portent for the future. (T.C. March)

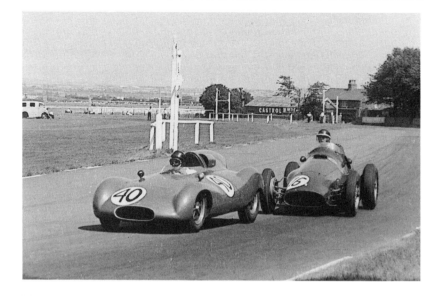

For years Bob Gerard had raced ERAs with immense success before moving on to a Mk II Cooper-Bristol in 1953. He was still racing the car in 1956, by which time it was fitted with an engine enlarged to 2246cc and is seen here in that year's International Trophy race. (T.C. March)

and sold it there. A second of these cars was built up for sports car racing by Bob Chase to be driven by Mike Keen, but sadly he crashed it with fatal results in the Goodwood 9 Hours Race.

It was to be another two years before a Cooper made any sort of impression in Formula 1, but that was to be with a very different motor car that revolutionized Grand Prix racing.

Connaught

Formed by Rodney Clarke in 1943 as Continental Cars based at Chobham in Surrey, this small firm moved to new premises on the Portsmouth road near Send in 1946. Originally Clarke had hoped to make Continental Cars a Bugatti specialist, but the Molsheim concern's failure to start production again after the war brought an end to that plan.

In 1946 Clarke had been joined by Mike Oliver, ex-RAF, who was initially employed as a salesman but became works manager when Continental Cars became Connaught Engineering, working on engine development with great success.

Connaught built a small number of sports cars based on Lea-Francis components and one of these was raced by Kenneth McAlpine who had entrusted maintenance work on his Maserati 8CM to Continental Cars. McAlpine and Clarke decided to go ahead with the development of a Formula 2 car under the name of Connaught. The newly formed Connaught Engineering took over manufacture of the sports cars and in June 1951 took over completely from Continental Cars.

Clarke soon displayed that he had remarkable talents as a designer and engineer. His first single-seater, the A-series, which first appeared in 1950, was beautifully engineered, but, like all British Formula 2 cars,

Above Le Patron Kenneth McAlpine at the wheel of the beautifully engineered, but underpowered, Connaught A-series, A1, in the 1952 British Grand Prix. He finished 16th. (Guy Griffiths)

Below Salvadori with the long-wheelbase, fuel injection works Connaught, AL9, in the 1953 British Grand Prix. He worked his way up to ninth place before retiring because of a broken radius arm. (T.C. March)

hopelessly underpowered. Clarke chose a simple twin-tubular structure, with tubular cross-members and the oil tank for the dry sump system carried in the main front cross-member. The engine was still basically the Lea-Francis but with a light-alloy cylinder block and, in due course, developed so that the capacity was 1960cc (79 × 100mm), although when the car was first raced in 1950 it retained a 1767cc engine. Transmission was by an Armstrong-Siddeley pre-selector four-speed gearbox.

By 1951, the A-series featured the full 1960cc engine, four separate equal-length exhaust pipes and the four Amal carburettors housed in an external 'plenum chamber' on 'balance-box', as dynamometer testing had revealed that long extensions from the carburettors to the inlet ports gave better power in the middle range. Although double wishbone and torsion bar suspension was retained at the front, there was now a de Dion axle at the rear. During 1951 the car ran only in a number of minor events, but a much fuller season was tackled in 1952. Very little was achieved during the year, although Dennis Poore held third place for much of the British Grand Prix and eventually finished fourth. For 1953 Connaught built two cars with longer 7 ft 6 in wheel base (the original wheelbase was 7 ft 0 in extended to 7 ft 1 in to make it easier to remove the engine), Hilborn-Travers fuel injection was adopted on the works cars and at some races they ran on nitromethane fuel additive. With fuel injection and nitromethane, power output was around 165 bhp, still rather lower than the Italian cars were developing and insufficient to be really competitive. Up to three works cars were fielded in 1953 races with a team headed by Roy Salvadori, then very much an up and coming driver, but except in minor British events no real success was gained. Perhaps the most successful A-series was Rob Walker's carburettor car usually driven by Tony Rolt which scored a string of successes in minor British races; in addition Rolt held fifth place in the 1953 British Grand Prix until eliminated by a broken half-shaft.

During the years 1954-56, the A-series Connaught continued to appear in British international events and together with the Cooper-Bristols made up the back of the grid at most British Formula 1 races. McAlpine had continued to race a works car during the early part of the 1954 season and private owners also continued to race the cars with some measure of success. An A-series owned by Sir Jeremy Boles gave young driver Don Beauman good racing experience and a measure of success that led to his inclusion in the Jaguar works team at Le Mans in 1955, but sadly he was killed in a crash in the Leinster Trophy in Ireland shortly afterwards. Mike Young installed a 2464cc Alta engine in his A-series in 1956, but in never achieved anything worth mentioning, and one of these cars had its engine reduced to 1484cc for the Formula 2 of 1957 onwards. Although by this time it was hopelessly uncompetitive, underpowered, overweight and generally obsolescent, it was not an illogical move because Connaught had built 1484cc sports cars, using in the main A-series components, and these were known as the

ALSR. In addition to these two Connaught sports cars, the 1484cc engine was used both by John Risley-Prichard in his 'Disco Volante'-bodied front-engined Cooper sports car and also in Tommy Sopwith's rear-engined 'Bobtail' Cooper.

For the 2500cc Grand Prix Formula, Clarke designed a very advanced rear-engine car featuring monocoque construction, with the Coventry Climax 'Godiva' engine. It really only consisted of a set of drawings and had made little progress before it became known that Coventry Climax was not going to make available the V-8 engine. This decision coincided with a degree of realism sinking into the Connaught concern, and Clarke concluded that he could not afford to produce other than what would be basically a very simple design. So the new B-series car featured a tubular ladder-type frame, with double wishbone and coil spring/damper front suspension and at the rear a de Dion tube located by a compound transverse link and with twin radius arms. Connaught had come to an arrangement with Geoffrey Taylor whereby the latest version of the Alta engine would be supplied to Connaught exclu-

The installation of the 2470cc Alta engine in the Connaught B-series chassis. Note the twin-plug ignition and the two twin-choke Weber carburettors with gauge wire filters over the intakes. (T.C. March)

sively. In its 1954 form this had a capacity of 2470cc (93.5 × 90mm). It retained the twin overhead camshafts driven by a single long roller chain from the rear of the crankshaft and there were two valves and two plugs per cylinder. The cylinders and crankcase were a single alloy casting inserted in the block to form four wet cylinder liners, and there was a one-piece forged crankshaft running in three main bearings. The engine was extensively developed by Mike Oliver and eventually produced a power output of around 240 bhp at 6,400 rpm. In its original form SU fuel injection was used. Transmission was by an Armstrong-Siddeley four-speed pre-selector gearbox mounted on the chassis close

Right *Testing at Silverstone: Jack Fairman at the wheel of the B-series Connaught. (Leslie Marr)*

Below *Another photograph of the B-series Connaught during testing at Silverstone: the wheels are off and the car is supported on a jack and wooden blocks. Designer Rodney Clark is to the left of the photograph. (Leslie Marr)*

to the rear axle. The most striking feature of the car was the stream-lined full-width bodywork, something that Clarke had conceived quite independently of outside influences, although it was of course developed contemporaneously with the Mercedes-Benz W196. The one-piece aluminium bodywork enclosed the driver to shoulder height and he sat well to the front of the car with his legs on either side of the engine. Unlike the Mercedes, this seating position coupled with a downward sloping bonnet gave the driver excellent visibility sideways and forwards, and there was a wide tail with a large stabilizing fin. Again, unlike the Mercedes bodywork, the Connaught B-series was perfectly functional, although it was expensive to make, very easily damaged and expensive to repair. When it was eventually abandoned, it was for economic rather than true racing reasons.

Clarke knew that the Company could not really afford the new Grand Prix Formula, for the cost of developing the B-series car, around £15,000, had already sapped the team's resources and to run a full team of cars in major events would cost £50,000 a year. There was no way that this could be managed. Instead, Connaught reconciled itself to running cars wherever it could afford to, with one usually driven by *Le Patron* Kenneth McAlpine, and it was hoped to sell cars to private owners. Orders were received from Leslie Marr, Rob Walker and Peter Whitehead. The first two were delivered, Walker's with conventional bodywork and exposed wheels, but Whitehead lost patience with all the delays and eventually cancelled his order.

When the B-series was first demonstrated to the press at Goodwood in 1954 it featured Borrani wire wheels. It was not raced until the Easter Goodwood meeting in 1955 and by then it was fitted with Connaught's own fuel injection system (soon to be abandoned in favour of twin-choke Weber carburettors) and Dunlop magnesium-alloy wheels and disc brakes. Rolt finished fourth in the Formule Libre Chichester Cup but retired in the main race of the day, the Richmond Trophy, with a broken throttle linkage. Two cars then appeared in the International Trophy at Silverstone in May, the prototype B1 driven by Jack Fairman, which retired again with a broken throttle linkage, and a new car, B2, driven by McAlpine, which retired with fuel injector trouble. Two months later three Connaughts, a works car and the newly delivered private cars of Marr and Walker, ran in the British Grand Prix at Aintree. All three trailed round at the tail of the field and all three retired. Reg Parnell with a works car came very close to winning the *Daily Telegraph* Trophy at Aintree in September, but four laps from the finish he was put out by engine trouble and had to push his car across the line into sixth place. Later that month Parnell drove the original car, B1, now fitted with an unstreamlined body, in the Gold Cup race at Oulton Park. He drove a good race to finish fourth behind Moss (Maserati 250F), Hawthorn (Lancia V-8) and Titterington (Vanwall).

So far the season had been a dismal succession of failures and mediocre performances. Connaught was very close to withdrawing from racing altogether, but then came the invitation to run in the Syracuse

In the paddock for the 1955 International Trophy at Silverstone are, second from left, Tony Rolt (who drove the B-series on its debut at the Easter Goodwood meeting that year) with, to his left, Mike Hawthorn and Rodney Clarke. (Leslie Marr)

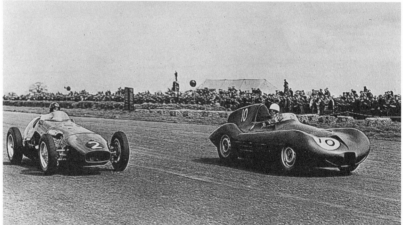

Ken Wharton (Vanwall) passes Ken McAlpine's B-series Connaught at Silverstone.

Grand Prix to be held on 23 October, coupled with the offer of £1,000 per car starting money. This was big money for Connaught and it could not refuse. The only problem was drivers; the Company could not afford an experienced pair, so Clarke took on a young dental student, Tony Brooks, who had driven for Aston Martin in three races that year and had also appeared with the works sports Connaught, and Les Leston, normally a 500cc Formula 3 driver but who also drove Peter Bell's private sports Connaught. Ferrari did not enter this race, but there was a strong team of Maseratis — and indeed, if Maserati had not promised to support the race with a strong team, it would have never taken place. Siracusa was a difficult, triangular, bumpy 3.4-mile circuit, lined for much of its distance by walls, with gentle curves, two slowish corners and a very slow hairpin. Although Brooks was allowed only very limited practice with his car, the newly rebuilt B1, he was third fastest in practice, and started from the front row of the grid alongside the Maserati 250Fs of Musso and Villoresi. Driving with the sublime confidence and skill for which he was later to become so famous, Brooks initially held third place in the race but soon passed Villoresi, closed up on Musso and took the lead on lap 11. Musso went back in front on the

The first unstreamlined B-series Connaught was Rob Walker's B4 seen here driven in the 1955 British Grand Prix at Aintree by Tony Rolt. As can be seen from the photograph on page 95, the style adopted for the works cars in 1956-57 was very similar. (T.C. March)

Leslie Marr's private B3, B-series Connaught, photographed in the same race at the same point on the circuit. This car was painted a light green, with paint made by Titanine, the aviation paint manufacturers, while the works cars were a darker, matt finish. Rob Walker's car was painted in his usual colours of dark blue with a white noseband, while Italian Piero Scotti's car, B7, which he acquired in 1956, was painted maroon rather than an Italian racing red. (T.C. March)

next lap, but then Brooks took the lead again and, striving to hold it broke the lap record. Musso then broke it twice. As the race progressed, so Musso's brakes weakened and the gearbox began to play up, allowing Brooks to pull steadily into the distance. At the end of the 214-miles, Brooks had a lead of 51 seconds from Musso and Villoresi had been lapped twice. Leston with the streamlined Connaught finished ninth, eight laps in arrears, after a spin and three pit stops for plug changes.

This was the first British win in any Grand Prix since Segrave's win with a Sunbeam at San Sebastian in 1924. It may not have been a significant win, for Ferrari had not been present and Maserati lacked its team-leader Jean Behra, but all the same it was a remarkable British victory. It gave hope to all the British constructors, it cheered immensely British enthusiasts, it established Brook's reputation and it gave Connaught the necessary will to carry on with its racing programme.

One remarkable development in 1956 was that Connaught negotiated the sale of B7 to Sicilian driver Piero Scotti. Scotti had something of a reputation as a sports car driver at the wheel of Ferraris and was by no means unknown. He arranged to buy the car on credit terms, but he was not happy with its performance and after the Belgian Grand Prix he ceased payments and the car was left at the works. When Connaught gave up racing and the cars were auctioned, B7 remained unsold and it was lent to the Science Museum in London. Twenty years ago I described this car as 'languishing' at the Museum, but despite squabbles as to its ownership it remains there and is one of the few surviving examples of a truly original and unspoilt Formula 1 car of the 1950s.

Connaught now decided to concentrate solely on the unstreamlined cars and in due course the streamliners were rebodied. They did, however, from time to time appear in streamlined form during the early part of the 1956 season. Mainly because of Connaught's very limited budget, the cars did not make many appearances during the year and were rarely successful. Archie Scott-Brown, that immensely talented but handicapped driver, appeared regularly for the team, although overseas organizers would not normally allow him to compete. He was only five feet tall, with broad shoulders, a normal trunk, but exceptionally short legs; his right arm was merely a stump of a forearm with no proper hand — just the palm and thumb. Scott-Brown was a blindingly fast, controlled driver and he did much to enhance Connaught's reputation during the year. He led the Richmond Trophy at Goodwood until half-distance when his Connaught's crankshaft broke with the result that Maseratis took the first two places, followed to the flag by a trio of Connaughts. Again he led the Aintree 200 race, but retired when a piston failed. Stirling Moss with a Vanwall won the International Trophy at Silverstone, but Scott-Brown took second place, ahead of another Connaught driven by Desmond Titterington. Following brake failures suffered by Titterington at Aintree and by Mike Oliver, having a rare drive, in the International Trophy, Connaught tried Girling disc brakes on one car at the British Grand Prix at Silverstone. In this race Scott-Brown retired when a drive-shaft broke, but Jack Fairman drove a steady but uninspired race to finish fourth behind two of the Lancia-Ferraris and a Maserati. The only overseas events tackled by the works team in 1956 were the Syracuse Grand Prix, held that year in April, where both Connaughts were slower than Brooks had been in 1955 and both retired, and the Italian Grand Prix at Monza. Here two cars were entered for Ron Flockhart, deputizing for Scott-Brown who had not been allowed to run, and Jack Fairman. The pair took third and fifth places.

In correspondence in *Autosport*, there were arguments as to whether Connaught should be slow and reliable or fast and break. Rodney Clarke replied in the following terms:

> 'The Connaught must be made more reliable and then we can drive it faster. I think most people would agree that those cars which went faster at the beginning of the race but later on dropped out would have done better to have gone a bit slower if this would have resulted in completion of the race. I think in this particular case Connaught [should be given] credit for being wise before the event (which is not always an easy task). 'It is not perhaps generally realized that most

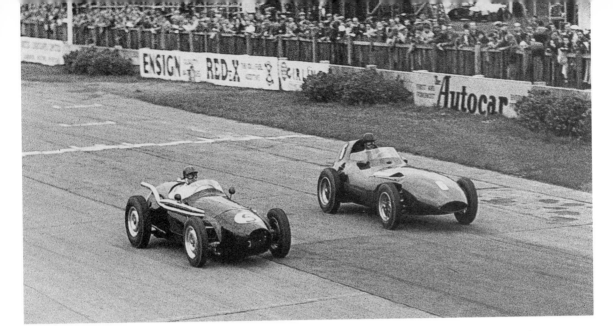

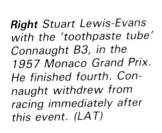

Above Jack Fairman (Connaught B-series) and Tony Brooks (Vanwall) pass the pits during the Richmond Trophy race at Goodwood on Easter Monday 1956. Fairman finished second, but Brooks retired because of Vanwall's not unfamiliar problem, broken throttle linkage.

team managers (unless they are fortunate enough to have a vastly superior car such as Neubauer had last year) have the option of making their cars seem either fast and fragile, or slow and reliable. It is merely a matter of mystic numbers whispered in the drivers' ears.'

By this time the writing was on the wall. Clearly the Alta engines were neither sufficiently powerful nor sufficiently reliable, and detailed modifications, including new and stronger con-rods, together with modifications to the valve gear, made little difference for 1957. Clarke had in hand the new C-series car with space-frame, strut and coil spring front suspension and inboard rear brakes, but it was never completed. Chassis B3, which Leslie Marr had sold back to the works in early 1956 after having raced it in the early part of the year in New Zealand with a Jaguar engine, was rebuilt with a very striking, dart-shaped body to give improved air penetration and was soon known as the 'toothpaste tube'.

Right Stuart Lewis-Evans with the 'toothpaste tube' Connaught B3, in the 1957 Monaco Grand Prix. He finished fourth. Connaught withdrew from racing immediately after this event. (LAT)

The team was now reduced to running purely for starting money and prize money and it was clear that this could not go on for long. At Siracusa, Ivor Bueb with a works car on his first Formula 1 drive finished fifth, whilst Lewis-Evans with the 'toothpaste tube' won the Richmond Trophy Formula 1 race at Goodwood after the failure of the Vanwalls. On that same day, Easter Monday, Ivor Bueb drove a B-series into third place in the Pau Grand Prix. Shortly afterwards Lewis-Evans was holding second place in the Naples Grand Prix when a front hub fractured. There was a suggestion that Alfred Owen should jack in his efforts with the BRM and that Tony Vandervell should give up the Vanwall and both should put their resources into Connaught, but this suggestion, almost needless to say, came to nothing. Instead, Connaught had to make do with very limited support from the Connaught Supporters Club and it was with their assistance that the team made its final Formula 1 appearance at Monaco. Here Lewis-Evans drove the 'toothpaste tube' into fourth place, but immediately after this race the team withdrew from racing. In October all the works cars, together with Rob Walker's, were auctioned.

Bernie Ecclestone bought two of the cars and tried racing them in 1958, but without works backing or any sort of development programme, it was a lost cause. The C-series car, still not completed, was not sold at the auction but was eventually driven in the 1959 United States Grand Prix by Bob Said, who retired after only one lap with handling problems. In the hands of various private owners the cars gradually sank down to the level of being mere 'bangers', but at least the popularity of historic racing has changed all that and the cars are now prized collectors' pieces.

BRM

Following the abandonment of the old 4500cc/1500cc Formula at the end of 1951, BRM had continued to race the V-16 cars and, albeit very slowly, had put work in hand on a new car for the 2500cc Formula, to be known as the P25. In the meanwhile, for the 1954 season, BRM built a lighter and shorter version of the V-16 known as the Mk II and this was raced until the end of 1955. In addition the team bought a new Maserati 250F car to keep the racing side active while the new car was under development. The car was driven to victory in the 1955 International Trophy at Silverstone by Peter Collins, and Mike Hawthorn finished third with it in the Argentine Grand Prix in 1956. After that it was sold to Jack Brabham who was horrified to find when he started to race it just what a deplorable condition it was in and he soon disposed of it.

The new P25 was built under the general design control of Peter Berthon, but the engine was the work of Stuart Tresilian, who had in fact conceived it on his own and at one time offered the design to Connaught. Although much of the emphasis on the new car was on power

The markedly oversquare engine of the P25 BRM in its 1956 form. (T.C. March)

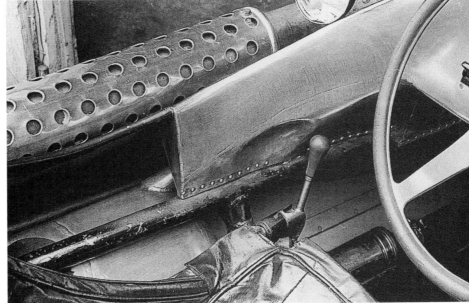

A cockpit shot of the P25 showing the left-hand gear-change with the rather crude depression to make room for the driver's hand and the protective shield over the exhaust pipe. (T.C. March)

Rear view of the BRM showing the single rear disc brake operating on the transmission. (T.C. March)

and simplicity, at the same time some of the worst features of the V-16 were retained. The engine was a four-cylinder design of 2497cc (102.87 × 74.93mm) with twin overhead camshafts driven by spur gears from the rear of the crankshaft, two large valves per cylinder, and two twin-choke Weber 58DCOE carburettors. In initial form, power output was 248 bhp at 9,000 rpm — at least this was the claimed output — and by 1956 it was said to have risen to 270 bhp. The transmission incorporated a four-speed gearbox mounted in unit with the final drive. The chassis was a multi-tubular structure, with a magnesium body skin, front suspension by double wishbones and at the rear a de Dion axle suspended on a transverse leaf spring and located by twin radius arms; front and rear Berthon had adopted the oleo-pneumatic struts used on the V-16 car. It was an odd and rather illogical decision, for this suspension layout had never really worked, and whilst there were Dunlop disc brakes, at the rear there was a single turbo-cooled transmission brake behind the gearbox and this proved hopelessly troublesome in practice.

For 1955 BRM had signed up Peter Collins, but he had to struggle with the V-16 until the new P25 was ready to race at Aintree in September. Because of an oil breather spraying oil over the rear of the car, including the tyres, he went off the road into a concrete post and the car non-started. Three weeks later he was in third place in the Gold Cup race at Oulton Park where he was forced to retire with apparent loss of oil pressure. Later BRM claimed that it was merely a faulty gauge.

So far the car had shown nothing but promise, but 1955 was to produce disaster after disaster and the team's reputation sank even lower that it had been during the days of the V-16 cars. BRM signed up Mike

Formally posed at Folkingham, the P25, team personnel and the transporter. Mike Hawthorn is second from the left with, to his left, Tony Brooks, Peter Berthon, Raymond Mays and Anthony Rivers-Fletcher and, to his right, Frank May. (T.C. March)

Mike Hawthorn testing the P25 BRM at Folkingham early in 1956. (T.C. March)

Hawthorn, who was very keen to drive a British car, and, as Number 2, Tony Brooks, the winner of the Syracuse Grand Prix at the wheel of a Connaught. As ever Raymond Mays was optimistic about the cars' prospects and a tremendous amount of 'hype' surrounded the team. This made it look even worse when things went badly wrong. The cars first appeared at Goodwood on Easter Monday and although Hawthorn led the race, the transmission failed on lap 23, the car went out of control, hit a ploughed earth infield and turned end over end, throwing out Hawthorn who was lucky to escape with a shaking and a lacerated ankle. Brooks' car was eliminated by loss of oil pressure. The team next appeared at Aintree where Hawthorn's brakes failed whilst he was leading and Brooks struggled on to finish second to Moss's private Maserati, although his brakes were pretty useless. A single car for Hawthorn ran in the International Trophy at Silverstone, and again it retired, this time with a sheered magneto drive. The cars non-started at Monaco because of a problem with the inlet valves which were distorting. As a result the cars did not race again until the British Grand Prix where Hawthorn took the lead at the start, but dropped back rapidly only to retire with oil leaking out of the final drive. Brooks ran well until a throttle connection broke which was 'repaired' in the pits, but after he had rejoined the race the throttle jammed open at Abbey Curve, the car went end over end and threw out the driver. The car was completely burnt out in the ensuing fire and Brooks was lucky to escape with burns and facial injuries. By this time both Hawthorn and Brooks had lost all confidence in BRM and neither was prepared to drive the car again. The Bourne team consequently withdrew from racing until 1957.

Against his better judgement and mainly because of the financial rewards offered, Roy Salvadori joined BRM for 1957 and was partnered by Ron Flockhart, who had been with BRM since 1954, but mainly as a test driver with his only racing miles with the P25 amounting to

The burnt-out wreck of Tony Brooks's P25 in the 1956 British Grand Prix. Brooks suffered burns and a broken jaw and would never again drive the P25. (T.C. March)

two laps in the 1956 British Grand Prix before retiring with slipped timing gears. In an effort to cure the braking problems, BRM had adopted Lockheed disc brakes and the bodywork now had the sides built up to shoulder height with aluminium skins.

At Goodwood on Easter Monday Salvadori spun both on the warming-up lap and during the race, a problem caused by locking brakes, while seized rear suspension caused Flockhart to spin, but he did manager to take third place. Apart from the brake problems, the handling of the cars was still appalling, so Mays sought the advice of Colin Chapman of Lotus. On Chapman's recommendation coil springs were fitted at the rear and the axle was henceforth located by a Watts linkage and these modifications were made in time for the Monaco race. However, the cars were still plagued with locking brakes and now Salvadori had lost all confidence, believing that the brakes were locking on when they were not, and he failed to qualify as a starter. The final straw came in a conversation between Salvadori and the Lockheed representative when that company's technician informed him that the team had been tampering with the brakes, rather than leaving them for the Lockheed experts to deal with. For Salvadori it was the final straw and he decided to leave the team. Flockhart stayed — he seemed completely inured to the incompetence of BRM and started the race only to retire with stripped timing gears.

BRM then pulled out of racing until the French Grand Prix, by which time it thought that it had resolved the brake trouble, and coil springs were now fitted at the front. Flockhart was badly injured after sliding off the road on oil dropped by Salvadori's Vanwall and the young American driver, Herbert MacKay Fraser, who had been brought into the team, retired with a leaking rear universal joint. The following weekend MacKay Fraser was killed in the Formula 2 race at Reims and, with Flockhart injured, BRM was completely without drivers for the British Grand Prix. There were innumerable drivers who wanted to compete in Formula 1, but very few prepared to do so at the wheel of the BRM. Former Connaught drivers Jack Fairman and Les Leston agreed to drive the cars, but both trailed round at the tail of the field and retired with engine trouble.

Just when BRM's fortunes were at their lowest ebb, there came a ray of hope. At Aintree Raymond Mays and French driver Jean Behra discussed the BRM at length and Behra expressed a wish to drive in the Caen Grand Prix which was to be held the following weekend. An urgent entry was made and two cars, one as a spare, were dispatched to France. During the practice at Caen, the Maserati of Harry Schell, Behra's teammate at Maserati, broke its engine, so it was agreed that Schell should drive the spare car. In the absence of any serious opposition, Behra and Schell swapped the lead, Schell broke the lap record twice and after the very tired engine of Schell's car broke, Behra went on to score an easy win. It may not have been much, but at least the BRM P25 had now won a race.

In September BRM made three entries for Behra, Schell and Flockhart in the International Trophy at Silverstone, a race postponed from its usual May date because of the petrol rationing following the Suez crisis. Apart from Brabham's 1.96-litre Cooper there were no other works entries at Silverstone (although Walker had also entered his 1.96-litre car for Brooks) and BRM took the first three places. It was another trivial success, but it led to suggestions that there should be a match race between Vanwall and BRM. In response to a telephone call from Gregor Grant, Editor of *Autosport*, Tony Vandervell rejected the idea out of hand, stating quite firmly that the whole purpose of building and racing the Vanwalls was to compete with the red cars of Italy and that if BRM was seriously to challenge the Vanwalls, every opportunity existed in Grand Prix racing. He added, 'I can assure BRM that they will get all the competition they want from those same red cars'. Before the end of the year BRM competed in the Modena Grand Prix, where both cars retired, and in the Moroccan Grand Prix at Casablanca where Maurice Trintignant took a very encouraging third place.

For 1958, the P25s were refined by the development of new multi-tubular chassis with detachable body panels and with modified front suspension to improve handling and braking. In line with international

In the absence of serious competition, BRM took the first three places in the 1957 International Trophy at Silverstone, postponed that year until September because of the fuel crisis following Suez. Here is the winner, Jean Behra. (T.C. March)

By 1958 the BRMs were beginning to find reliability. This is Harry Schell in the British Grand Prix in which he finished fourth. (T.C. March)

regulations, the engines had to be converted to run on Av-gas and in this form power output eventually reached 272 bhp at 8,500 rpm. Now that Maserati had withdrawn from Grand Prix racing, BRM was able to sign up both Jean Behra and Harry Schell. Although both drivers tried desperately hard to achieve success, the team was still plagued by ill-luck and incompetence. In the Richmond Trophy race at the Easter Goodwood meeting, Behra's car lost its brakes when a servo piston caused them to jam off and he ploughed straight into the chicane, wrecking the front of the car. Schell's car retired in the pits with the brakes jammed on and then caught fire from oil dripping out of the overheated gearbox. This is what might be described as the middle phase of BRM brake problems — there were many more failures to come in the future and it was miraculous that BRM never killed one of its drivers. Behra led the International Trophy at Silverstone, but his goggles were shattered by a stone and after a pit stop to have fragments of glass removed from his eye, he rejoined the race to finish fourth. Most of BRM's finishes during the year were in fourth, fifth or sixth places, not particularly encouraging, but in the Dutch Grand Prix at Zandvoort early in the season, a circuit on which the cars seemed to go remarkably well, Schell and Behra took second and third places behind Moss's Vanwall.

Further improvements were made to the cars for 1959, including a body of reduced frontal area, the oil overheating problem which had caused a number of retirements during 1958 was cured and the team reverted to Dunlop disc brakes. Now that Vanwall had retired from serious racing, it could and should have been a very successful year for BRM. However, it was now the era of the Cooper and the rear-engined car. Jean Behra had left to join Ferrari, whilst Schell and Flockhart remained with the team and were joined by Joakim Bonnier. Stirling

Moss agreed to drive a works BRM in the International Trophy at Silverstone, but was yet another victim of BRM's brake traumas and had a narrow escape when a broken pipe caused complete brake failure. Moss was convinced that the real problem with the BRM was poor preparation and he came to an arrangement with Alfred Owen of the Owen Racing Organisation whereby a car would be loaned to the British Racing Partnership, the team run by his father Alfred Moss and his manager Ken Gregory. This was painted in BRP's rather unpleasant pale green colour finish. It was a slap in the face for Raymond Mays who had naturally urged Owen not to agree to this arrangement, for if the world's greatest driver failed to achieve anything with the BRM, then clearly it was the BRM at fault, and if he did well with the car, then clearly BRM's own standards of preparation would be shown to be totally inadequate.

Once again the cars went magnificently at Zandvoort. In practice for the Dutch Grand Prix, Bonnier was equal fastest with Jack Brabham (Cooper) and throughout the race struggled with the Cooper opposition, never falling below second place and eventually scoring BRM's first Grande Épreuve victory, 14 seconds ahead of Brabham. Although it was a marvellous win for the team, it hardly vindicated all the wasted years that BRM had spent in Formula 1 and the marque still lacked credibility.

During the remainder of the year it was back to the old level, with the works drivers retiring or finishing fourth, fifth, sixth or seventh. The fortunes of the BRP-entered car were rather different. Moss had the choice of the BRM or his Rob Walker-entered Cooper and drove the BRM in just two races. At Reims he spun on wet tar and was unable to restart, but he took a very encouraging second place in the British Grand Prix at Aintree. The German Grand Prix was held on the banked Avus circuit in Berlin and here the BRP car was driven by Hans Herrmann, one-time Mercedes team-member. A brake pipe failed as Herrmann was slowing down for the south corner. The car rolled end over

In 1959 the British Racing Partnership arranged with Alfred Owen to race a car in its pale green colour. Here is Stirling Moss on his way to second place in the British Grand Prix at Aintree. The car was written off with Hans Herrmann at the wheel in the German Grand Prix at Avus.

end, throwing the driver out and allowed photographers to take some of the most dramatic motor racing pictures of all time. The BRM was a complete write-off, but fortunately Herrmann escaped serious injury.

BRM had read the writing on the wall and by the Italian Grand Prix the new BRM P48 appeared in practice. The fortunes of this rear-engined car will be discussed in greater detail in Chapter 6.

Vanwall

Tony Vandervell, founder and owner of Vandervell Products, manufacturers of the famous Thin Wall-type bearings, had been a long-time devotee of motor racing. In early post-war days he had enthusiastically supported the BRM project and had acquired a V-12 Ferrari to race against it, hoping that it would prove a spur to development and progress for the engineers at Bourne. In all, Vandervell imported four Ferraris, but by the time he was racing the last of these, in 1953-54, he had long since severed his relations with BRM, thoroughly sick of that organization's inefficiency and ineptitude. The last of the Thin Wall Specials, as Vandervell's Ferraris were known, was a potent 4.5-litre unsupercharged V-12 car, much modified, which dominated Formule Libre races in Britain. It was driven by a host of famous drivers, for Vandervell was always prepared to pay for the best talent, but its most stirring drives came in 1954 when young Peter Collins was at the wheel.

By this time Vandervell's own Vanwall project was well advanced. Norton development engineer, Leo Kuzmicki, had suggested to Vandervell that his new car should be powered by a four-cylinder engine, which would consist in effect of four Norton twin-cam single-cylinder Manx racing engines on a common crankcase. This layout was developed by Vandervell and was used with an aluminium version of the Rolls-Royce B40 crankcase with a separate cylinder head based on Norton valve design. In its original form the Vanwall Special, as the

The Guv'nor, Tony Vandervell, with Giuseppe Farina at the wheel of the Ferrari 'Thin Wall Special' in 1952. (Guy Griffiths)

car was known, had a capacity of 1998cc (85.93 × 86mm) and power output was as high as 235 bhp at 7,500 rpm. Vandervell contracted with Cooper Cars of Surbiton to build him a chassis, following more or less standard Ferrari practice, ie a tubular ladder-type frame, and with Ferrari suspension components. When it was first raced, the most striking feature of the car was the external surface radiator of Clayton-Still 'wire-wound' tubing mounted across the nose. Obviously Vandervell had been hoping that the car would be ready to race during 1953, the last year of the 2000cc Formula 2, but it could not be ready in time. When it first appeared in 1954, it was already obsolescent.

Both the Vanwall and the Thin Wall Special were entered by Tony Vandervell for Alberto Ascari, the 1953 World Champion, to drive at the Easter Goodwood meeting. A mere six days before the race, Ascari telegraphed Vandervell to say that he had to withdraw because Lancia, to whom he was contracted, needed him to drive in the Mille Miglia sports car race. The cars were therefore withdrawn from the Goodwood race meeting, but the organizers, the BARC, did not announce the withdrawal hoping that Ascari would change his mind and attend the meeting. The result was a lot of unnecessary ill-feeling and disappointment for spectators.

In the meanwhile, testing of the car had continued, and in the absence of any other driver available, Tony Vandervell had used Alan Brown, a well-known Formula 2 Cooper-Bristol and Formula 3 Cooper 500cc driver, but no Formula 1 ace. When the car was first ready to race in the International Trophy at Silverstone in May, Vandervell still had no team driver, so the drive was again offered to Alan Brown. Brown drove steadily in appallingly wet weather conditions in the first heat to finish sixth and became the first Formula 2 car home. In the final, however, he retired because of a broken oil pipe.

For Vandervell this was nevertheless a most encouraging start and the pace of development work at Vandervell's factory at Park Royal was speeded up. Peter Collins was now signed to drive the car on a regular

Although of 2-litre capacity, the 'Vanwall Special' did not make its debut until the International Trophy at Silverstone in May 1954. It was distinguished by an external tubular radiator. Driven by Alan Brown, it retired because of a broken oil pipe. (T.C. March)

basis. The next appearance of the Vanwall Special was at the British Grand Prix at Silverstone in July 1954. By then the capacity of the engine had been increased to 2236cc and it had an aluminium duct over the external radiator. Starting from the third row of the grid, having turned in a very competitive practice time, Collins ran well for 17 laps until a cylinder head joint developed a leak. By the Italian Grand Prix Vanwall had ready a full 2490cc (96 × 86mm) engine and it was intended to race this. However, during test running prior to the race, the engine broke a valve which caused extensive damage. This meant that Collins had to drive the car with the 2.3-litre engine. The external radiator had now been replaced by a conventional radiator, based on a standard Morris Oxford unit. Collins, driving with considerable verve, was holding fifth place in the race, but was forced to make a pit stop with a broken pipe to the oil pressure gauge. The pipe was sealed and he rejoined the race to finish seventh. It was still an encouraging result.

Tony Vandervell was very anxious to persuade Mike Hawthorn to join the team and as Enzo Ferrari was prepared to release him from his Ferrari contract for this meeting, Vandervell made entries for both Hawthorn and Collins at the September Goodwood meeting. In the Formula 1 race Collins drove the Vanwall Special and finished second to Moss with his Maserati. Collins won the Formule Libre race with the Thin Wall Special whilst Hawthorn drove the Vanwall Special into third place behind Moss with his private Maserati. The team then contested the autumn meeting at Aintree and here Hawthorn drove the Vanwall Special in both the Formula 1 and Formule Libre races. In the former Hawthorn finished second, again to Moss with his Maserati, and in the Formule Libre event, after Collins had retired the Thin Wall and the V-16 BRMs had run into brake problems, Hawthorn was again in second place, but locked up his brakes and spun on to the grass. With the radiator intake blocked by mud and grass and the car beginning to overheat, Mike had no alternative but to retire. The final race for the team that year was to be the Spanish Grand Prix on the Pedralbes circuit at Barcelona. During practice all three British drivers, Moss, Hawthorn and Collins, crashed, and Collins' accident with the Van-

By the 1954 British Grand Prix at Silverstone, the capacity of the Vanwall had been increased from 1988cc to 2236cc and there was a shield over the tubular radiator. Now the car was driven by Peter Collins, and it is seen here on the starting grid before the race. (T.C. March)

The external radiator had been abandoned by the Italian Grand Prix where Peter Collins, delayed by a broken pipe to the oil pressure gauge, drove a fine race to be classified seventh. (LAT)

wall caused such extensive damage to the tail of the car that it could not be repaired in time to start the race.

Although Vandervell had entered the new Formula with a car of only 2000cc, development had been rapid and by the end of the 1954 season the Vanwall's potential was only too obvious. There was still a very long way to go before the car could be regarded as a race-winner, but certainly Vandervell's ideas were working out well. He had high hopes of signing up both Hawthorn and Collins for 1955 for his new two-car team. Mike was quick to join the team; following the death of his father in a road accident, and the need to devote more time to the family garage business at Farnham, he welcomed the opportunity of spending longer periods in England than was possible with Ferrari. For some totally obscure reason, and quite out of character, Peter Collins procrastinated in making a decision, and in fact continued negotiations with Vandervell even after he had signed up to drive the new BRM. He was usually a remarkably open and straight person in his dealings and the reasons for his odd behaviour on this occasion are difficult to comprehend. By the time Collins had given Vandervell a negative decision, it was rather late in the day to contract another suitable driver, but Vandervell was able to sign Ken Wharton, a very competent all-rounder who had been successful not only with single-seaters and sports cars but also in trials and rallies. In addition the team was joined by David Yorke as team manager.

From now onwards the cars were known simply as Vanwalls and there were a number of major changes. The most significant was the adoption of Bosch fuel injection with the injectors feeding into the inlet ports and the Amal motorcycle carburettor bodies retained to provide the throttle slides and inlet bell mouths. One of the major weaknesses of the Vanwall Special in 1954 had been the roadholding which was not really up to the power offered by the Vanwall's engine. Unfortunately very little development had been made in that direction and this remained the weakest area of the car in 1955.

It would have been a miracle if Vanwall had achieved anything significant in Championship races in 1955, especially at a time when Mercedes-Benz was so dominant, but the team should have done reasonably in lesser events where the opposition was limited to Ferrari and Maserati, which were not at their best. The season started with the International Trophy race at Silverstone where two cars were entered for Hawthorn and Wharton. It proved a complete disaster. Hawthorn's car retired after only 15 laps when an oil leak developed in the gearbox, spreading oil over his legs and the rear brakes. Wharton made a pit stop early in the race because of throttle linkage problems and after work in the pits to ensure that the throttle opened properly, he rejoined the race with a view to turning in one or two fast laps. Unfortunately, at Copse he was forced off-line by another car, mounted the grass, hit a marker drum and the car crashed, bursting into flames and leaving a trail of blazing fuel along the track. Wharton was badly burned and the car was severely damaged. After this race, of the two then competing British marques, Connaught and Vanwall, the Connaught team, who had entered two of its streamlined cars at Silverstone, looked by far the better bet for the future. Although both had retired, they had run well in the early stages of the race and were only eliminated by minor troubles.

Next came the Monaco Grand Prix where there was now only a single car for Mike Hawthorn. Once again the Vanwall failed to shine and was eliminated when the linkage between the throttles and the fuel injection pump failed. The team next appeared in the Belgian Grand Prix, with once again a single car for Hawthorn. During practice Tony Vandervell decided to drive the car from the garage to the circuit, but cooked the clutch and spoilt the final practice session for Hawthorn; the mechanics had to work overnight to fit the new clutch. Early in the race Hawthorn retired the Vanwall with an oil leak from the gearbox.

By this stage Hawthorn was thoroughly disillusioned with the team, perhaps a little unfairly, and he had received an invitation to return to Ferrari. The contract between Vandervell and Hawthorn was terminated, fairly amicably, for Hawthorn was again to drive a Vanwall on

Mike Hawthorn with the Vanwall was in fourth place in the International Trophy at Silverstone in May 1955 when he was forced to retire because of a gearbox oil leak that spread all over his legs and the car's rear brakes. (T.C. March)

'B. Bira' (Maserati) passes the wreck of Wharton's burning Vanwall at Silverstone in May 1955.

one more occasion. Now Vandervell faced a really serious driver problem. The team missed the Dutch Grand Prix, the French Grand Prix was cancelled, and the team next appeared in the British race at Aintree where Ken Wharton was now fit enough to drive and Harry Schell had joined the team. It has often been written that Schell was not really a top-flight driver who was likely to win races. Certainly he was not World Championship material and in fact he never did win a Grand Prix, but he was always at the forefront of racing, be it during his time at Vanwall or at the wheel of Maseratis or Ferraris. In an ideal world he would have been number two in the Vanwall team to a driver of the calibre of Moss or Fangio. Schell stalled his engine at the start, but fearlessly fought his way through the field, only to have the throttle pedal break off its mounting. Wharton had driven a very quiet race but had been forced to stop at the pits because of a fractured oil pipe. Schell took over his car and it was still running at the finish, albeit in ninth place. Because of the cancellation of races following the Le Mans disaster, there was only one more round in the Championship, the Italian Grand Prix in September, so Vandervell was forced to run the cars in minor British Formula 1 races. At the Crystal Palace on August Bank Holiday Monday, Schell won his heat in the short Formula 1 race and finished second to Mike Hawthorn, at the wheel of Stirling Moss's Maserati, in the final. Shortly afterwards Schell and Wharton took the first two places in the Formula 1 event at Snetterton, ahead of Moss with his Maserati, but Moss was not at all well that day. Schell retired in the Formule Libre race the same day because of a leaking fuel tank.

Both cars ran well in practice for the Italian Grand Prix, but both were early retirements. Wharton was eliminated by the fracture of the bracket supporting the fuel injection pump and Schell was eliminated by a broken de Dion tube, a result of the bumpy banking used at Monza

A fine shot of Harry Schell at the wheel of the Vanwall at the 1955 British Grand Prix. (T.C. March)

in 1955. There were two more British events before the end of the season. In the Gold Cup race at Oulton Park the cars were driven by Schell and Desmond Titterington (an up and coming young driver who replaced Wharton, injured in the Tourist Trophy sports car race at Dundrod). Schell retired because of drive-shaft trouble, but Titterington drove a very fine race to finish third behind Moss (Maserati) and Hawthorn (Lancia D50). The final race of the season was at Castle Combe in Wiltshire where the sole driver was Harry Schell who won both the Formula 1 and Formule Libre races.

By 1956 the Vanwall had been completely transformed. Colin Chapman, already renowned for his Lotus sports car designs, agreed to design a new multi-tubular space-frame chassis, incorporating the existing engine, transmission and front suspension, but with a completely new de Dion rear axle located by a Watts linkage. Frank Costin evolved a completely new body with a long penetrating nose, high tail and superb aerodynamics, including full aerodynamic under-shielding and with the exhaust recessed into the body to reduce drag. A one-piece wrap-around perspex windscreen enclosed the cockpit and all the panels were held in place by flush-fitting Dzus fasteners. Steady development work on the engine, with Harry Weslake collaborating with Leo Kuzmicki, resulted in a substantial increase in power and the five-speed gearbox now incorporated Porsche synchromesh. However, Vandervell still faced two major hurdles; only the racing season would prove whether the cars had the reliability to match their undoubted performance and sophistication, and the team was still unable to attract top-line drivers. Tony Vandervell had hoped for Stirling Moss, but had to settle for Harry Schell and Maurice Trintignant.

Although Moss had refused to join the Vanwall team, returning to Maserati instead, when Modena did not enter the International Trophy at Silverstone he agreed to drive a car, and ran away from the Lancia-Ferrari opposition to score a fine victory. The race was not over a full Grand Prix distance, but it certainly was yet another good pointer to the future. Schell retired because of a cracked fuel injector pipe.

Unfortunately the Championship races did not bring the team anything in the way of success. At Monaco, Trintignant crumpled the nose of his car against another driver's rear wheel and was forced to retire

Harry Schell with his Vanwall in the 1956 Silverstone International Trophy. (T.C. March)

In the 1956 Belgian Grand Prix Harry Schell, with the almost completely redesigned Vanwall, chases Pilette's Lancia-Ferrari into the Mirabeau. He finished fourth behind two of the Lancia-Ferraris and Moss's Maserati. (LAT)

due to overheating. As for Schell, early in the race he spun while avoiding another car and hit a wall, badly damaging the front of the car. Next came the Belgian Grand Prix at Spa-Francorchamps, where Schell drove a very encouraging race, demonstrating that the Vanwall had the speed to match the continental opposition, although its road-holding was still not in the same league on the fast bends that characterized the Ardennes circuit. He finished in fourth place, behind two Lancia-Ferraris and a Maserati, and only nine miles behind the winner in this 315-mile race. Trintignant again retired early in the race, because of mixture problems resulting from fuel injection trouble.

It had been agreed that Trintignant would be released from the team at Reims so that he could drive the new Bugatti 251 on its début. Originally Vanwall planned to run three cars, for Schell, Farina and Colin Chapman of Lotus — Allowing Chapman to have a drive in the car that he had helped to create could well lead to some sensible design suggestions and development improvements for the near future. Unfortunately Farina was injured in a sports car race, but his place was taken

by Mike Hawthorn, because mechanical problems had caused BRM to miss the French Grand Prix. Poor Chapman was not able to start the race, for brake trouble during the second day's practice had caused him to run into the back of Hawthorn's car and the British designer's Vanwall could not be repaired in time for the race. Hawthorn showed no real form in the race, having just finished competing in the previous night's 12 Hours sports car race as a member of the winning Jaguar team, so when Harry's Schell's car ran into gearbox problems, he took over from Mike.

Schell turned in a magnificent performance, rapidly climbing through the field and hounding the leading trio of Lancia-Ferraris which were forced to line up near enough abreast on the straight to prevent him overtaking into the lead. After many laps of this fantastically close battle, Schell dropped back because of problems with the fuel injection pump. Once this had been repaired, he rejoined the race but was now way down the field and finished tenth. What Schell had displayed was not only the fact that he was a much faster and braver driver than many of his contemporaries would admit, but that the Vanwall had the potential speed to beat the Italian cars, although the team was still a long way away from finding the necessary reliability.

In contrast, the British Grand Prix proved something of a débâcle. Again Vandervell entered three cars, for Froilan Gonzalez, who had flown specially from the Argentine, Schell and Trintignant. None of the Vanwall drivers was impressive in practice and Gonzalez's race stopped at the fall of the Union Jack; a universal joint in a rear drive-shaft broke and the Vanwall just lurched forward a few inches. After a pit stop by Schell for a rear shock absorber to be replaced, both he and Trintignant were eliminated by fuel starvation problems caused by the silicate sealing of the joints in the fuel tank dissolving and clogging the fuel filtering system. Vanwall was not ready to run in the German Grand Prix at the beginning of August and there remained only one race in the Championship series, the Italian Grand Prix on the combined road and banked circuit at Monza in September. Once again three cars were entered for Taruffi, Schell and Trintignant. Both Trintignant and Taruffi retired early in the race, the former because of a broken mounting for a coil spring in the front suspension and the latter because of a gearbox oil leak. For many laps Schell held a brilliant second place, the Vanwall looking dangerously unsafe as it jumped and cavorted over the bumpy banking of the circuit. Hot oil began to leak from the gearbox over Schell's legs, but the Franco-American kept plugging away until the gearbox finally seized and he was forced to walk back to the pits, soaked in hot oil.

Vanwall had reached the point where it was so very close to a breakthrough to real success. A number of changes were made to the cars for 1957, including the adoption of coil springs at the rear in place of the original transverse leaf spring, and constant development work resulted in the power output rising to 285 bhp at 7,300 rpm. Stirling Moss agreed to join the team and he was backed up by Tony Brooks

whose brilliance had been undiminished by his miserable season with BRM in 1956. What was so very sad and rather heartless was that Vandervell had obstinately decided upon an all-British team and refused to renew Harry Schell's contract.

The 1957 season was to see a momentous struggle for supremacy between Maserati and Vanwall, with Vanwall eventually coming out on top, Vandervell fulfulling his great ambition of beating 'those bloody red cars' and the Lancia-Ferraris largely relegated to the role of also-rans. Vanwall decided to contest the Syracuse Grand Prix in April, primarily because the only British race before the main Championship series started in Europe was the Easter Goodwood meeting (the International Meeting at Silverstone was postponed to September following the Suez crisis). In the opening laps of the race Moss and Brooks led from the Ferrari and Maserati opposition, but on Moss's car the high-pressure pipe between the Bosch injection pump and the cylinder injector nozzle broke; after this had been replaced in the pits, Moss rejoined the race in a desperate effort to make up lost ground, setting a new lap record and eventually finishing third behind two Lancia-Ferraris. Brooks was eliminated by a split water pipe; water leaked over the sparking plugs causing a misfire and the water loss in turn caused engine overheating and cracked the cylinder head. Moss and Brooks appeared again at the Easter Goodwood meeting but both drivers suffered broken throttle linkages which resulted in Moss retiring and Brooks finishing sixth after setting a new lap record.

By the Monaco race in May, the problem of the breakage of the pressure pipes in the fuel injection system had been solved by the adoption of Palmer 'Silvoflex' high-pressure flexible rubber fuel pipes. For Monaco the cars were fitted with lower power output engines (275 bhp) to give better torque and wider power spread to suit this slow circuit and both were fitted with truncated nose cowlings to prevent a recurrence of the minor damage that had caused overheating in 1956. In the opening laps Moss led from the Lancia-Ferraris of Collins and Hawthorn, but on lap 4 Moss went straight into the barriers at the chicane, an accident which he has always blamed on brake failure. Collins hit another barrier, but Fangio and Brooks avoided the accident, manoeuvring through the poles scattered across the road at a crawl, whilst Hawthorn hit one of the rear wheels of the Vanwall and collided with the Lancia-Ferrari of Collins. Fangio went on to win the race, unchallenged by Brooks who had wisely decided to settle for second place, having lost the clutch on his Vanwall. He drove the remainder of the long race making clutchless gear changes and finished the race with a severely bruised left hand.

Because of the cancellation of the Dutch and Belgian Grands Prix, the next race was the French Grand Prix held in 1957 on the Circuit des Essarts at Rouen. Vanwall found itself in serious driver trouble because Brooks had suffered bad injuries in a crash at Le Mans and Moss was unable to drive because of sinus trouble. Already Vandervell had arranged for Roy Salvadori to drive one car and now, with Moss out of action, Stuart Lewis-Evans, who had driven a works Connaught with considerable success, was brought into the team. Neither Van-

After the pile-up which eliminated Moss's Vanwall and the Lancia-Ferraris of Collins and Hawthorn, Brooks brought this Vanwall across the line in second place behind Fangio's Maserati at Monaco in 1957. For this 'round the houses' race, the Vanwalls were fitted with short noses, protected by nudge bars.

wall ran particularly well, mainly because the drivers were too unfamiliar with them to get the best from them; Salvadori retired because of broken valve springs, whilst Lewis-Evans was eliminated by a very odd problem. As the race progressed, so he found the steering of his car getting heavier and heavier; when he pulled into the pits the trouble was diagnosed as a cracked cylinder head which was causing the engine compression to pressurize the water system which in turn resulted in the expansion of the scuttle-mounted header tank so that it pressed up against the steering column.

The following weekend at Reims the Vanwall team produced the superb-looking streamlined car evolved by Frank Costin. Without Moss to drive it, there was no prospect of it showing good form and although Lewis-Evans tried it in practice at Reims, it was not raced and failed to appear again. Lewis-Evans made a remarkably good start and led the race, driving with a calm and relaxed style until he started to slow after 20 laps because of oil from the engine breather working its way into the cockpit and over his goggles and gloves. He eventually finished third with Salvadori in fifth place.

Barely a week later the European Grand Prix was held at Aintree, and whilst both Moss and Brooks were back in the team, the latter still far from fit, a third car was now entered for Lewis-Evans whose two performances in France had so impressed Tony Vandervell. Moss was fastest in practice, quickly took the lead from Behra who had led away from the flag, and steadily built up a lead. By lap 20 Moss had a lead of nearly 10 seconds, but as he came past the pits a very slight misfire could be heard from the Vanwall's engine. This misfire became progressively worse and Moss was obliged to make a pit stop, losing the lead to Behra. He rejoined the race in seventh place, stopped again at the pits next time round, and Brooks, still far from fit and trailing well down the field, was called in for the team leader to take over. As the race progressed so Moss clawed his way up the field, whilst Lewis-Evans was also gaining ground on the Ferraris. Fangio was off-form — as was his car — and retired his Maserati without ever challenging for the lead. Moss rose to third place behind Behra and Hawthorn, but with a little over 20 laps to go there seemed very little possibility that he would be able to catch the two red cars in front. For once, however, there was a switch of fortune in Vanwall's favour, for Behra was unexpectedly eliminated when his Maserati's clutch disintegrated and Hawthorn's Lancia-Ferrari punctured a tyre on debris from the 250F. Now the Vanwalls were in first and second places, but it was not to last long, for after only another two laps Lewis-Evans stopped out on the course because of throttle linkage problems, that recurring Vanwall shortcoming. Moss, having time to make a precautionary refuelling stop, won the race comfortably from Musso's Lancia-Ferrari. Lewis-Evans, having made a bodged repair followed by a pit stop for proper attention to the throttle linkage, rejoined the race to finish seventh, but was subsequently disqualified for completing the race without the bonnet in place.

This page and opposite
Vanwall's breakthrough
finally came in the 1957
British Grand Prix at
Aintree (given the title
European Grand Prix that
year). After his own car
had failed, Moss took over
from Tony Brooks,
gradually working his way
through the field and
benefiting from
retirements to take the
lead. In the closing laps of
the race he made a
precautionary refuelling
stop. Moss, not without a
little difficulty, climbs out
of the high-sided cockpit
of the Vanwall, while Len
Butler places the funnel in
the tank. Then, while
Moss supervises, Tony
Brooks offers him a
'Coke'. Behind the nose of
the car are G.A.V. and
John Eason Gibson of the
RAC. Refuelling almost
completed, Moss prepares
to climb back in, and goes
on to take the chequered
flag to score Britain's first
Grand Epreuve victory
since Segrave's win in the
1923 French race.

It had been a long uphill struggle for Vandervell and his team, but he had finally beaten the Italians, and now the challenge was to maintain the superiority. Even before the Vanwall team left Park Royal for the German Grand Prix at the Nürburgring, held a fortnight later, it knew that its prospects of success were slim. The team had never raced at Nürburgring before and had no experience of how to set the cars up for this difficult mountainous circuit's bumps and turns. As it was, Fangio drove a masterly race to win from the Lancia-Ferraris of Hawthorn, Collins and Musso. Moss with the leading Vanwall could do no better than take fifth place, while Brooks was right back in ninth place, having been physically sick in the cockpit. Lewis-Evans was also sick and retired when he spun on oil from the gearbox breather blowing on to his rear tyres.

Because of the cancellation of two Championship rounds earlier in the season, the Pescara Grand Prix was included in that one year as a Championship race and Vanwall entered three cars for Moss, Brooks and Lewis-Evans. The Ferrari challenge was limited to a single car for Musso, as Enzo Ferrari was still writhing under criticism of the tyres used on his cars following de Portago's fatal crash in the Mille Miglia, but there was a full team of four Maseratis. That Vanwall now had the upper edge was clear, for Moss took the lead on the second lap and went on convincingly to win this 289-mile race from the Maseratis of Fangio and Schell. Lewis-Evans finished fifth, but Brooks retired on the first lap because of engine problems.

Next came the Italian Grand Prix, the most crucial event so far as Vandervell was concerned, for it gave him the chance to beat the Italians on home territory. In practice Moss tried his Vanwall with a perspex cockpit cover but this was soon abandoned because of the noise level. The Lancia-Ferraris lacked the speed to challenge Maserati and Vanwall, but the Modena and Park Royal teams scrapped furiously. Both Brooks and Lewis-Evans ran into mechanical problems, the former much delayed by throttle linkage problems and eventually finishing eighth, whilst Lewis-Evans was eliminated by a leaking cylinder head core plug.

The start of the 1957 Italian Grand Prix with Moss leading away from Luigi Musso (Lancia-Ferrari), Jean Behra (Maserati V-12), Lewis-Evans and Brooks.

Moss, however, won the race by a margin of over 40 seconds from Fangio's Maserati with the Lancia-Ferrari of von Trips in third place. In addition, Brooks set a new lap record of 124.04 mph. In the World Championship Moss took second place with 25 points to the 40 of Fangio. There was one minor race for the Vanwall team before the end of the year, the Moroccan Grand Prix at Ain-Diab set out in the sandy wastes near the capital of Morocco. It was an advance event for the holding of a World Championship race there in 1958 and one that Vandervell had to compete in. Moss was unable to take part in the race because of influenza; whilst Brooks retired because of magneto trouble, Lewis-Evans finished second to Behra's Maserati. It was something of a disappointment after those three magnificent wins, but it was not in itself a race of great importance.

The biggest problem for Vanwall in 1958 was the ruling of the Fédération Internationale de l'Automobile that all cars should use Av-gas aviation fuel of 100/130-octane rating. The reason for the ruling was that the oil companies, who gave so much support to motor racing, felt that they were getting insufficient benefit because the cars were running on special brews not normally available. The suggestion that the cars should run on straight pump petrol was unacceptable to all the entrants, and the choice of Av-gas was merely a compromise. The development of the cars to run on the new fuel was a long and slow process, causing Vanwall to miss the first round of the 1958 World Championship, the Argentine Grand Prix. A number of other changes were made to the cars, including the lightening of chassis components and the reprofiling of the tail of the cars by Frank Costin. Moss, Brooks and Lewis-Evans all remained with the team.

For financial reasons Maserati had now withdrawn from racing, but Ferrari had bounced back in strength with the new Dino V-6 cars which had appeared with smaller than 2500cc engines at Modena and subsequently at Casablanca with one car having a full capacity 2417cc (85 × 71mm) engine. The V-6 car, largely the work of Vittorio Jano and developed from the Scuderia's very promising Formula 2 car, had the six cylinders in a 65° V formation with twin overhead camshafts per bank of cylinders chain-driven from the nose of the crankshaft. As raced in 1958, the Dino's power output was 275 bhp at 8,300 rpm. This engine was used in conjunction with a four-speed and reverse gearbox mounted on the right-hand side of the differential assembly and in unit with it. The gear-change without gate was on the right-hand side of the cockpit. The chassis featured large diameter tubular lower members with a smaller diameter tubular superstructure. At the front, suspension was by unequal length wishbones, coil springs and Houdaille vane-type dampers and anti-roll bar. At the rear there was a de Dion axle with the tube running behind the gearbox and located by a central sliding guide on the tube centre-line, with location by two forward-facing radius arms from each end of the tube to the chassis frame, with the springing by a transverse leaf spring and, once again, Houdaille vane-type dampers. The Dinos were distinctively stumpy looking, with a perspex cover over the carburettor intakes replaced later in the season by a large metal scoop that emphasized the stumpiness of the lines and gave the impression of a very bulging bonnet. In 1958 the Ferrari team consisted of Mike Hawthorn, Peter Collins and Luigi Musso, together with Phil Hill and Wolfgang von Trips.

The year 1958 was to witness a season-long battle for supremacy in the World Championship between Mike Hawthorn with his Ferrari and Stirling Moss with the Vanwall, and although Moss was to score more outright wins than Hawthorn, he was to miss the World Championship by the narrowest of margins. There was, however, a wild card in the deck, in the shape of the Cooper-Climax. In the absence of Vanwall, Stirling Moss drove a 1.96-litre Cooper-Climax for Rob Walker in the Argentine Grand Prix and by dint of driving through patches of oil and onto the grass to conserve the tyres, Moss won the race from the Ferrari of Luigi Musso. It was to prove a very similar story at the Monaco Grand Prix. All three Vanwalls retired, as did many other faster cars, and in a race of attrition the victor was the Cooper-Climax of Maurice Trintignant, again entered by Rob Walker.

By the Dutch Grand Prix at Zandvoort the Vanwall team was back in its stride again; Stirling Moss led throughout and set a new lap record. At this race his car was fitted with what was to become the standard 'wear', Borrani wire wheels at the front and the new light alloy 'wobbly web' wheels at the rear. Both Brooks and Lewis-Evans retired. Another victory followed in the Belgian race at Spa-Francorchamps. Although Moss set the pace, and showed all signs of dominating the race, he

The beautifully constructed centre-lock Borrani wire wheel of the 1958 Vanwall.

This view of the engine of the 1958 car shows clearly the air throttles, the Bosch fuel injection pump together with the Palmer Silvoflex high-pressure injection piping and Silvoflex throttle control rod which were adopted after problems early in 1957.

missed a gear-change at high revs, pistons and valve heads touched and the car was out of the race with bent valve heads. However, this was a circuit on which Tony Brooks always starred, revelling in the fast swoops and curves, and he came through to score a fine victory, despite signs of a seizing gearbox in the last few laps which allowed Hawthorn's Ferrari to close. Just as the Ferrari crossed the finishing line the engine blew up and the other Vanwall of Lewis-Evans, which took third place, finished with a broken front wishbone, the result of

Above The start of the 1958 British Grand Prix with Moss (who retired with engine problems) leading away from Peter Collins (No 1, Ferrari, the race winner), Harry Schell (No 20, BRM, who finished fifth), Mike Hawthorn (No 2, Ferrari, who took second place) and, on the outside, Roy Salvadori (Cooper) who finished third.

Right Stuart Lewis-Evans on his way to fourth place in the 1958 British Grand Prix. Note the improved enclosure of the exhaust system on the 1958 cars and whilst there are still wire wheels at the front, there are 'wobbly web' alloy rear wheels. (T.C. March)

a minor collision with one of the Ferraris. Then the tide of fortune turned again. Mike Hawthorn won the French Grand Prix at Reims, repeating his victory of 1953, but the Ferrari team was sadly shattered by the death of Luigi Musso who crashed during the race. Next came the British Grand Prix at Silverstone where the Ferraris were dominant yet again, and Peter Collins and Mike Hawthorn took the first two places. Although Moss had managed to finish second in the French race, and he was fastest in practice at Silverstone, he made no impression on the leading Ferrari and retired with engine trouble. Lewis-Evans finished fourth and Brooks, who had been off-form throughout the race, was seventh and a lap in arrears.

Next came the German Grand Prix and the Vanwall team was now fully equipped to deal with the special problems of the Nürburgring. In practice Brooks and Moss were second and third fastest (only the two cars were entered in this race) and Moss led until he retired with magneto trouble on lap 4. Brooks then lay third behind the Ferraris of Hawthorn and Collins, but closed on them rapidly, taking the lead on lap 10. On only the following lap Collins crashed with fatal results, and shortly afterwards Hawthorn retired with clutch trouble. The Nürburgring was another circuit at which Brooks shone and he would probably have been leading the race from the start but for the fact that he naturally deferred to Moss as team leader. Moss also set a new lap record. With the disappearance of the Ferrari opposition, the Coopers of Salvadori and Trintignant took second and third places.

The balance of success in Vanwall's favour continued in the Portuguese Grand Prix at Oporto later in August where Moss took the lead from Hawthorn early in the race and built up a substantial advantage which he held to the finish, whilst Lewis-Evans took third place. Brooks retired after spinning and stalling his engine. Second place went to Mike Hawthorn with the Ferrari, but it was a rather controversial second place and one that was to have a momentous impact on that year's Drivers' World Championship. On the last lap of the race Hawthorn spun because of brake trouble and stalled. Because the circuit was uphill at this point, it was impossible for Hawthorn to push the car in the race direction, but encouraged by Moss, who stopped on his slowing-down lap, Hawthorn pushed the car along the pavement against the direction of the race until the engine fired and he could rejoin the circuit to take the chequered flag. After the race an enquiry was held as to whether Hawthorn should be disqualified for pushing his car against the direction of the race, and Moss was a key witness in giving evidence to the fact that Hawthorn had not pushed the car on the circuit, but on the pavement, and accordingly Hawthorn's second place was allowed to stand.

Next came the Italian Grand Prix at Monza where all three Vanwalls were on the front row of the grid, together with Hawthorn's Ferrari. Initially the Vanwalls led, but then Phil Hill's Ferrari went ahead until it threw a tread and Moss resumed the lead. Unfortunately he retired early in the race because of a seized gearbox and Lewis-Evans also retired because of overheating. Despite a short pit stop to check an oil leak, Brooks came through to take second place from Hill when the Ferrari driver stopped for a further tyre change. When Hawthorn's Ferrari began to run rough, Brooks closed on the Maranello car, taking the lead ten laps from the end and winning by 22 seconds.

There remained one only World Championship event that year, the Moroccan Grand Prix which would settle the Drivers' World Championship. The leader, Hawthorn, had gained 40 points from six races,

Stirling Moss leads away in the Moroccan Grand Prix, the last Championship race of 1958, from Phil Hill's Ferrari. Although Moss won the race and set fastest lap, he was pipped by Hawthorn for the World Championship by one point. (LAT)

the maximum number of races which could count towards the Championship. Moss had only finished in five races from which he had accumulated 32 points, so if he won (8 points) and also made fastest lap (1 point) he would then achieve a higher score than Hawthorn, unless Hawthorn finished second (6 points). However, if Hawthorn, whose six best performances out of the eight finishes that made up his score, gained more points in this event than one of those already counting in his score, this would be substituted and he would win the Championship. If Hawthorn failed to improve on his score and Moss won but failed to make fastest lap, they would be even on points whereupon a seventh event would be taken into consideration and Hawthorn would become Champion.

Moss drove one of the finest races of his career, leading from start to finish and also setting a new lap record. It was Vanwall's fourth successive win that year and also its sixth in 1958. However, it was simply not good enough, for Hawthorn finished second, but only because his team mate Phil Hill had allowed him to slip by into second place towards the end of the race. Any joy from Moss's victory and Vanwall's win in the Manufacturers' Championship (which had been inaugurated

Above *Although Vandervell withdrew from serious racing at the end of 1958, a small team still worked on the cars and Tony Brooks drove this lower, lighter car in the 1959 British Grand Prix, but retired early in the race because of an engine misfire.*

that year) was completely destroyed by Lewis-Evans's crash when the engine of his Vanwall seized, the car went off the road, tore its petrol tank against a tree and caught fire. Lewis-Evans received critical burns to which he succumbed six days after the race. Tony Vandervell was now 60 years old, the strain of building and developing his racing team

Right *Tony Brooks with a second lightweight Vanwall in the 1960 French Grand Prix at Reims. He retired early in the race with transmission trouble, probably caused by a start-line incident.*

Junk! The 1960 light-weight car and the 1957 streamlined body (above) and a great heap of components (below right) seen in the Western Avenue factory shortly before it was demolished for redevelopment and Vandervell Products moved to Maidenhead.

had proved immense and he was terribly distressed at Lewis-Evans's death. Reluctantly he decided to withdraw from serious motor racing. In fact the writing was in any event on the wall, for 1958 had seen two victories by the lightweight rear-engined Coopers, and whilst many people were not yet convinced that a rear-engined car was the way to

go, any future Vanwall Grand Prix car would have to be a complete redesign, substantially lighter than its 1957-58 predecessors.

In 1959 one of the 1958 team cars was rebuilt into a smaller and much more compact car and was driven by Tony Brooks in the British Grand Prix and Aintree. By this time the rear-engined Coopers were supreme and after a slow race Brooks retired with an engine misfire. The following year Vanwall tried again and both the 1959 car, VW5, and a new car, VW11, appeared in so-called low-line form with independent rear suspension by double wishbones designed by Colotti and with a Colotti five-speed gearbox mounted behind the rear axle. Again Brooks was the driver when the car appeared at the French Grand Prix but it retired early in the race with gearbox trouble, probably the result of a shunt on the start line. This was not quite the end of the Vanwall line because Vandervell also experimented with a car based on a rear-engined Lotus chassis powered by a Vanwall engine, and finally in 1961 there appeared a new rear-engined Vanwall with capacity increased to 2.6 litres and intended for the Inter-Continental Formula. John Surtees drove this car in the International Trophy race at Silverstone and after holding second place behind Brabham's Cooper, he spun and restarted to finish fifth. It was a sad note on which to end the racing career of the marque that had caused the vanquishment of Italian red and set on its way the dominance of British Racing Green.

5

Drivers

The Italians

In the early 1950s the outstanding motor racing figure was undoubtedly Alberto Ascari, himself the son of a leading Alfa Romeo driver who had been killed in the 1925 French Grand Prix at Montlhéry, when Alberto was but seven years old. Guided by his mentor, Luigi Villoresi, Ascari became the greatest Italian driver of post-war years. There was an irony in the relationship between the older Villoresi and Ascari, for Villoresi's own brother Emilio had been killed at the wheel of an Alfa Romeo Tipo 158 in 1938. During 1948 and 1949 both Ascari and Villoresi had driven Maseratis for the Scuderi Ambrosiana, but in 1950 both joined Ferrari and remained there until the end of the 1953 season. In 1951 Ascari had finished second in the World Championship to Fangio, and would have taken the title if Ferrari had not suffered tyre trouble in the last round of the Championship at Barcelona. During the years 1952-53, when the World Championship was held to Formula 2 rules, Ascari's driving was superlative, unmatched by any other in the team, and there was no other team that could compete on level terms with the all-dominant Ferraris. In 1952 Ascari won his first World Championship, missing the Swiss Grand Prix because he drove a Ferrari at Indianapolis, but winning every other of the season's Championship races. In 1953 he again won the Championship, but was fourth in the French race, retired in the German race and spun off in the Italian Grand Prix under immense pressure from the Maseratis.

Froilan Gonzalez (left) and Alberto Ascari (right) at the 1951 British Grand Prix when they were both members of the Ferrari team. Ascari was one of the greatest drivers of all time and known worldwide. When he was killed in 1955, even British newsvendors had posters proclaiming 'Ascari killed'. (Guy Griffiths)

During the remainder of Ascari's racing career, he appeared to slide into something of a decline. At the end of 1953 both Ascari and Villoresi decided to leave the Ferrari team to join the new Lancia team, and the reasons were not difficult to see. Complacent after two year's domination of racing, Enzo Ferrari seemed totally unaware of the threat from Mercedes-Benz which was expected to return to racing in 1954, and he seemed content to race updated version of the Tipo 500 Formula 2 cars. Vittorio Jano's new Lancia Grand Prix car was not ready to race until the autumn of 1954 and in the meantime Ascari won the Mille Miglia road race for Lancia, filling in with drives for Maserati and Ferrari. His driving was characterized by a disregard for the mechanics of his cars and he retired on his few appearances with engine trouble. When Ascari drove for Maserati, as he did at Reims and Silverstone, so did Villoresi but when Ascari drove for Ferrari, as he did at Monza, Villoresi appeared with a Maserati. The new Lancias appeared in the Spanish Grand Prix and although they retired early in the race, Ascari appeared to show his old form.

It was a form that he repeated in the early races of 1955, and then came the fatal Monaco Grand Prix. The race was to prove a titanic battle between the Mercedes-Benz W196 cars and the Lancias, and after both Fangio and Moss had retired, Ascari took the lead, only to have a brake lock on that lap causing his car to plunge into Monte Carlo harbour.

A superb portrait of Giuseppe Farina, the 1950 World Champion, with his Alfa Romeo 158 at the 1950 Italian Grand Prix at Monza. Apart from being one of the fastest drivers of his generation, Farina was one of the hardest and most difficult to beat.

Afterwards, a broken nose apart, Ascari appeared unhurt, but a few day's later he borrowed Castellotti's Ferrari Monza sports-racing car for a few laps at Monza and for reasons that have never been clearly established, crashed with fatal results. The Ferrari Monza was a pig of a car with appalling handling and more than its fair share of tyre problems. The most likely cause of the accident was either a tyre failure or an inter-action between the tyre and ripples on the rather worn surface at Monza. After Ascari's death, Villoresi gave up serious racing, but still again appeared occasionally at the wheel of a Maserati.

The other great Italian driver of post-war years was Giuseppe Farina, who had been racing since pre-war days and was the winner of the 1950 World Championship at the wheel of an Alfa Romeo. When Alfa Romeo withdrew from racing at the end of 1951, Farina joined Ferrari and was second in the World Championship in 1952 and third in 1953. Born in Turin on 30 October 1906, Farina was a hard, ruthless and determined driver but also a noted stylist. At the 1953 Argentine Grand Prix his Ferrari was involved in a horrific accident when he mowed down a crowd of spectators who had strayed over the safety barriers to watch the race from the edge of the track. Just how many onlookers lost their lives is not clear, but some reports put the figure as high as ten. But Farina seemed little affected by the accident and raced again on the same circuit a fortnight later. During the years of the 2500cc Formula, Farina's power was spent although he did take second place in the 1954 Argentine Grand Prix. He crashed in the Mille Miglia, reappeared at the Belgian Grand Prix, had another bad crash during testing at Monza and did not race again until 1955. After running in a few events in that year, he withdrew from racing. He was entered in the 1955 Italian Grand Prix, with one of the Lancia V-8 cars which Ferrari had just acquired, but non-started after tyre trouble in practice. Farina, now 49, decided to withdraw from racing although he made unsuccessful attempts to qualify at Indianapolis in both 1956 and 1957. He died in June 1966 when he crashed his Lotus-Cortina near Chambéry in France while driving to the French Grand Prix.

It would be impossible to mention the 'old guard' of Italian drivers without reference to Piero Taruffi. Taruffi, whose greatest claim to fame is a win in the 1957 Mille Miglia, was a remarkably versatile driver who occasionally drove Formula 1 Maseratis in 1954-55, who had been Technical Director of the Gilera motorcycle team, who set records with his Tarf twin-boom cars and wrote a standard work on the art of motor racing.

During the early years of the 1950s there was a growing band of young and promising Italian drivers, but in the main their efforts were dogged by ill-luck and disaster. Perhaps the best-known driver of the period was Luigi Musso, who — after showing considerable promise with Maserati sports-racing cars, including a second place in the 1954 Targa Florio in which he finished second (despite being violently ill and sick in the cockpit) — was taken in to the Maserati Formula 1 team. He finished second in the 1954 Spanish Grand Prix and was the mainstay, along

Eugenio Castellotti, a rising star so tragically killed in a testing accident early in 1957, with Senora Fangio (although they never actually married) and the reigning World Champion at the 1956 British Grand Prix. In the background is William Boddy, editor of Motor Sport *(T.C. March)*

with Jean Behra, at Maserati in 1955. For 1956 Musso joined Ferrari and over the next couple of seasons his skill and speed improved immeasurably. He became very much the hero of Italy, the one leading Italian driver in an era dominated by Argentinian and British drivers. Like a number of others, he did rather tend to overrate his ability and always demanded, but did not always get, preferential treatment from Enzo Ferrari. By 1958 Musso was at the peak of his ability, but by this time he was burdened by gambling debts and the threat of action from 'heavies'. He was killed in the 1958 French Grand Prix.

With almost equal skill and speed, which was extinguished far too soon, was Eugenio Castellotti. After impressing with private sports cars, Castellotti joined the Lancia sports-racing team in 1953 and drove that team's Formula 1 cars in early 1955. After many of the faster cars had fallen by the wayside, he brought his Lancia across the line in second place in the 1955 Monaco Grand Prix. He tigered furiously with the Mercedes opposition at the wheel of the sole Lancia entered in that year's Belgian Grand Prix, then became a member of Scuderia Ferrari and stayed with the Ferrari team, enjoying mixed fortunes, until he was killed in a testing accident at Modena early in 1957. It is an odd fact that the accident was not fully reported and to this day there seems to be some real doubt as to what precisely happened.

Another promising Italian was Sergio Mantovani, more of a gentleman amateur than a dedicated professional driver, but one with considerable skill and judgement who drove works Maserati 250Fs in 1954 and early 1955. He crashed badly early in 1955 in the Turin Grand Prix held in Valentino Park and had to have a leg amputated above the knee. This was the end of his Grand Prix career, although he did occasionally appear afterwards at the wheel of OSCA sports-racing cars and today is still closely associated with the sport.

Juan Fangio with one of the Ferrari mechanics at the 1956 British Grand Prix. Alfa Romeo recognized Fangio's potential in 1950, his genius became acknowledged universally when he won the World Championship in 1951 and from Ascari's death until his retirement from serious racing at the end of 1957 his supremacy was unchallenged. (T.C. March)

The Argentinians

In the early 1950s a phenomenon of motor racing was the strong contingent of Argentinians who were competing. This was partly because under the Péron government motor racing was actively encouraged and there were in fact driver training schemes including a sponsored team that competed in Europe. A member of this team, the Squadra Achille Varzi (named after a famous Italian driver of an earlier age), was the great Juan Fangio. Fangio's skills with his Maserati led to an invitation to join the Alfa Romeo team for 1950 and he became World Champion with Alfa Romeo in 1951. For a while afterwards his career went into a decline, for he agreed to drive Maseratis in 1952 following Alfa Romeo's withdrawal from racing. After driving the V-16 BRM at Dundrod in April, he flew to Paris and then drove on to Monza to take part in the Autodromo Grand Prix. He started from the back of the grid without practising, crashed badly and broke his neck, so putting himself out of racing for the rest of the year. In 1953 he again drove for Maserati, but whilst there was no lack of power under the Maserati bonnets, the cars lacked Ferrari's roadholding and despite tigering all year with the Maranello opposition, Fangio's only race win was at Monza in the autumn of that year, as much through the intervention of his teammate Marimon as for any other reason.

When Mercedes-Benz returned to motor racing in 1954, team manager Neubauer was only too well aware that because he could not simply rely on German drivers, as the Daimler-Benz directors would have liked, an outsider was needed to lead the team. So Fangio was signed on and, but for him, the Mercedes-Benz season starting at Reims in July would have been a complete disaster. Already that year Fangio had won the Argentine and Belgian Grands Prix for Maserati, and with victories added at Reims, the Nürburgring, Bremgarten and Monza, he clinched his second World Championship. In 1955, partnered in the Mercedes-Benz team by Moss, Fangio was all-dominant. After Mercedes' withdrawal from racing he joined Ferrari, an unhappy year in which he came close to a nervous breakdown because of Ferrari politics and team in-fighting, but returned to Maserati in 1957 to win the World Championship yet again. Fangio was a driver of immense restraint, very great judgement and considerable speed. In 1957 his drives in the French Grand Prix at Rouen and in the German race at the Nürburgring, so much more skilful, so much faster than any of the opposition, put him on a pedestal above all other drivers at that time. To all intents and purposes Fangio retired at the height of his powers at the end of 1957, although he did drive in the Argentine races early in 1958 and in the French Grand Prix later that year.

One of the most prominent of the Argentinians was Froilan Gonza-

He may have been known as 'the Pampas Bull', but it was a reference to Froilan Gonzalez's physical bulk rather than his temperament. Apart from being a driver of superb judgement and determination, Gonzalez was a kind and gentle man whose career, to all intents and purposes, came to an end with a bad crash in practice for the 1954 Tourist Trophy on the Dundrod circuit. (Guy Griffiths)

Tony Vandervell arranged for Froilan Gonzalez to fly over from the Argentine to drive a Vanwall in the 1956 British Grand Prix. Here he waits calmly on the starting grid. Sadly, the car moved only a few inches at the start because a universal joint in a drive-shaft broke. (T.C. March)

lez, often referred to in the press as 'the Pampas Bull'; in reality this was a misnomer, because whilst he was a forceful and determined driver on the track, he was in fact a very sympathetic and emotional man. Gonzalez' appearances in Formula 1 during the period under review were soon over. He had first driven for Ferrari in 1951 and scored an epic victory in that year's British Grand Prix with the previous year's model, the single-plug V-12 car, but he left to drive for Maserati in 1952-53. He always drove with great consistency, but scored very little in the way of success, apart from a second place in the 1952 Italian Grand Prix, a race of some importance in itself as it was the first time the new Formula 2 Maseratis had made any impact on the racing scene. Gonzalez returned to Ferrari in 1954 and he again scored an epic victory, winning the British Grand Prix and defeating the Mercedes team. At that year's Tourist Trophy race, he crashed badly during practice and to all intents and purposes this was the end of his racing career. He sometimes drove in Argentine events until the late '50s, but his last European race was the 1956 British Grand Prix where he was flown over specially to handle the Vanwall. He found the very light steering and handling characteristics of the car strange, his practice times were disappointing and at the start of the race his car jerked merely a few inches forward before breaking down with drive-shaft problems.

The career of Onofre Marimon was cut short in its prime. Marimon was another sponsored Argentinian driver who drove a quasi-works Maserati finished in blue and yellow Argentinian colours in 1953. His most significant contribution to the team that year was when he joined in, a lap in arrears, with the harassment of race-leader Ascari in the Italian Grand Prix until the reigning World Champion spun and Fangio was able to slip by to score his only win of the year. Marimon became a full member of the Maserati team in 1954 and once Fangio had left to drive for Mercedes, he was team-leader. It was a position that he viewed with great pride and he suffered badly when Stirling Moss was invited to join the team. It was at the next race, the German Grand Prix, that Marimon crashed with fatal results, simply trying too hard to assert his position as team-leader. It was a sad death and it was one that badly shook Marimon's fellow Argentinians.

A driver of immense potential, Argentinian Onofre Marimon, protégé of Fangio and Gonzalez who became Maserati team-leader after Fangio left to drive for Mercedes-Benz following the 1954 Belgian Grand Prix. Sadly, he was killed in practice for the 1954 German Grand Prix when his car left the road at high speed.

Europeans and others

Thanks to Mercedes-Benz, which was keen to retain German drivers in the team, both Karl Kling and Hans Herrmann were prominent in Grand Prix racing in 1954-55. Neither was capable of winning or coming anywhere near the lap times achieved by Fangio. In any event Herrmann's career suffered a severe jolt when he crashed badly in practice at Monaco in 1955 and did not race again that year. Later Herrmann drove the BRP-entered BRM in the 1959 German Grand Prix at Avus and crashed badly, writing the car off when the brakes failed. Herrmann was much more of a sports car driver and he had a long and distinguished career with Porsche that lasted until his victory in the Le Mans 24 Hours race in 1970. Herrmann also drove Maseratis for Scuderia Centro-Sud, but this private team always ran obsolescent cars and never gave any of its drivers a chance to show their real form.

Another German driver to appear for Centro-Sud was Wolfgang Seidel, a very middling driver of competence but no stirring inspiration, whose main successes were at the wheel of Ferrari sports cars. There was, however, one German driver destined to rise above the ranks of the others, Wolfgang von Trips, who established a fine reputation with Porsche sports cars before joining Scuderia Ferrari. He was with Ferrari during the unsuccessful years of the front-engined Dino cars in 1959-60, and he appeared to be destined to win the World Championship in 1961 with the new rear-engined cars that dominated that year's racing. Sadly he was involved in a collision in the Italian Grand Prix with Jim Clark's Lotus; his car was catapulted into the crowd, several spectators and von Trips were killed and the result was that American Phil Hill won that race and that year's Championship.

Undoubtedly the most successful French driver of the 2500cc For-

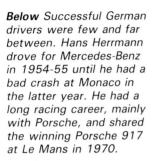

Below *Successful German drivers were few and far between. Hans Herrmann drove for Mercedes-Benz in 1954-55 until he had a bad crash at Monaco in the latter year. He had a long racing career, mainly with Porsche, and shared the winning Porsche 917 at Le Mans in 1970.*

Below right *Wolfgang ('Taffy') von Trips established himself with Porsche sports cars before joining Ferrari. He stayed with Ferrari through the lean years, 1959-60, but was killed in the 1961 Italian Grand Prix in a collision with Jim Clark's Lotus. It is likely that he would have won the World Championship that year.*

mula was Maurice Trintignant who enjoyed a long and distinguished racing career and scored substantial successes. At the start of the 2500cc Grand Prix Formula, Trintignant agreed to drive a car for Louis Rosier's private Ferrari team but he scored a totally unexpected victory in the Buenos Aires Grand Prix that year and was immediately invited to join Ferrari. During 1954 Trintignant scored many successes in minor events and stayed with Ferrari in 1955, winning that year's Monaco Grand Prix after the failure of the Mercedes and Lancia teams; it was Ferrari's only Championship Grand Prix of the year. For a couple of years after that, Trintignant's career slipped into a backwater, but he bounced back at the wheel of Rob Walker's Coopers in 1958 and again won at Monaco. Trintignant was a driver who took an immensely relaxed view of his racing, always dependable, always reliable, never the fastest driver around, but the ideal number two man in any team.

Trintignant's temperament contrasted fiercely with that of fellow Frenchman Jean Behra, another driver who vastly overrated his own ability. From 1952 through to the end of 1954, he drove for the French Gordini team, displaying considerable speed and skill, but never achieving much except in minor races because of the terrible unreliability of the French cars. When Moss left to drive for Mercedes in 1954, Behra was invited to join the Maserati team and he stayed with them until the end of 1957. As team leader in 1955, he was simply not up to the job, but he proved an admirable number two to Moss in 1956, a role that he accepted with resigned reluctance, and to Fangio in 1957. During the latter year he provided immense inspiration for the BRM team by suggesting that he drove one of its cars in the non-Championship Caen Grand Prix which he won; he subsequently signed up for BRM in 1958. For 1959 Behra joined Scuderia Ferrari and was firmly convinced that he should be team leader. In this highly political team, run

Maurice Trintignant, who became mayor of Vergeze, had a long racing career with Gordini, Ferrari and the Rob Walker team. His greatest successes were wins at Monaco in 1955 with a Ferrari and in 1958 with a Cooper-Climax, but both were 'lucky' wins in that he survived races of attrition. (Guy Griffiths)

Above *Joakim Bonnier became a vastly experienced driver, starting his racing career with Alfa Romeos (for which he was agent in his native Sweden) before driving for Scuderia Centro-Sud, BRM (for whom he scored their first World Championship race victory at Zandvoort in 1959) and later, Porsche. He was killed at the wheel of a Lola at Le Mans in 1972. (Nigel Snowdon)*

Right *A former racing motorcyclist and always an exciting driver to watch, Jean Behra, after three sessions with Gordini, joined Maserati for three years and then BRM and Ferrari. Sadly, he always overrated his own ability and was killed at the wheel of his Porsche sports car at Avus in 1959. Here he is seen at Silverstone with a Gordini. (Guy Griffiths)*

on a basis of divide and rule, there was no room for team leaders and no room for egos other than Ferrari's. Behra was immensely strained by the atmosphere there; his relations with the other drivers deteriorated and he fell out with team manager Tavoni, this disagreement ending with a punch-up at Reims. Thereafter Behra was in the wilderness, but he raced a sports Porsche and died in a crash at a supporting race to the 1959 German Grand Prix.

Joakim Bonnier enjoyed an immensely long career in Formula 1, from 1957 through to 1967, but this Swedish driver's international career started earlier. He was an Alfa Romeo dealer in Sweden and in 1956 he raced both a 1900 saloon and also one of the ex-works *Disco Volante* sports-racing cars. From this he progressed to a Maserati 250F and to living in Switzerland where he spent the remainder of his life. In 1959 he became a member of the BRM team, scoring BRM's first World Championship victory at Zandvoort. It was in fact to prove the only World Championship victory that he ever scored. However, he was later a member of the works Porsche Formula 1 team in 1961-62 and in 1966 he raced a 3-litre Cooper-Maserati. Motor racing was very much in the affable Swede's blood, whether he won or lost, and he was still racing in 1972, running his own team of Lolas in endurance racing. Sadly, Bonnier was killed at Le Mans.

The Marquis Alfonso de Portago, a Spanish nobleman, was a magnificent all-round sportsman who travelled through life looking down-and-out and scruffy, as though he was a mechanic belonging to one of the less well-heeled teams, but was an accomplished horseman and skier. However, whilst he might well have been able to compete at the top levels in these sports, he never quite made the grade in Formula 1. During 1956-57 he raced Lancia-Ferraris for Scuderia Ferrari but his career came to a premature end, as did the race in which he was competing, when he crashed fatally in the 1957 Mille Miglia.

Right Spanish nobleman the Marquis Alfonso de Portago was no star in the motor racing world, but was a brilliant all-round sportsman. He skied and rode as well as he drove, and his position and influence did much to ensure his place with the Ferrari team. Here he is seen with Peter Collins to his left before the fateful 1957 Mille Miglia in which de Portago, his co-driver Edmund Nelson and a number of spectators were killed. Peter Collins looks unhappy, for he had no love for the 1,000 mile road race.

Below Siamese Prince Birabongse, always entered as 'B. Bira', had been racing since pre-war days and that was his great period when he achieved immense success with ERAs, the ex-Seaman Delage and the ex-Whitney Straight Maserati. Here 'B. Bira' is seen at the wheel of his 4½ litre V-12 OSCA at Goodwood in 1951. (Guy Griffiths)

Few drivers had a longer racing career than Siamese Prince Birabongse, always entered as 'B.Bira' by his cousin Prince Chula. B. Bira had a distinguished racing career starting with ERAs in the 1930s, then moving on to the ex-Dick Seaman Delage rebuilt by Giulio Ramponi. In postwar days Bira always drove Maseratis and OSCAs, initially 1.5-litre supercharged 4CLT/48 cars entered by Enrico Platé but later buying his own Formula 1 OSCA. He reverted to Platé-entered cars during the years 1952-53 and competed in Formula 1 in his last year of racing with one of the old A6GCM cars powered by a 250F engine, and finally with his own Maserati 250F. Bira gave up racing early in 1955 and sold his car to West Country driver Horace Gould. It was this car, chassis number 2504, that was the first car of the 2500cc Formula to run in historic racing car events organized by the Vintage Sports Car Club. After he retired from racing, Bira disappeared from view for many years, although latterly he took part in the number of historic parades. He died in London in very straitened circumstances.

The Brits

In 1958, when racing was to all intents and purposes a straightforward dual between Ferrari and Vanwall, these two teams had the cream of the world's drivers, all British. Heading the Vanwall team was Stirling Moss, a driver who, from the date of Fangio's retirement to his own bad accident at Goodwood in 1962, towered above all others. Moss remains a household name in 1990 and has probably gained more distinction than anything else for being the man who never won the World Championship. He took second place in 1955, 1956, 1957 and 1958, and was third in the Championship in 1959, 1960 and 1961. He displayed a rare combination of talent, exceptional judgement, restraint, speed, skill and temperament. He was a man who could have succeeded at many sports and in an earlier age he would probably have been a champion horseman. From the time when he first raced a Cooper 500cc car in 1948, Moss already, despite his youth, towered above his rivals. He was the driver who put the HWMs on the map (together with that very underrated driver Lance Macklin) and he had a burning desire to achieve success at the wheel of a British car. After two seasons with HWM he switched to the ERA G Type — a disastrous failure — and in 1953 tried to race a Cooper-Alta of very special design devised by John Cooper, technical editor of *The Autocar* and Formula 3 designer Ray Martin. The car was also a disastrous failure and Moss and his family saw no alternative but for him to acquire a foreign Formula 1 car for 1954.

With financial support from BP, Moss acquired a Maserati 250F and by the middle of the year was a member of the works team. His close collaboration with the technical personnel at Maserati meant that a strong and enthusiastic bond was built up and Maserati believed in 1954 that it had found a great team leader for the future. He so nearly won the Italian Grand Prix, leading beyond challenge when an oil pipe

broke, and it seemed that he was the one man who could beat the Mercedes opposition in 1955. However, Neubauer of Mercedes, who had
seemed to be unaware of Moss's talent in 1954, knew that he needed
a really sound back-up for Fangio and the team, because of the shortcomings of the German drivers, and Moss knew that he could have
a learning curve with Mercedes that he would never obtain elsewhere.
Throughout 1955 Moss drove in Fangio's wheel-tracks, being allowed
(in all probability) to win the British Grand Prix but elsewhere having
to settle for a secondary role, but consistently out-performing the Argentinian in sports car races. The year 1955 saw one of Moss's greatest
triumphs, albeit not in Formula 1, when, with Denis Jenkinson alongside him in the cockpit, he won the arduous 1000-mile Mille Miglia
road race with a Mercedes-Benz 300SLR. Carraciola had won the race

with a Mercedes in 1931, but such intimate knowledge of the course was needed that Italians were quite convinced that in post-war days no one but an Italian would ever win the race. Moss changed that and his driving skill, aided by Jenkinson's navigation and system of signals for indicating the road, set new standards in road racing.

Moss returned to Maserati in 1956 but perhaps his greatest years were in 1957-58 when he led the British Vanwall team. Together with Tony Vandervell, he was the man who put British Racing Green on the map and he scored a magnificent trio of victories in 1957, followed by a year-long duel with Hawthorn for the World Championship in 1958. It has often been said that it was unreasonable that Moss should have finished second in the World Championship, having won more races during the year than his rival Hawthorn. However, it seems totally illogical to suggest that a victory should have been awarded to a man who scored less points (albeit only one) under the rules then prevailing. After Vanwall withdrew from racing, Moss was able to pursue a racing career as the underdog and loner, choosing to team up with Rob Walker at the wheel of the private entrant's Coopers and Lotus 18s. Two of Moss's finest victories came in 1961 when he drove his outdated four-cylinder Lotus to victories at Monaco and the Nürburgring, defeating the might of the much more powerful Ferrari team. The only man who could be argued to challenge Moss's supremacy as a driver is Jim Clark and because of Moss's so serious accident at Goodwood in 1962, which brought his career to an end, it can be said that the two drivers never raced against each other on level terms. Moss is still great, still an enthusiast, and still taking part in historic racing. I had the opportunity of seeing him driving an Elva with considerable enthusiasm at Elkhart Lake in 1988.

The mature Moss, seen in 1960, when he enjoyed such a brilliant season at the wheel of Rob Walker's Lotus 18.

Throughout the 1950s there was much argument as to who was the greater British driver, Moss or Hawthorn. John Michael Hawthorn, son of garage-owner Leslie Hawthorn, had entered racing in 1951 with Riley cars and graduated to the international scene in 1952 with a Cooper-Bristol bought for him to drive by Bob Chase. With the Cooper, Hawthorn displayed tremendous skill and ability, but he had a distinct advantage, not revealed at the time, that his car was running on power-boosting nitromethane fuel additive; he also had another driving force, his father, who was always most obsessive in his desire for his son's success and always pushed Hawthorn too hard. Hawthorn appeared to feel a sense of release after his father died in 1954 and he then became more than ever the joker in the pack, full of his own brand of school-boy humour and practical joking, which amused some of his friends, but certainly did not do too much to improve his relations with others in the racing world.

In 1953 Ferrari had signed up young Hawthorn and he proved his worth to the team by a furious battle with Fangio in the 1953 French Grand Prix which resulted in a first World Championship victory for the young Englishman. Most of Hawthorn's career was spent with Ferrari but he signed for Vanwall in 1955, leaving the team halfway through

Mike Hawthorn had an immense talent, but until his death in a road accident, his father, Leslie, was always his driving force. Here Mike is seen with his works Ferrari at Silverstone in 1953. (Guy Griffiths)

the season when it was clear that the new British car was not competitive; he tried again with BRM in 1956, but it was a year of disaster. Throughout 1957 Hawthorn was handicapped by driving the uncompetitive Lancia-Ferraris, but for 1958 Ferrari had produced the new Dino 246 cars and on some circuits these were more than a match for the Vanwalls. As has been described earlier, Hawthorn won the 1958 World Championship by the margin of one point, and it was a victory partly attributable to the fact that in the Portuguese Grand Prix, after Hawthorn had spun and pushed his car along the pavement against the flow of the race, Moss spoke up in his support.

The year 1958 was traumatic for Hawthorn, for not only was his teammate Musso killed in the French Grand Prix, but his closest friend Peter Collins died in the German Grand Prix and Hawthorn witnessed the crash. Hawthorn struggled through the remainder of that season and scored the Championship win, before announcing his retirement from racing. In January 1959 he was killed when he crashed his own 3.8 MkII Jaguar saloon on the Guildford bypass. Hawthorn's racing career spanned a mere eight seasons, from starting as a novice to his retirement as World Champion, but it was not an easy eight years for him, for apart from the death of his father in a road accident, the harrassment by the British press over his eligibility for National Service, and the death of his friend Collins, he was very much involved in the 1955 Le Mans disaster, from which he suffered pointless and unjustified criticism, a criticism which resulted, at one stage, in the organizers of the German Grand Prix refusing to accept his entry. What one must say with the benefit of hindsight is that Hawthorn as a driver was obviously of World Championship class, but he could not stand at the same level as Moss.

During the years 1957-58, alongside Hawthorn in the Ferrari team was Peter Collins, another of the great drivers of his era. Collins, like Moss, started in 500cc racing, and later graduated to the HWM team for whom he drove in 1952-53. Like Hawthorn, Collins had spells with Vanwall (in 1954) and BRM (in 1955). He was given a works Maserati in the 1955 Italian Grand Prix and it seems that he would have been able to choose between Ferrari or Maserati for 1956. He chose Ferrari, and stayed with the team until his death. At Maranello, Collins was always regarded with great affection, especially by Laura Ferrari, and always treated as a member of the family. His early successes included a brilliant win in the Belgian Grand Prix and there has always stood out over the years his gesture at Monza in 1956 when he handed over his Ferrari to Juan Fangio; it may well have been that if Collins had not made this voluntary gesture, he would have been ordered to hand his car over but, as things stood, if he had stayed at the wheel he could very well have won the World Championship, whereas his generous gesture assured Fangio of his fourth such title.

In 1958 Vanwall had one of the strongest Grand Prix teams of all times, for alongside Moss there were Tony Brooks and Stuart Lewis-Evans. Brooks had entered racing as a dental student, just a keen amateur entered by his friend, Hely, with a Fraser Nash Le Mans Replica, before he was invited in 1955 to drive the private Formula 2 Connaught of

An enigmatic Peter Collins before the start of the 1956 British Grand Prix at Silverstone in 1956. Despite his inherent good nature, it sometimes seemed that motor racing — and Hawthorn's sense of humour — were all just too much for him. (T.C. March)

John Risely-Prichard and the works sports Connaught. When Connaught decided to enter the Syracuse Grand Prix, lured by starting money of £1,000 per car, it never expected to win and was looking for two cheap and competent drivers to handle the cars. Tony Brooks fitted the bill admirably; he won the race with consummate skill, defeating the Maserati team, and assured his future as a racing driver rather than as a dentist. After a thoroughly miserable season with BRM in 1956 he joined Vanwall for two brilliant seasons. During those two years Brooks was always content to play number two to Moss, taking over the role of the fighter and the winner only when Moss's car had fallen by the wayside.

When Vanwall withdrew from racing, Brooks was the one who was still willing to drive Tony Vandervell's latest and uncompetitive project, but he signed for Ferrari in 1959, enjoying a less than happy year before moving to the private Yeoman Credit team in 1960 and completing an almost equally miserable year with BRM in 1961 before retiring from racing. Brooks was a remarkably calm, responsive, intuitive and skilful driver. He would and could fight hard, and performed best of all on the more difficult circuits such as Spa-Francorchamps, where he won almost every race in which he drove, whether he was at the wheel of a Formula 1 car or a sports Aston Martin, and the Nürburgring. Brooks did, however, insist that his car must be completely right and that he must have absolute confidence in it. If he felt unhappy about it, he unhesitatingly made for the pits to have the trouble resolved. He was never the sort of driver who would plug on to finish at the tail of the field with a defective car believing that to finish was the most important thing.

Small, frail and suffering from stomach ulcers, Stuart Lewis-Evans was originally in partnership with his father 'Pop' Lewis Lewis-Evans, and they both drove Cooper-Nortons in Formula 3. His skill impressed and he drove works Aston Martins — but really lacked the stamina for endurance racing — and also Connaughts, before being asked to step into the Vanwall team as a substitute driver at Reims and Rouen in 1957. He seemed to settle down at once in the Vanwall and showed immense form at both circuits, impressing Vandervell so much that he was invited to join the works team. Although never a driver that could be regarded in quite the same bracket as Moss or Brooks, often his practice times were every bit as good and he would set a startling pace in the race. There is no doubt that with Moss, Brooks and Lewis-Evans, Vanwall had the very best team of drivers imaginable. It was a terrible blow to Vandervell when Lewis-Evans crashed at Casablanca at the end of 1958, suffering fatal burns.

In a short book of this kind it is not possible to mention every prominent British driver of the period — there were so many. It would, however, be impossible to pass over the 1950s without reference to Roy Salvadori, perhaps the most versatile driver of the era and certainly the most commercially minded. Salvadori's career never really reached the heights, because he divided his activities between a very successful motor business and racing — and when he raced, he expected to be paid for it. He would drive in five different races in a day and he has calculated that his income in the 1950s was in excess of £20,000 per annum, £10,000 of which was sponsorship from Esso fuel and oil. Salvadori is best remembered for his drives in British events with the Gilby Maserati 250F in 1954-56, but he was for a short while a member of the BRM team in 1957, but withdrew because he was so disillusioned by the way the team was run, and drove works Coopers from 1956 onwards. This meant a prominent role in Formula 1 races in 1958, but at the end of that year, during which he had scored some quite good successes, both he and Jack Brabham agreed with John Wyer that they would drive for Aston Martin in 1959.

However, for 1959 Coventry Climax announced that it would be making available a new 2495cc version of the FPF engine and Brabham decided, now that Cooper had raised additional finance from Esso, that he would stay with that team. He tried to persuade Salvadori to stay at Cooper too, but Salvadori had been driving for Aston Martin since 1953. He had a very close relationship with the team manager John Wyer and felt that he could not go back on his word. The result was that Brabham won the World Championship in 1959-60, whilst Salvadori enjoyed two lucrative years, but absolutely nothing in the way of success. One of the great 'what-ifs' of motor racing is what would have happened if Salvadori had stayed with Cooper. Brabham only won the Championship by a narrow margin in 1959 and it is more than likely that if Salvadori had continued to drive for Cooper, there would have been times when he finished ahead of the Australian and it is very likely that Tony Brooks — who finished second — would have won the World Championship that year.

The later years of the 2500cc Formula saw three young English drivers break on to the scene and, eventually, to leave behind reputations that matched or almost matched that of Moss. Graham Hill, a Lotus employee, first drove for Team Lotus in Formula 1 in 1958 and had a thoroughly misarable time at the wheel of the front-engined cars until 1960 when he joined BRM. All his great successes were to come with BRM during the 1500cc Formula. Hill was not a natural driver, but a hard worker who deserved everything that he did achieve, and he achieved a very great deal, including two World Championships, by determination and resolution. Both John Surtees and Jim Clark had their first Formula 1 drives with Team Lotus. Both showed brilliance, Clark after only a limited background in motor racing, but Surtees with vast experience and already a World Champion on two wheels. Clark's flair and brilliance, willingness and determination during his racing career has only been matched by one other post-war driver, Stirling Moss, but fortunately they never ever raced on equal terms against each other so invidious comparisons can be avoided. For most of his racing career, Clark drove comparatively under-powered Formula 1 cars, for his career was concentrated during the years 1961-65 when the 1500cc Formula was in force, and it was during those years that he won his

A very bashful Graham Hill, seen in 1960 when he was driving during his first — and unsuccessful — season for BRM. What Graham Hill lacked in natural talent, he more than compensated for by sheer determinaion and guts.

Jack Brabham with Jim Clark at the time the latter was learning to fly an aeroplane. Clark became the great stylist, with sublime smoothness and skill, and without him Team Lotus would have taken so much longer to achieve real success. (Nigel Snowdon)

The only man to win World Championships on both four wheels and two — John Surtees, who first appeared in Formula 1 for Lotus in 1960. (Nigel Snowdon)

Jack Brabham, World Champion in 1959 and 1960, with John Cooper. Brabham made Cooper's success and when he left them in 1962 to run his own team, it started their downfall. (Nigel Snowdon)

World Championships. John Surtees drove only briefly for Lotus before moving on to Reg Parnell (Racing) and then to Ferrari. One of the great sadnesses of the last year of 2500cc Formula 1 was the Belgian Grand Prix in which two of the most promising drivers, Chris Bristow, always regarded as a World Champion in the making by those who should know, including Stirling Moss, and Alan Stacey, who raced despite the handicap of an artificial leg, were both killed.

The 'Colonials'

After Jack Brabham came to the United Kingdom in 1955, he became inseparably associated with Cooper and in many ways he carried out a personal take-over of the Cooper team. Brabham, now Sir Jack Brabham and with three successful racing driver sons, combined a dour, blunt attitude with the ability to weld together far greater achievement in the Cooper team than those diverse characters John and his father Charles could have managed alone. Jack Brabham was a tireless worker, an innovator and a skilled practical engineer, and these qualities combined with his skilful and hard driving were to make him World Champion in 1959 and 1960. After 1961 he left to set up his own team, which went on to achieve remarkable success, with Brabham himself again winning the World Championship in 1966 and finishing second in 1967. Without him Cooper went into a sad decline.

In 1959, young New Zealander Bruce McLaren had joined the Cooper team and he stayed with Cooper right the way through until the end of the 1965 racing season. McLaren was another inspired driver, but also rapidly became a skilled engineer, who would listen to advice and knew exactly where he was going in life. Initially he lacked the

New Zealander Bruce McLaren was another who combined the talents of driver, tester and, later, constructor. He joined the works Cooper team for 1959 and stayed with them until the end of the 1965 season. (Nigel Snowdon)

experience and weight to influence the Coopers, and undoubtedly if the team had listened to him more it would have been a lot more successful during the years of the 1500cc Formula. In 1966 McLaren set up his own racing team which was to prove immensely successful in both Formula 1 and Can-Am racing. Notwithstanding McLaren's tragic death during a testing accident at Goodwood in 1970, the McLaren team continued to flourish for several years until it was eventually taken over by a consortium headed by Ron Dennis and became the strongest force in Formula 1.

The Americans

During the 1950s and 1960s there was a strong contingent of American drivers in Europe. With one exception most of these had had successful careers with privately-entered sports-racing cars in the United States, most had come over to Europe to try their hand at European endurance racing and most had shown sufficient skill to be invited to join works teams. The exception was Harry Schell, whose parents had run a team in pre-war days, the Ecurie Lucy O'Reilly Schell. Harry's father was French and his mother American. He combined an immensely long racing career with running a bar in Paris, and he was not only a very determined, forceful driver, but he was also known perhaps best of all for his sense of humour and practical jokes. Schell's greatest years in Formula 1 were 1956-58. He had first driven for Vanwall in 1955, when the cars were not really competitive, but by 1956 they had the speed, if neither the roadholding nor the reliability, to match the Italian opposition, and Schell's fearless determination took on the Italians and thoroughly shook them until his car broke, espe-

Franco-American Harry Schell, notorious for his practical jokes and always a stalwart 'number 2', steeped in motor racing from the cradle and a member of the Maserati, Vanwall and BRM teams amongst others. He was killed in a practice crash at the 1960 International Trophy at Silverstone. (Guy Griffiths)

cially at Spa, Reims and Monza that year. Sadly Vandervell did not want to retain his services so he became third-string for Maserati in 1957, then, when it withdrew from racing, he left to drive for the BRM. He was killed in practice at the International Trophy Meeting at Silverstone in 1960.

The most important American driver to appear in European racing was Phil Hill, who had achieved a fine track record in the United States with Ferrari sports-racing cars, privately entered, and who had first competed in Europe, at Le Mans, in 1953. He drove in several races, all sports car events, in Europe in 1956, joined the works Ferrari team in 1957 and first drove in Formula 1 in 1958, when he was very much the junior boy of the team. Hill was with Ferrari during the lean years, 1959-60, when the Dinos became increasingly outclassed, but he won the World Championship in 1961 when Ferrari was running the V-6 1500cc unsupercharged cars. At the 1961 Italian Grand Prix, Wolfgang von Trips led the World Championship with 33 points to Hill's 29. Sadly, as already mentioned, von Trips was killed in a collisiion with Clark's Lotus and Hill went on to win the race and the Championship. By 1962 Hill's racing career was in decline and he had a thoroughly miserable year with Ferrari. He drove for ATS in 1963, but both he and his team-mate Giancarlo Baghetti had their careers destroyed by those unreliable and badly built cars. He was with Cooper in 1964 (another miserable season) and thereafter only drove in Prototype events. Hill's career was successful, but sad.

Dan Gurney, later the builder of Formula 1 and Indianapolis cars,

The Ferrari team after Tony Brooks's win in the 1959 French Grand Prix. On the left is the quiet, unassuming Phil Hill who drove in Formula 1 for Ferrari for five years; next to him is Dan Gurney who became a successful racing car constructor, then Englishman Tony who had won the race and was close to winning that year's World Championship. (LAT)

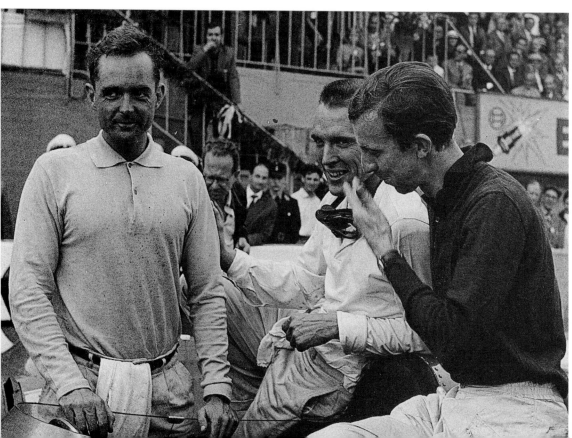

must also be mentioned as a prominent driver in the 2500cc era. He was a leading member of the BRM team in 1960 but his career never really shone in Formula 1. Kansan Masten Gregory was one of the most successful American drivers, with a career that extended in Europe from 1958, when he drove Scuderia Centro-Sud Maseratis, and 1959, when he was a member of the works Cooper team, right the way through to a reappearance in European events with the works Alfa Romeo sports car team in the early 1970s. Gregory was a driver of laid-back manner and a spectacle-wearer (unusual for a racing driver because eyesight is so very important), and became well-known for all the wrong reasons. He twice jumped out of Tojeiro sports cars entered by Ecurie Ecosse, just before they were about to crash through brake failure, and it was he who was dicing with Archie Scott-Brown at Spa in 1958 when Archie crashed fatally. But no one should underestimate the Kansan's ability, for he was determined, accurate and forceful but, as events were to prove, a more suitable member of a long-distance sports-racing car team than a Formula 1 organization.

During the 1950s there was plenty of scope for private owners in Formula 1, provided that they were prepared to rely on starting money and some prize money, running at the back of the field most of the time and leading a frugal hand-to-mouth existence. Prominent 'privateers' were West Country driver Horace Gould, commonly known as the 'Gonzalez of the West Country', who raced a Cooper-Bristol before graduating to a Maserati 250F, two of which he owned. He was even on occasions regarded sufficiently highly at the Maserati works to be

Concentration: Phil Hill with his 1500cc V-6 Ferrari in the 1961 Monaco Grand Prix, won by Stirling Moss with the outdated Lotus 18. Hill won that year's World Championship.

A fine study of Dan Gurney at the wheel of his works BRM at Oulton Park in 1960. The photograph clearly reveals the rather shoddy construction of the rear-engined BRM P48. (T.C. March)

loaned a works car when there were problems with his own. The first of his cars was sold to young Bruce Halford who later graduated to a private Lotus 16 which he still owns and enters regularly in VSCC events. These privateers, British, Italian, French and even Spanish, were part of the life-blood of Formula 1 and their role in the era should never be forgotten.

6

The rear-engine revolution

1957-60

During the years 1957-60 the face of Formula 1 racing was changed for ever, and the basic concept for the racing car of today was laid down. Three men were responsible for this revolution. To adapt a cliché, two of these, Charles and John Cooper, had greatness forced upon them, whilst the other, Colin Chapman, sought greatness and finally achieved it. The concept and development of the rear-engine racing car was that of the Coopers, father and son, but engineering genius Chapman, albeit with initial reluctance, adopted the Coopers' basic ideas and refined and improved them beyond recognition.

The take-off point for the new breed of racing cars came in the Formula 2 race at the British Grand Prix meeting at Silverstone in July 1957. There had been announced a new 1500cc Formula 2 for 1957 onwards and almost six months before that Formula came into official being the BRDC organized a race for the future Formula which attracted a very large entry, but only two that were not sports cars. One of these was the Beart-Rodger-OSCA which was strictly speaking a very narrow sports car running without wings and not a true single-seater, whilst the other was the new Cooper which had only just been finished in time for the race.

The development of the Formula 2 car had been the result of a steady progression. Cooper Cars of Surbiton was run by Charles Cooper, who in pre-war days had been mechanic to Kaye Don, together with his son John. Charles Cooper was an artisan, but at the same time autocratic and reactionary in his views rather than radical, while John was a superb all-round mechanic who could become inspired. Both were dependent, perhaps more than they ever cared to admit, on their draughtsman-designer Owen Maddock who had joined the company in 1949. Cooper's success had been founded on 500cc motorcycle-engine-powered single-seater racing cars (the category became known as Formula 3 from 1950 onwards); it was a field in which Cooper had gradually attained complete ascendancy and the Company had become the first serious British manufacturer of racing cars. From 1949 onwards the Coopers had built a number of front-engined sports cars and in 1952-53 the very successful Cooper-Bristol Formula 2 car, also front-engined. In 1954 they had produced the Cooper-Jaguar, their last front-engined racing car, characterized by a chassis constructed from curved tubing. Production of this in Mk II form continued in a very small way in 1955, a year marked by a major development from Cooper cars.

During 1954 Colin Chapman had been racing with immense success his Lotus Mk VIII sports-racing car, with a sophisticated multi-tubular space-frame chassis and a very aerodynamic body designed by Frank Costin. That same year the Kieft firm had run a sports car at Le Mans powered by the new Coventry Climax FWA single overhead camshaft 1098cc engine developing 72 bhp at 6,300 rpm. In August of that year Dickie Steed, adopted son of the Editor of *The Times*, had installed one of these Coventry Climax engines in a Lotus Mk VIII chassis/body unit. In 1955 Chapman produced the improved Mk 9 car which was available both with the MG and the Coventry Climax engine, and works cars were entered in both forms. There followed the Lotus Eleven built in substantial numbers, by far the most successful car in its category and so popular with amateur drivers that its popularity was to lead to the death knell of the old 500cc Formula 3.

By 1954 Cooper Cars had lost any sense of direction as to where to go in the future, relying on sales of 500cc cars and of course the small number of Cooper-Jaguar cars built. It had watched with considerable interest the progress of the Lotus and the Coventry Climax engine and the decision was made to enter the 1100cc sports car category the following year. Relying on their existing practices, the Coopers built a rear-engined car with a chassis very similar to that of their Mark IX 500cc car, based on curved tubes, with a two-seater all-enveloping body, a central driving position and the passenger seat on an outrigger to the left. The Coventry Climax engine was used in unit with a Citroen-ERSA four-speed gearbox. The most remarkable feature of the Cooper was its cut-off, concave tail, which led to it being known as the 'Bob-tail', or more accurately the 'Camm-tail', because the aerodynamic advantages of a cut-off tail had been suggested by an assistant to Sir Sydney Camm, Hawker's chief designer. During 1955 the new Cooper-Climax probably achieved just as much success and popularity as the rival Lotus, but Chapman's 1956 Eleven car tipped the balance of the scales in favour of Lotus. In addition to the Climax-powered Coopers, there were also two Bristol-powered cars, one built up by Jack Brabham and one for Bob Chase who entered it for Mike Keen. Keen was killed with this car in the 1955 Goodwood 9 Hours race.

In 1956 Coventry Climax laid down a small number of FWB single-cam engines, with the capacity stretched to 1460cc (76.2 × 80mm) and a power output of 100 bhp at 6,000 rpm. In addition, a new twin overhead camshaft engine was promised for 1957. The 1460cc engine was used in Cooper and Lotus sports-racing cars and also the new Cooper formula 2 car. This single-seater closely followed the design of the sports model, with the same wheelbase and track, but a narrower curved-tube chassis frame, the same transverse leaf front and rear suspension and the Climax FWB engine in unit with the Citroen-ERSA gearbox. Although Colin Chapman's Lotus Eleven led initially at Silverstone and set the fastest lap, Salvadori at the wheel of the works Cooper came through to take the lead and score an easy victory. A number of other Formula 2 events were held during the year, including the very important Gold Cup race at Oulton Park, and Coopers completely dominated these.

It had been known that Colin Chapman was developing a Formula 2 car and it eventually appeared on the Lotus stand at the 1956 Earls Court Motor Show, but it was in many ways a mock-up, for both the engine and gearbox were dummies. The new Lotus, the 12, was derived from the Eleven sports-racing car, but double wishbone and coil spring front suspension now replaced the swing-axles previously favoured by Chapman (and double wishbones were also adopted on the sports-racing cars in 1957), while the prototype featured a de Dion rear axle assembly, similar to but simpler than that used on the Eleven. As a result of early tests this was abandoned in favour of Chapman's new independent strut-type suspension. With this system the drive-shaft located the wheel laterally, and there was a forward-facing radius arm and coil spring damper with all three members leading into an aluminium casing just behind the wheel. As usual Chapman adopted a multi-tubular space-frame chassis design, but to improve the stiffness he incorporated the crankcase of the Coventry Climax engine in the chassis. The power unit was the new twin overhead camshaft Coventry Climax FPF engine of 1475cc (81.2 × 71.1mm) with two new twin-choke SU carburettors and an initial power output of 141 bhp at 7,000 rpm. The transmission was an entirely new Chapman design, incoporating ZF gears and a limited slip differential. The gear change for the five-speed gearbox was formed by a gate consisting of a series of 'Z's so that the driver pushed the gear lever to the right to change up the box and pressed it to the left to change down. The 12 was a superbly styled car, with beautifully balanced lines and set off by Chapman's new magnesium-alloy disc-type wheels, which became popularly known as the 'wobbly web' style. Team Lotus ran only in Formula 2 during 1957 but it soon became obvious that these sophisticated front-engined cars were no match for the rather more basic rear-engine cars from Surbiton. For 1957 a number of changes were made to the Formula 2 Cooper, now known as the Mk II or T43, including a wheelbase 2 in longer, much smoother bodywork and, of course, the Climax FPF engine.

Cooper's entry into Formula 1 was decided at a test session at Goodwood in March 1957. In late 1956 Alf Francis, Stirling Moss's mechanic, had joined Rob Walker to take charge of his racing section, and at this test session Roy Salvadori had agreed to drive Walker's Formula 1 Connaught and his Formula 2 Cooper. The original proposal for an enlarged engine came from Salvadori and following a conversation between Salvadori, Francis and John Cooper, Walker agreed to underwrite the cost of an enlarged 1960cc version of the Climax twin-cam FPF engine. This was installed in a special car prepared for the Monaco Grand Prix, a race specifically chosen because of its low-speed characteristics.

It was originally planned that Roy Salvadori should drive at Monaco, but he was committed to BRM so Jack Brabham was the driver. During practice the brakes locked, Brabham hit a barrier of sandbags and tele-

Above and right At Monaco in 1957 Rob Walker entered a Cooper with a 1960cc Climax engine for Jack Brabham, who rose to third place when the fuel pump mounting failed; Brabham pushed the car across the line to finish sixth and last. It was a serious pointer and at the British race both Cooper and Walker entered cars. Salvadori (above) pushed the works car across the line to finish fifth, scoring Cooper's first Championship points under the 2500cc Formula (at this time points were only awarded down to fifth place, so Brabham had scored nothing at Monaco). Brabham (right) retired the Rob Walker car with clutch failure. (T.C. March)

graph posts and the car was only too obviously not going to be repaired in time for the race. However, Walker had also entered a Formula 2 Cooper for Les Leston, so the 2-litre engine was transferred to the Formula 2 chassis. Despite an illegal push-start after a refuelling stop, Brabham with the Cooper-Climax held third place in what had been a race of attrition, until the car failed on lap 100 because of a broken fuel pump mounting. Brabham eventually pushed the car across the line

Tony Brooks (Rob Walker-entered Cooper) and Dennis Taylor (private Lotus) side by side in the final of the International Trophy at Silverstone in September 1957. The Lotus was a very advanced concept, but a blind alley in development. In 1957 the Lotus 12s ran in Formula 2 form only. (T.C. March)

into sixth place. During the remainder of the year the cars appeared in 1.96-litre form in the French, British, Caen and Moroccan Grands Prix, together with the International Trophy at Silverstone. The best performances were a fifth by Roy Salvadori in the British Grand Prix at Aintree, although Salvadori again pushed the car across the line after gearbox failure; then in the minor Caen Grand Prix in France the following weekend Salvadori took second place behind Behra's BRM. Both of Salvadori's successes were with works cars, but no other successes were gained that year.

1958

For 1958 the Commission Sportive Internationale (now FISA) had ruled that from that year methanol fuel would be banned and that 100/130-octane Av-gas aviation spirit would have to be used. Another change made at this time was a reduction in race distance from a minimum of 500 kms or 3 hours to 300 kms or 2 hours. Not only would the cars achieve better fuel consumption on Av-gas, but with shorter race distances they needed to carry a smaller fuel load and this in itself was a factor that encouraged the development of smaller and lighter cars, such as the Cooper and Lotus. All the existing manufacturers, Ferrari apart, had problems in converting their engines to run on Av-gas. Tony Vandervell had calculated that he would need all the time available before the first round in the 1958 World Championship at Monaco which was planned as the team's first outing that year. However, the Argentine Automobile Club made a late application to stage the Argentine Grand Prix on 19 January 1958 and the CSI consented. Neither Vanwall nor BRM was able to run in the race because of the preparations needed to run on Av-gas, and both entered objections to the running of the event. It was eventually decided that the event would go ahead, but the appeals would be heard at the Monaco Grand Prix!

Already Rob Walker and Stirling Moss had agreed that the latter would drive for Walker whenever his contract with Vanwall permitted, so Walker made an entry of his 1.96-litre Cooper in the Argentine race. Modified to run on Av-gas, the Climax engine developed 180 bhp, only a marginal drop against its previous best running on alcohol-based fuels. The principal opposition in the Argentine came from Scuderia Ferrari with the new Dino 246 cars, which had already been running on Av-gas since late 1957 and whose strong team of drivers included Hawthorn, Collins and Musso.

Because the Cooper had wheels attached by fixing studs and any wheel change would take an impossibly long time, the Walker team decided that every effort would be made to run through the race non-stop. The Ferrari team did not believe that Cooper could do this, and indeed Moss almost failed! Despite an eye problem (caused by Katie Moss accidentally poking him in the eye) and despite gearbox trouble during the race when for a whole lap the gearbox jammed in second gear, Moss, after holding third place, dropped back, but then passed the Ferraris of Musso and Collins and the Maseratis of Fangio and Behra, both of which had to make refuelling stops. Although Rob Walker's team prepared for a pit stop, standing with the spare wheels ready, Moss kept on circulating, and despite the rear tyres wearing through to the canvas, he carried on gently, aiming for the oily patches on the circuit and doing everything possible to conserve his tyres, whilst behind him Musso was charging hard, eroding his lead. Moss carried on to achieve a quite remarkable victory, the first World Championship win for Cooper by a margin of 2.7 seconds, and the first World Championship race win by a private entry.

In January 1958 Cooper had revealed its new Mark III T45 car which now featured coil spring and wishbone front suspension, the engine lowered by canting it to the right and towards the nose of the car, step-up gears which enabled the rear of the engine to be dropped to a level mounting, and a gearbox now incorporating a ZF limited slip differential. In addition, as a result of constant persuasion from both Cooper and Colin Chapman, Coventry Climax had been persuaded to produce just four FPF engines of 2207cc (88.9 × 88.9mm) developing approximately 194 bhp at 6,250 rpm on Av-gas. Two of these engines went to Cooper and two to Lotus, but Rob Walker produced his own stretched FPF with a capacity of 2015cc to be used by Moss in a new T45 chassis.

In the absence of the Vanwalls, Cooper scored a good measure of success early in the season, with Brabham and Salvadori in 1.96-litre works cars finishing second and third behind Hawthorn's Ferrari in the Richmond Trophy at Goodwood, and Moss winning the Aintree 200 with Walker's 2-litre car from Brabham's 1.96-litre version. In the

International Trophy at Silverstone Ferrari was again the winner, with Peter Collins at the wheel, but Salvadori took a fine second place with his 1.96-litre Cooper. Colin Chapman had also by this time agreed that Lotus would enter Formula 1, initially with the existing 12 model, fitted like the Coopers with enlarged FPF engines, and the International Trophy race was the first Formula 1 race for Team Lotus.

At Monaco Stirling Moss was of course leading the Vanwall team, so Walker's new Mark III car with its 2015cc engine was entered for Maurice Trintignant, whilst works cars were driven by Brabham (2.2-litre) and Salvadori (1.96-litre). Walker also entered a second car with a 2015cc engine for Ron Flockhart, a vastly experienced driver both with BRM and in sports car racing. It proved yet another race of attrition, for all the Vanwalls retired and when Hawthorn's Ferrari was eliminated by a broken fuel pump mounting, Trintignant took the lead to win at an average of 67.99 mph, repeating his victory for Ferrari on the same circuit three years before when there had been a similar level of attrition. Jack Brabham took fourth place.

It was quite remarkable for Cooper to have achieved two World Championship race victories in succession, but as the season progressed, because many of the races were held on faster circuits and the 'major' teams got their act together, so Cooper successes became few and far between. As for Lotus, it was to achieve nothing virtually all season. In the Dutch race Roy Salvadori with the works 2.2-litre Cooper finished fourth behind the winning Vanwall and two BRMs, while on the very fast Spa-Francorchamps circuit, scene of the Belgian Grand Prix, Cliff Allison brought his Lotus 12 with its 2.2-litre Climax engine across the line to take a remarkable fourth place, a position that could in fact have proved a victory if the race had been one lap longer, for all three cars in front, two Vanwalls and a Ferrari, could not have completed another lap — but this was to be Lotus' only Formula 1 success of the year.

At the French Grand Prix, Colin Chapman revealed the new Lotus 16, a much more sophisticated front-engined car, developed from the 12 but different from it in so many ways. At this stage Chapman still had faith in the front-engine layout, and it was to be another 18 months before he revised his ideas. Once again Chapman designed a multi-tubular space-frame with Costin-type bodywork (the body was not actually designed by Frank Costin) and the sleekest and prettiest lines, making it look like a mini-Vanwall. At the front there was the usual Lotus wishbone suspension, but there was a modified strut layout at the rear with longer, oval-section radius rods. Girling disc brakes were mounted outboard at the front and inboard at the rear. To achieve the lowest possible body line, the Climax FPF engine was both canted at 62° to the right, and offset 5½° from the chassis centre-line; a developed form of the Lotus gearbox used in the 12 was installed. One unusual feature of the car was that there was ducting on both sides of the body shell, with the exhaust pipe feeding through the right-hand side and discharging ahead of the right-hand rear wheel and with two long oil pipes acting as the main cooler running through the ducting on the left-hand side.

Beautiful though these cars may have been, they were simply failures. Apart from the fact that they were built to the lowest possible weight level and the team was constantly plagued by frame failures, the 16 suffered other problems, including overheating, and the ducting of the exhaust simply did not work. During 1958 the 16s were driven by Graham Hill (he had the sole 16 entry at Reims), Cliff Allison and Alan Stacey, but the only finishes during the whole season for the 16 were a fifth amongst the Formula 1 entries by Cliff Allison in the German Grand Prix (but much lower down than fifth on the road behind Formula 2 cars), a fifth by Graham Hill in the Italian Grand Prix at Monza (he had finished sixth but rose to fifth after the Maserati 'Piccolo' of Gregory/Shelby had been disqualified) and 12th Formula 1 place by Graham Hill in the Moroccan Grand Prix.

During the remainder of the year the Coopers enjoyed a measure of success, although they were outclassed in the Belgian Grand Prix at Spa-Francorchamps and the French Grand Prix at Reims. Salvadori took an excellent third place in the British Grand Prix at Silverstone behind the Ferraris of Collins and Hawthorn, and in the German Grand Prix he took second place behind Tony Brooks (Vanwall) in a disastrous race which cost the life of Collins and during which so many cars retired. At Monza Salvadori was elevated to fourth place with the 2.2-litre car following the disqualification of the Maserati referred to above, but he was many laps in arrears.

For 1959 there were two significant developments. Vanwall withdrew from serious racing and, following Maserati's withdrawal at the end of 1957, there would have been a lacuna in Formula 1 but for the growing strength of the Climax-powered cars, especially the Coopers, which would prove the dominant cars of the year. The second important development was that Coventry Climax had now produced a full 2495cc

(94 × 89.9mm) engine which with careful development was soon producing 240 bhp. There was obviously going to be a shortage of these engines during the early part of the year, so certain private owners opted for buying Maserati units (see Chapter 7) and the British works teams, Cooper and Lotus, reconciled themselves to running the 2.2-litre units during the early part of the year.

1959

Cooper's car for 1959 was the T51 MkIV which first appeared with Jack Brabham at the wheel in the International Trophy at Silverstone in May. Cooper had now a three-driver team consisting of Brabham, the rather wild American driver Masten Gregory and young New Zealander Bruce McLaren. Sadly, Roy Salvadori was no longer in the team as he had left to drive the new Aston Martin which was to prove a complete failure. Originally John Wyer of Aston Martin had agreed terms with both Salvadori and Brabham, and faced with the loss of both their drivers, the Coopers went to Esso in something of a panic to see whether it could help provide the finance to resolve the situation. Esso came up with the money, but in a famous conversation between Brabham and Salvadori, Brabham confirmed that he would stay with Cooper, notwithstanding that he had told Wyer he would drive for Aston Martin, but Salvadori, who had driven for Aston Martin since 1953, felt too heavily committed to the Feltham team and thus sealed the fate on his serious Formula 1 career.

Following Vanwall's withdrawal from racing, Stirling Moss had agreed to drive Coopers for Rob Walker, whose Alf Francis-prepared cars combined the FPF 2.5-litre engine with a Colotti gearbox. Throughout the year the Walker team was to be plagued by transmission problems, the result of poor quality parts provided by Colotti's sub-contractor. Walker had also agreed to try a Cooper powered by the BRM P25 engine, but after one race, the Aintree 200, this car was abandoned. Moss was also later to drive BRMs in two races that year, in the International Trophy at Silverstone and the British Grand Prix at Aintree.

Tony Brooks had agreed to drive for Ferrari, alongside Phil Hill, Jean

Future World Champion Jack Brabham works on his car in the paddock at the British Empire Trophy at Oulton Park in 1959. (T.C. March)

Private entrant Bruce Halford with his Lotus 16, in Formula 2 form, in the 1959 British Empire Trophy at Oulton Park. Despite the ingenuity of the design, these cars were never successful — until much later in Historic Racing Car events.

Behra and Cliff Allison (who had then left Lotus). Later in the year Dan Gurney also appeared for that team. The Ferraris were developed versions of the cars that Hawthorn had driven to win the 1958 Drivers' Championship, but the Dinos were now little more than dinosaurs, unable to match the performance of the Coopers except on the very fastest circuits. Brooks, however did come very close to winning the World Championship as the result of wins on the two high speed circuits. Reims and Avus.

Lotus remained an almost insignificant also-ran, with the prettiest cars in racing but the least effective. For 1959 a number of changes were made to the 16s. During 1958 they had been tried with the engine canted to the left at the reduced angle of 17° and this became standard in 1959. The chassis frame had been completely redesigned and there were substantial modifications to both front and rear suspension. Outside exhausts were now adopted and the bodies were more slippery and shapely than ever. Formula 1 team drivers were Graham Hill and Innes Ireland and the team ran in both Formula 1 and Formula 2. Very little was gained in Formula 2, the best performance being a second place on aggregate by Hill at Brands Hatch in August, and the team's performances were even worse in Formula 1. The only finishes in the points were a fourth place by Innes Ireland in the Dutch Grand Prix at Zandvoort and sixth by the same driver in the United States Grand Prix in December.

There were no Argentine races in 1959, so the start of the season was at the Goodwood meeting at the end of March on Easter Monday. Despite problems in practice and a sticking throttle and gearbox trouble in the race, Moss, driving really hard, scored a win with Rob Walker's car in the Formula 1 event, the first win for the 2.5-litre FPF engine.

At the Aintree 200 Moss drove the Cooper-BRM. Most of the Coopers had some problem or other and victory went to Jean Behra with his Ferrari Dino. Another Cooper victory, however, followed in the International Trophy at Silverstone where Brabham was the winner with the new MkIV car distinguished by its very slender nose, beating Salvadori with the new Aston Martin into second place. It seemed as though the Aston Martin could provide real problems for Cooper in 1959, but in fact the bearing trouble that plagued these cars would have meant that it would not have lasted if the race had been over full Grand Prix distance.

Moss with his Rob Walker car took the lead early in the Monaco Grand Prix but was eliminated by crown wheel and pinion failure. Brab-

Right Jack Brabham drove hard in practice and the race at Silverstone in May 1959, taking pole position and leading throughout, although as can be seen from the photograph, the roadholding of the Mark IV Cooper was still not all that it might be. (T.C. March)

Below With his Ferrari Dino, Phil Hill finished fourth at Silverstone, but by this stage the Dinos had, almost overnight, become dinosaurs except on the fastest circuits. (T.C. March)

ham assumed the lead with the works car and scored a fine win, his first in a World Championship race and also the works team's first World Championship victory (the previous wins of course being by Rob Walker) from Brooks's Ferrari. In this race the Ferrari Dinos were distinguished by abbreviated noses to prevent a damaged nose cone blocking off the air flow to the radiator during the thrash of the opening laps. Maurice Trintignant brought his Rob Walker car home third. The Dutch Grand Prix was to provide an unexpected win for Joakim Bonnier with the works BRM after a titanic struggle with Moss and Brabham, and while Moss was eliminated yet again by transmission problems, Brabham took a fine second place. Masten Gregory brought his works Cooper home in third place.

One of two races where the Ferraris' speed was to assert itself was in the French Grand Prix at Reims, the next round in the Championship following the cancellation of the Belgian Grand Prix. Because of the problems with the Colotti gearbox, Moss elected to drive the BRM which had been loaned to the British Racing Partnership. In practice for this race, Cooper tried a Formula 1 car with a streamlined body which incorporated the nose from a Monaco sports car with the centre section from one of the 'Bob-tail' sports cars. Brabham found that the aerodynamics of the streamlined car did not work, for at speed on the straights the front end became airborne and the car wandered badly, so he drove a normal car in the race, which was run in exceptionally hot conditions. Tony Brooks led throughout to win for Ferrari, whilst Phil Hill brought another Ferrari across the line in second place. It was here that Jean Behra was sacked from the Ferrari team after losing his temper and striking team manager Tavoni. It was a very sad end to the Formula 1 career of France's finest driver since the war, and only a month later poor Behra was killed at the wheel of his private Porsche in a 1500cc sports car race at the Avus circuit on the day before the

Although Brooks won the high-speed 1959 French Grand Prix with his Ferrari, Brabham was dominant at Aintree and scored a clear victory with his Cooper-Climax. It was only Brabham's second World Championship race win and he went on to win that year's Drivers' World Championship. (T.C. March)

Right Maurice Trintignant, who finished fifth with Rob Walker's Cooper-Climax in the 1959 British Grand Prix at Aintree, leads Bruce McLaren who finished third with a works car. (T.C. March)

Right Another view of Brabham's Cooper at Aintree in 1959. This photograph emphasizes just how the lines of the Cooper — and its construction — had improved over the years. (T.C. March)

Below Graham Hill with his fragile Lotus 16 leads Carroll Shelby's Aston Martin at Aintree. Hill finished well down the field, but Shelby was forced to retire his Aston Martin. (T.C. March)

German Grand Prix. The French race was one of the two events in 1959 in which the British entries were eclipsed. Moss spun his BRM on wet tar and was unable to restart and Brabham finished third, battered by flying stones flung up by Gendebien's Ferrari which eventually finished fourth, but led him for much of the race.

In 1959 the British Grand Prix was held at Aintree and once again the British entries were dominant. Brabham made a brilliant start and led away in the opening laps, while Gregory battled with Moss, who had again chosen to drive the BRM. Heavy on fuel and heavy on tyres, Moss was obliged to make pit stops for both and finished second to Brabham's Cooper which had run through the race non-stop, although the tyres were very thin towards the end. McLaren finished third with his works car, sharing fastest lap with Moss.

Almost as though it were a move to protect the established teams, Ferrari and BRM, from the newcomers, the organizers of the German Grand Prix decided to hold the race on the Avus track in Berlin. This 'circuit' which incorporated very steep banking at one end together with two sides of a dual carriageway and a simple hairpin bend at the other, was in fact totally unsuitable for a Grand Prix. In pre-war days the circuit had featured the steeply banked curves at both ends, but one of the curves was now in the eastern sector of Berlin, so the track was used in a truncated form. Because of the high speeds anticipated it was decided to run the race in two 155-mile heats with the results decided on the aggregate. It was calculated that the Coopers were something like 15 mph slower than the Ferrari opposition. Moss, at the wheel of the Walker Cooper, was eliminated on only the second lap, but both Brabham and Gregory mixed it with the Italian cars at close to 180

This is Innes Ireland's Lotus 16, about to be passed by Bruce McLaren in the 1959 British race. (T.C March)

mph. Ferraris took the first three places in that heat and Brabham finished fourth with Trintignant sixth. It was much the same story in the second heat where McLaren again mixed it with the Ferraris until transmission problems intervened and the Ferraris took the first three places. It was with a great sigh of relief that Cooper returned to England knowing that the next race would be on a road circuit far more suited to the car's characteristics.

This race was the Portuguese Grand Prix held on the fast Monsanto circuit at Lisbon. Moss was fastest in practice with the Walker Cooper, set fastest lap in the race and scored a fine victory with Masten Gregory with his works car in second place and Trintignant, with the second Walker car, fourth. Brabham was eliminated when he was forced off line by a slower driver and hit the straw bales. McLaren also retired. Next came the Italian Grand Prix at Monza where Moss was again fastest in practice and, driving an intelligent race to conserve his tyres, won from the Ferrari of Phil Hill. Brabham took third place. Whilst Cooper had clinched the Manufacturers' World Championship, the outcome of the Drivers' Championship was still undecided and this could have been won by Moss, Brabham or Brooks, each of whom had won two Grands Prix.

Before the final round of the Championship there were two minor races, the first of which was the Gold Cup at Oulton Park, Britain's finest road circuit. It was a race completely dominated by the Coopers and although Brabham jumped the start, Moss went ahead and scored a fine victory from Brabham with third place going to young Chris Bristow at the wheel of a Cooper entered by British Racing Partnership. In the Silver City Trophy at Snetterton, Brabham finished second with his private 2.2-litre Cooper to the works BRM of Ron Flockhart.

The final round in the Championship was the United States Grand Prix held at Sebring. Moss led away at the start, pursued by Brabham

Stirling Moss drove a fine race with Rob Walker's Cooper to win the Gold Cup race at Oulton Park at the end of September 1959, passing Jack Brabham who had jumped the start but was not penalized. Moss is seen at Esso Bend. (T.C. March)

At Oulton Park young Chris Bristow drove a Cooper Formula 2 chassis with the engine from Moss's former Cooper Monaco sports car entered by the newly formed Yeoman Credit team and took a fine third place on his Formula 1 debut. (T.C. March)

One of the last Team Lotus entries of the Lotus 16 was in the Gold Cup race and Graham Hill finished fifth. (T.C. March)

and McLaren, whilst Brooks's Ferrari was rammed by his team-mate von Trips. Brooks made a precautionary pit stop for the car to be checked and with that stop went his hopes of victory in the Championship. Brabham moved up into second place behind Moss, but early in the race Moss's gearbox broke yet again and he was out of the race and the Championship battle. Out in front McLaren and Brabham still led, whilst Brooks was driving swiftly and smoothly to make up lost ground. On the final lap of the race Brabham's engine died on him and he waved on McLaren, who accelerated away to win his first Championship Grand Prix, while Trintignant took second place with his Walker car. Brooks finished third while Brabham pushed his car over 400 yards to take the chequered flag in fourth place, having run out of fuel because of a slight leak. Brabham won the World Championship from Brooks with Moss in third place.

1960

During 1959 it had become increasingly obvious that the rear-engine way was the only one to go and all the teams, including Ferrari and Aston Martin (whose project did not get beyond the construction of a chassis), had plans for rear-engine cars well under way. One of the first to introduce a new rear-engine car was BRM whose new P48 appeared in practice for the Italian Grand Prix at Monza in 1959. This retained the existing engine, which developed 272 bhp at 8,500 rpm on Av-gas, together with the same gearbox linked to the engine by a new bell housing. The front part of the multi-tubular space-frame was almost identical to that of the front-engine cars, save that the pedals and seating position were moved forward. Double wishbone suspension was retained at the front, whilst there was a new rear layout incorporating Macpherson struts with single wishbones and radius arms. Overall the dimensions were very similar to those of the front-engine cars, with the wheelbase 2 in longer at 7 ft 6 in, the same front track and a rear track 2 in wider at 4 ft 4 in. For 1960 Joakim Bonnier stayed with the team, but he was joined by Graham Hill and Dan Gurney. In the first races of 1960 in the Argentine, BRM used the front-engine cars and although they could do no better than fifth place by Bonnier in the Argentine Grand Prix, in the Buenos Aires City Grand Prix, held that year at Cordoba, Gurney took second place. The rear-engine BRMs made their racing debut at Goodwood on Easter Monday.

The most dramatic switch in design approach was that of Colin Chapman who after struggling for three seasons with his front-engine cars, abandoned them completely and introduced a rear-engine design which represented a major step forward in technical progress. This new car, the Lotus 18, was, as far as Chapman was concerned, his first Formula 1 design, for he always regarded the front-engine cars as mere Formula 2 designs. The new car was constructed from 18-gauge tubing but also incorporated certain 16-gauge mild steel tubing. At the front there was a fully triangulated front suspension bay, carrying a forward sub-frame supporting the radiator, oil tank and body mounts. To the rear of this front frame and the scuttle panel was a cross-braced chassis bay, with braced engine bulkhead and two tubes converging with the rear suspension pick-up points. A detachable Y-section frame could be unbolted to allow engine and gearbox removal.

Within this tight, almost square-shape chassis, Chapman managed to incorporate a 22-gallon fuel tank mounted above the driver's legs and a 9½-gallon tank behind and to the right of the driver's seat. At the front there was a new layout of unequal-length double wishbones whilst at the rear there was a new double-link system with lateral location of the wheels provided by fixed-length half-shafts which also formed the upper members of the double-link system, with a long tubular wishbone pivoted beneath the gearbox. The wheels at the rear were located longitudinally by twin parallel radius rods. The glass-fibre bodywork was a distinctive squarish shape and so very different from the

Three views of the installation of the Coventry Climax 2.5 litre engine in the rear of the Lotus 18 chassis. For Colin Chapman to build a rear-engine car was a radical and an unexpected move. (T.C. March)

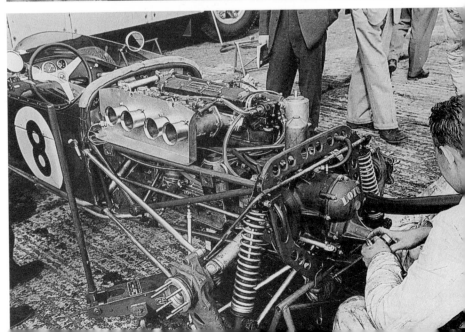

One of the new rear-engine designs to be raced throughout 1960 was the BRM P48. Here the new car is seen at Silverstone driven by Dan Gurney who retired because of engine trouble. (T.C. March)

bodywork of all the other cars competing that Team Lotus was able to re-enter Formula 1 in 1960 not only with a new car, but with a new image. At the front the Girling disc brakes remained outboard, but they were inboard at the rear, and there were the familiar 'wobbly web' wheels. The new car first appeared with Alan Stacey at the wheel at the Boxing Day Brands Hatch meeting in Formula Junior form where, mainly because of the very low-powered engine fitted, its performance failed to reflect its potential. However, Chapman had succeeded in producing a brilliant design that would prove equally effective in Formula 1, Formula 2 and Formula Junior.

Shortly after the Brands Hatch meeting, the first of the Formula 1 cars was flown to Buenos Aires for the Argentine Grand Prix. During 1960 the principal Formula 1 drivers were to be Innes Ireland and Alan Stacey (until his tragic death), together with John Surtees and Jim Clark. In addition, very early in the season a car was supplied to Rob Walker for Stirling Moss to drive. Initially the Walker Lotus was fitted with the usual Lotus gearbox, but subsequently 18s raced by Walker's team used Colotti transmission which necessitated the use of outboard rear brakes. Despite the immense potential of the 18 it was to be plagued by misfortune and tragedy during the year, although it was also to prove Lotus' first successful season in Formula 1.

At the beginning of 1960 Cooper continued to race its familiar 1959 cars, but by May the team was testing the new 'low-line' Cooper-Climax which besides being of much lower construction also featured a straight-tube chassis frame, new double wishbone and coil spring rear suspension and a five-speed gearbox. Coopers were run by many teams, including Yeoman Credit (formerly the British Racing Partnership), whose cars were distinguished by a large induction scoop on the left-hand side of the nose and excessively large tail fin, 'Tommy' Atkins, who entered a Maserati-powered car for Roy Salvadori, Scuderia Centro-Sud, also with Maserati-powered cars, and the Scuderia Eugenio Castel-

Innes Ireland scored a fine victory with a new rear-engine Lotus 18 in the 1960 International Trophy at Silverstone. (T.C. March)

lotti, which entered Coopers powered by four-cylinder Ferrari *Super Squalo* engines. This latter project, albeit unsuccessful, had some Ferrari money in it, for Enzo Ferrari was very anxious to dip his toe in the water of rear-engine car development without getting it too wet! Ferrari was to continue to race the front-engine Dinos in 1960, now fitted with independent rear suspension, but, as will be seen, Ferrari was also to experiment himself with rear-engine cars during the year.

In the Argentine Grand Prix the real sensation was Innes Ireland with the Lotus 18; he led until he spun, the BRMs came to the front, then Moss with the Walker Cooper took the lead. When Moss retired with a broken wishbone, Bonnier with the front-engined BRM led from Innes Ireland and Bruce McLaren (Cooper). The BRM retired, Innes Ireland had steering problems (and eventually finished sixth) and McLaren won the race. It was only too clear, however, that in a year in which Cooper now confidently expected to be supreme, there was a very real challenge from other teams. The next race was the Formule Libre Buenos Aires City Grand Prix, held at Cordoba, 500 miles from the capital city. After the works cars of Brabham and McLaren had led, both ran into problems and the race was eventually won by Maurice Trintignant with his Walker-entered Cooper. It was only after their experiences in South America that Cooper planned the low-line T53 cars.

The writing was clearly on the wall when Innes Ireland with the works Lotus 18 won both the Goodwood and Silverstone races early in the season and Moss followed this up by a fine victory for Rob Walker with his newly delivered 18 in the Monaco Grand Prix. At Silverstone Brabham with the new T53 Cooper had to settle for second place and at Monaco, whilst he passed Moss for the lead when rain began to fall, he crashed at Ste Devote. Second place at Monaco went to Bruce McLaren with his works low-line Cooper and Phil Hill finished third with a front-engined Dino. However, one of the most interesting developments at Monaco was the appearance of a rear-engine Ferrari. This car, with a multi-tubular chassis, 7 ft 7 in wheelbase and standard Dino 246 engine with new combined five-speed gearbox and final drive unit, was driven by Richie Ginther into sixth place. It was in practice for this race that Cliff Allison, the former Lotus driver, at the wheel of his Ferrari, crashed badly and suffered injuries which effectively brought his racing career to an end.

So far in 1960, Brabham, the reigning World Champion, had not scored a single Championship point, but all came right in the Dutch Grand Prix at Zandvoort. There was a terrific battle between Brabham and Moss, which continued until Brabham's Cooper flicked up a lump of concrete kerbstone that smashed into the Lotus, wrecking a front wheel. As a result of this accident, Brabham was unchallenged. Ireland took second place with his works 18 and, after a pit stop for a new wheel to be fitted, Moss finished fourth and set fastest lap.

The Belgian Grand Prix was the next round in the Championship and it was to prove a tragic race, especially for Lotus. In practice the Walker Lotus 18 suffered a hub failure, as a result of which Moss crashed badly and was out of racing until the Portuguese Grand Prix in August. At almost the same time, but on a different part of the circuit, Mike Taylor also crashed badly with his Lotus 18, driven by Ireland in the Argentine and which he had recently bought. The problem on this car was the failure of a steering column weld. Taylor was very seriously injured and he subsequently obtained financial damages from Lotus. In the race Alan Stacey lost control of his works Lotus 18, apparently because he was struck by a bird, and crashed with fatal results. In addition young Chris Bristow at the wheel of his Yeoman Credit Cooper, battling wheel for wheel with Mairesse's Ferrari, made a terrible error of judgement, took Burnenville corner on the wrong line, crashed through the wire fence and was killed instantly. These terrible accidents tended to overshadow the race itself which proved a 1-2 for Cooper with Brabham leading McLaren across the line.

A gaggle of 18s in the 1960 Dutch Grand Prix at Zandvoort. Innes Ireland (who finished second) leads Moss (who took fourth place with the Rob Walker car) and Stacey (who retired). (LAT)

Even on the high-speed Reims circuit, the Ferraris were outpaced by the Coopers. Here Brabham, who scored yet another victory, leads Phil Hill whose Ferrari with its crumpled nose disappeared up the escape road at Thillois in a cloud of smoke shortly after this photograph was taken. He rejoined the race, but finished at the tail of the field. (LAT)

But the Reims circuit used for the French Grand Prix was one of the very few on which the Ferraris showed real form in 1960. For the first 29 laps Brabham battled with Phil Hill and von Trips (Ferraris), but both Maranello cars suffered mechanical trouble and Brabham went on to win his third consecutive Championship race, having set a new lap record of 135.8 mph. McLaren and Gendebien, with a Yeoman Credit Cooper, had their own battle for second place, but McLaren's engine lost its power ten laps from the finish and Gendebien finished second. In this race, without Moss at the wheel of the Walker car, the Lotus 18s were never in the picture.

By now the Cooper team was at the peak of its 1960 form. Jack Brabham took pole position in practice for the British Grand Prix, with Graham Hill in his much developed rear-engine BRM second and McLaren third. As the race progressed so a pattern developed, with Brabham leading the field from the Lotus 18s of the two youngsters included in Team Lotus at this race, John Surtees and Jim Clark, and Innes Ireland, with McLaren trailing in fifth place. At the fall of the Union Jack, Hill had stalled his BRM on the line, but driving with inspiration he fought his way through the field until lap 55 when he managed to slip past Brabham into the lead. 'Black' Jack was nothing if not a fighter and he stayed firmly on the BRM's tail until just six laps from the finish when Hill made a mistake at Copse Corner; taking the apex too tightly as he lapped a slower car, his brakes played up and the BRM spun on to the grass. Brabham, not without his own problems of fluctuating fuel pressure, went on to score an easy victory from the Lotus 18s of Surtees and Ireland with McLaren in fourth place.

There were three more Championship races in 1960, but the British teams were to compete in only two of these. For reasons best known to themselves, the Automobilclub von Deutschland had decided to give the World Championship a miss and run the German Grand Prix as a Formula 2 race. Brabham scored another minor victory in the Silver City Trophy at Brands Hatch on August Bank Holiday Monday, setting

Above Jack Brabham's continued success in 1960 became almost boring and here in the British Grand Prix at Silverstone he scored yet another victory.

Right At Silverstone Graham Hill drove one of the finest races of his long career with the rear-engined BRM. After stalling on the grid he came through to take the lead from Brabham, only to spin off and out of the race. (T.C. March)

Right By 1960 several different teams were running Cooper cars in Formula 1. At Silverstone the Yeoman Credit team had three entries and this car was driven by Tony Brooks. (T.C. March)

Above Jack Brabham
(Cooper) in the 1960
Portuguese Grand Prix at
Oporto.

Right A view of one of the
Yeoman Credit Coopers,
stripped of its body panels
at Oulton Park in 1960.
(T.C. March)

Fine cockpit shots of Innes Ireland (Lotus) and Graham Hill (BRM) in the Gold Cup race at Oulton Park, 1960. (T.C. March)

fastest lap as well, before the team moved on to Oporto for the Portuguese Grand Prix. Here Moss made his racing return, but he spun in the race and was disqualified because he ran against the direction of the road to restart his car. So it was to be another victory for Jack Brabham, his fifth in succession, with McLaren in second place. The next best performance came from Jim Clark who finished third, the nose of his car patched after a practice accident.

The organizers of the Italian Grand Prix had decided to incorporate the banked track into the Monza circuit for their round of the Championship. On the basis of their experience at Avus in 1959, with the Manufacturers' Championship in the bag for Cooper and the almost certainty that Brabham would win the World Championship, the British teams did not enter. In the absence of serious opposition, this 311-mile race was won by Phil Hill with the front-engined Ferrari Dino at 132.07 mph, with team-mates Ginther and Mairesse in second and third places and Wolfgang von Trips fifth at the wheel of Ferrari's new rear-engine Formula 2 car. Two minor Formula 1 races followed in Britain. Innes Ireland won the Lombank Trophy at Snetterton with Jim Clark in second place, and Stirling Moss with his Walker car was the victor in the Gold Cup race at Oulton Park, followed home by Jack Brabham.

The final round of the Championship was the United States Grand Prix held at Riverside Raceway in November. Completely outclassed and in the knowledge that the cars could do nothing but fail, Ferrari missed the race. Stirling Moss with his Rob Walker Lotus 18 took pole position in practice and won the race from the works Lotus 18 of Innes Ireland. Third place went to Bruce McLaren with the works Cooper, and in fourth place came Jack Brabham, who also set fastest lap. Brabham had led initially, but the fuel tanks had been topped to the brim to avoid the problem suffered at Sebring the previous year. As the fuel warmed it expanded and leaked from a breather, blowing back over the engine and causing the exhaust pipe to ignite. Brabham had stopped at the pits for the problem to be investigated and he rejoined the race in ninth place. After another pit stop caused by the same problem, fuel dripping out of the overflow, he finished a poor fourth. He did, however, have the Drivers' Championship in the bag and for the second year running Cooper, too, had won the Manufacturers' Championship.

Postscript

The United States Grand Prix was the last race to the 2500cc Formula, but not the last race for cars of this capacity. Because all the British teams had opposed the introduction of the 1500cc Grand Prix for Formula 1 for 1961, there was also run in the UK a series of races to the so-called Inter-Continental Formula with a maximum capacity of 3000cc. The Formula faded out at the end of 1961, by which time the British teams were getting into their stride in Formula 1.

Because of the reluctance of British constructors to adapt to the new Formula, engine development was slow. The new V-8 Coventry Climax engine did not appear until the German Grand Prix in 1961, when the first unit was installed in Brabham's Cooper, and a new V-8 BRM did not appear until the Italian Grand Prix that year (but was not raced until the Brussels Grand Prix on 1 April 1962), so Formula 1 in 1961 was dominated by the new rear-engine Ferraris, cars that only too obviously aped their earlier British counterparts. During that year there were two major exceptions to Ferrari domination, the Monaco and German Grands Prix, both of which were won by Stirling Moss with an outdated four-cylinder Climax-powered Lotus 18. Those two races, if no others in his career, established Moss as the greatest driver of the era.

During 1962 the dominant marque was BRM and the dominant driver Graham Hill at the wheel of the Bourne cars. This combination won four of the nine Championship races that year, Clark with his Lotus won another three and there was one victory each for Bruce McLaren (Cooper) and Dan Gurney with the new flat-8 Porsche. Jim Clark and Lotus were to win their respective Championships in both 1963 and 1965, establishing beyond any shadow of doubt the complete ascendancy of Britain in Grand Prix racing, but all the time BRM, having risen from the ashes of despondency and despair, was their most serious challenger. In contrast Cooper, bereft of inspiration once Brabham had left to run his own team, gradually slid downhill, achieving less and less success and finally being taken over in April 1965 following Charles Cooper's death the previous October. The team enjoyed a brief renaissance with Maserati-powered cars in 1966-67, but disappeared from racing altogether at the end of 1968. By this time Lotus and Jack Brabham's own Brabham team were the dominant marques and the wheel had turned full circle with Ferrari being the challenger and not the challenged.

7

The also-rans

During the years of the 2500cc Grand Prix Formula there were a substantial number of contenders who never achieved real success. Sometimes these were, to all intents and purposes, amateur efforts that lacked finance, design ability and an able driver. Others were major contenders who should have achieved something worthwhile, but were not able to get their act together. Certain of the British constructors referred to in Chapter 4 fall into the category of 'also-rans', but each in its own way made a contribution to the rise of British Racing Green. It is also sad that Gordini has to be regarded as an 'also-ran', but although the team did achieve success in minor events, it could never make a breakthrough at Championship level.

France

Bugatti

The great French builder of racing and high performance cars never managed to get back into production after the war — although a handful of cars was built — partly because of the French Government's imposition of fiscal penalties on small quality manufacturers and partly because the company was making its money in other fields. Following Ettore Bugatti's death, the destiny of the company was guided by his younger son Roland and with former chief mechanic Pierre Marco acting as his mentor and 'misguiding' light. Bugatti and Marco were keen to build a new competition car and schemed a basic design that could run in both Formula 1 and sports car racing.

The veteran Italian designer, Giaocchino Colombo, amongst whose successful designs can be counted the Alfa Romeo Tipo 158 and the first post-war V-12 Ferraris, was commissioned to design the new car, typed the 251, which with vast optimism was originally hoped to be ready to race in 1954. Needless to say, the project progressed much more slowly. The design was unconventional by any standard, for it featured a straight-eight engine mounted transversely at the rear of the chassis — the rear-engine layout revealed advanced thinking and prescience (albeit to no purpose), but resulted in a car of exceptional width and very short wheelbase; the latter was 7 ft 2 in and the track 4 ft 3 in. The 2430cc (75 × 68.8mm) engine had twin overhead camshafts driven by a train of gears from the centre of the crankshaft, twin plugs per cylinder, a crankshaft in two halves, each with four throws and bolted together through a spur gear so that they could be bolted in different planes, and four twin-choke Weber carburettors. It was supposed to develop 275 bhp at 9,000 rpm, but the true output was much lower. The idea behind the rather odd crankshaft arrangement was that by bolting it in different planes, the balance, firing order and induction pulses of the engine could be varied, so that the engine characteristics could be adopted to suit the circuit on which the car was being raced. The cylinder block was cast in magnesium alloy and had wet cylinder liners. The transverse mounting of the engine was such that the inlet ports faced forwards and the exhaust rearwards. The radiator was mounted at the front of the car with the water running through the frame tubes to the engine. At the rear of the engine, an aluminium housing contained the spur gears and to the right of this there was a five-speed gearbox with Porsche synchromesh.

A de Dion axle provided the suspension front and rear with the rear axle having the de Dion tube located behind the axle centre-line in a sliding central trunnion and located fore and aft by double radius arms. On each side of the car of a rocker arm was pivoted transversely above the axle assembly with the outer end connected to the end of the de Dion tube by a vertical link and the inner end to the opposite side of the chassis. The tubular connection contained a coil spring unit, the lower part of the coil being attached to the chassis. The idea was that the load on a rising wheel was transferred through the chassis frame and acted on to the linkage on the opposite side, pushing that wheel on to the road at the same time that the other wheel was pushed upwards. A similar system was used for the front with the wheels pivoted for steering on a tubular beam axle located by a central sliding guide and with double radius rods at each wheel. Although the team was

Roland Bugatti at the wheel of the Type 251 Bugatti with Pierre Marco standing alongside the car. This was the 251 actually raced at Reims in 1956.

planning to use disc brakes of its own design, normal drums were fitted. Two cars were built, one, the rather bulbous prototype which was used for all the testing, and the other with sleeker and more shapely bodywork. Both were distinguished by the bodywork extending across the front wheels and by a radiator grill with a horseshoe emblem enclosing the symbol 'B'. The newer car had a longer wheelbase because in testing the first car had shown a distinct tendency to weave at speed.

An entry was made for the 1956 French Grand Prix at Reims, but before practice it was only too evident that the car would not prove competitive and there was much dispute within the team as to whether the car should actually be run. Maurice Trintignant was released by the Vanwall team to drive at Reims, using the newer car in practice and the prototype in the race. Trintignant retired at one-third race distance because the throttles had become jammed with dust collected by the air intakes. The team's grandiose plans to run a full team of the cars and to field a sports version at Le Mans disappeared. The Type 251 Bugattis passed into the Schlumpf collection and now form part of the French National collection at Mulhouse. Bugatti itself was acquired in 1966 by Hispano-Suiza.

DB

During the post-war years, DB, run by Charles Deutsch and René Bonnet, had built a long line of successful 750cc sports-racing cars, with a good record of success in the Index of Performance at Le Mans and one of their cars driven by Laureau and Armangnac had actually won on handicap in the 1954 Tourist Trophy Race on the Dundrod circuit in Northern Ireland. Back in 1951 DB had produced an experimental Formula 2 car based on two 750cc Panhard engines but this was never raced. During 1954 the company had built the 'monomilles' 850cc Panhard-engined single-seaters as part of a racing drivers' school project and in 1954 the team decided to adapt one of these cars for Formula 1. There was of course a 750cc supercharged category as an alternative to the conventional 2500cc and the 'monomille' with a 750cc engine and fitted with a single Roots-type supercharger slotted into this category, although its potential was decidedly limited. The car was displayed at the Paris Salon in October 1954 and two were entered in the Pau Grand Prix held on Easter Monday in 1955. They were essentially very simple cars, with a box-section chassis based on twin tubes, independent suspension at the front by wishbones and a transverse leaf spring, and at the rear by trailing arms and torsion bars. The power unit was the familiar overhead valve flat-twin engine mounted transversely ahead of the front suspension. There were special magnesium alloy disc wheels manufactured by Messier and disc brakes at the front. The cars were high in construction, with the driver seated well to the front, and their roadholding was almost non-existent. At Pau the cars were driven by Claude Storez, who gave up the hopeless pursuit of the leaders, and Paul Armagnac, who finished last, 16 laps in arrears. DBs were never seen in Formula 1 again.

Gordini

In post-war days there was very little serious support for motor racing in France and the one bright star in an otherwise dark sky was Amédée Gordini, who from early post-war years through until 1957 raced a team of cars on remarkably limited finance and with a fair level of success considering the handicaps he faced.

In pre-war days Gordini had raced Fiats with the support of the Simca organisation, the company that manufactured Fiats under licence in France, and it was a relationship that continued after the war. All early post-war Gordinis used engines based on production Simcas, but in 1951 he obtained the approval of Simca to go ahead with the production of a 1496cc (78 × 78mm) four-cylinder engine with twin overhead camshafts driven by a train of gears from the front of the engine. These cars were run in both Formula 1 and 2, in the latter events of course with the supercharger removed. Simca withdrew its support at the end of 1951 and for 1952 Gordini managed to scrape together enough money to build a new 1987.8cc (75 × 75mm) six-cylinder engine with a claimed power output of 175 bhp, although it is clear that the actual power output was much less. This was used in unit with a four-speed gearbox and the chassis was a new tubular structure with torsion bars front and rear. As well as racing the single-seaters, Gordini also built sports cars and these made frequent if only fleeting appearances (because of their unreliability) in most of the European long-distance races. Throughout 1952-53 very little success was gained, but it was not failure all the way. In 1952 Robert Manzon finished third in the Belgian Grand Prix, Jean Behra scored a surprise victory over the Ferrari team in the non-Championship Reims Grand Prix, and Manzon was fourth in the French Grand Prix at Rouen. During 1953 the only successes were victories by Maurice Trintignant in minor events, the Grand Prix des Frontières at Chimay and the Circuit of Cadours.

For the 2500cc Formula, Gordini used the six-cylinder engine enlarged

That very underrated French driver Robert Manzon at the wheel of his six-cylinder 2-litre Gordini in the 1952 International Trophy at Silverstone. He won his heat, but retired at the end of the first lap of the final with transmission problems. (T.C. March)

The six-cylinder Gordini engine, seen here in 2-litre form. (Guy Griffiths)

to 2473cc (80 × 82mm) in which form it had already been raced in sports cars and, running on alcohol fuel, had a power output of around 212 bhp. Undoubtedly the Gordini was the lightest of the 2500cc cars, but it was one of the least well endowed with power and one of the most archaic in design, for the chassis had been only slightly modified and retained a rigid rear axle. Very early in the year the team scored a remarkable victory at Pau, for Gonzalez's works Ferrari broke its crankshaft whilst leading, and Behra went on to win the race. Behra and Simon took second and third places in the International Trophy at Silverstone, Behra was third at both Bari and Caen, while Pilette was second at Chimey, and Behra and Pilette first and second in the Circuit of Cadours.

It was only too evident that the six-cylinder Gordini had no future and it was also only too evident that Gordini was so crippled financially that his prospects of producing anything more competitive were

In the 1954 Pau Grand Prix, Jean Behra turned in a very determined performance to score a victory and defeat strong Ferrari and Maserati opposition.

At Pau the Gordini équipe anxiously monitors Behra's performance. Amédée Gordini holds the stop watch, while to his right is Behra's younger brother.

not good; nevertheless somehow he scraped together the money and a new Gordini eventually appeared in mid-1955. This featured a very neat straight-eight engine of 2498cc (75 × 70mm) with twin overhead camshafts gear-driven from the front of the crankshaft, four twin-choke Solex carburettors, single-plug ignition and a claimed power output of 256 bhp at 7,300 rpm (but the true output was in the region of 230 bhp). There was a five-speed gearbox with synchromesh on the upper four ratios in unit with the engine. Once again the chassis was a simple ladder-type tubular structure with independent suspension front and rear by torsion bars which controlled a pair of L-shaped links pivoted to the side and cross members of the chassis, together with Messier hydraulic dampers. Thus the wheels moved up and down in a true vertical plane without wheelbase or track variation. The wheelbase was 7 ft 3.625 in with a front and rear track of 3 ft 10.625 in. The new car featured very neat, smooth bodywork that extended out to form a full-width nose. Originally it had been hoped that the new car would race in the 1955 French Grand Prix, but following the cancellation of this race, it was eventually driven by Jean Lucas in the Italian race at Monza where it retired after only eight laps.

During 1956 Gordini raced both the eight-cylinder and six-cylinder cars and early in the season Robert Manzon scored a surprise victory with a six-cylinder car in the Naples Grand Prix after the retirement of the works Lancia-Ferraris. Throughout 1956 no success was gained, apart from sixth place (12 laps in arrears) by Pilette at Monaco and a win by da Silva Ramos in the 48-mile Formule Libre Autumn Cup at Montlhéry at the end of the year.

Gordini had reached the end of the road, completely without financial support and at the end of his resources, and after running cars at Pau and Naples in 1957 he finally withdrew from racing and took a job as a development engineer with Renault. Gordini's withdrawal

André Pilette with the straight-eight Gordini, featuring independent suspension front and rear and Messier disc brakes, in the 1956 International Trophy at Silverstone. He retired because of final drive problems. (T.C. March)

from the racing scene was a sad blow, for the pale blue cars always looked and sounded superb — especially the cars entered in the 1956 British Grand Prix which featured a weird system of eight equal-length exhaust pipes ending just in front of the left-hand rear wheel — but it was always sad that their speed did not match their appearance. At Renault Gordini was responsible for the high-performance version of the Dauphine saloon, named the Dauphine-Gordini. He played a part in the development of Alpine sports-racing cars and, when Renault entered Formula 1 in 1977, the cam covers of its turbocharged cars bore the name 'Gordini'.

Italy
Alfa Romeo

The great Milan company had withdrawn from Formula 1 at the end of 1951 but throughout the next few years there were constant rumours that Alfa Romeo would be returning to Grand Prix racing with a car to be known as the Tipo 160. The engine design was largely based on Alfa's unraced Tipo 512 flat-12 rear-engine car designed by Colombo under the direction of Wifredo Ricart. The engine capacity was 2483cc (68 × 57mm) with twin overhead camshafts per bank of cylinders, magnesium alloy cylinder block and a roller-bearing built-up crankshaft. Alfa Romeo talked of a power figure of around 285 bhp at 10,000 rpm. The basic plan was for a front-engined car with four-wheel drive and the driver sitting at the extreme rear of the car behind the rear axle-line. Sketches of how this car was to look appear in *Alfaromeo* by Luigi Fusi (1965, third edition 1977). It has been said that a test rig was built and driven by tester Consalvo Sanesi at Monza, but there seem to be very real doubts as to whether the car proceeded to this stage. In any event, the project was abandoned and Alfa Romeo did not re-enter racing seriously until 1967 with its next Formula 1 car not appearing until 1979.

Arzani-Volpini

This car was built by Gianpaolo Volpini to a design jointly by himself and Egidio Arzani at the commission of a young amateur driver called Mario Alborghetti. Volpini had extensive experience in building small-capacity cars, but this was his first and only foray into Formula 1. The Arzani-Volpini was a rebuild and a development of the Milano, which was itself a developed version of the Maserati 4CLT/48 'San Remo' which first appeared at Monza in 1949. Two cars were raced in 1950, one with a tubular chassis, and it seems that the Arzani-Volpini was based on this car. The engine now had a capacity of 2496cc (94 × 90mm) and retained the familiar Maserati twin overhead camshafts driven by a gear-train from the nose of the crankshaft and was fitted with four single-choke Weber 48DOM carburettors. Power output was said to be 240 bhp, but there is nothing to substantiate this figure one way or the other. The chassis was a ladder-section structure of oval tubing, with front suspension by lower wishbones and longitudinal torsion bars, and at the rear a transverse leaf spring and parallel trailing arms. The body-work, built on a lightweight superstructure on the main frame, was neat and purposeful, although the styling certainly seemed to have been inspired by that of the Ferrari *Squalo*.

Sensibly the team decided that a low-key approach to racing should be followed and an entry was made in the Turin Grand Prix, a minor race held on the Valentino Park circuit in Turin at the end of March 1955. Unfortunately the car was not ready in time, so it was entered in the Pau Grand Prix a fortnight later. Alborghetti was incredibly slow in practice, slowest of all except for one of the supercharged 'monomille' DBs. He drove a very slow race, making three pit stops then, on lap

Mario Alborghetti at the wheel of the Arzani-Volpini shortly before his fatal crash in the 1955 Pau Grand Prix. The lines of the car suggest that its mother had been frightened by a Ferrari Squalo.

19, he crashed heavily into the straw bales at the tight Station corner, apparently without making any attempt to round it. Alborghetti was killed and nine spectators were injured. Quite why he crashed is just one of those mysteries of motor racing. The car was subsequently entered in the Italian Grand Prix at Monza in September where it was to be driven by Luigi Piotti, but for unknown reasons it was withdrawn and the car was never raced again.

Maserati 'Piccolo'

Although Maserati had officially withdrawn from racing at the end of 1957, development work still continued and apart from building a 3-litre V-12 sports-racing car, the team also built a new and lighter version of the 250F, the 250F/3 'Piccolo' ('diminutive') — something of a misnomer bearing in mind how large the new 250F was compared with the new breed of British lightweight cars. The project had been underwritten by an American enthusiast, Temple Buell, who had intended running a team of two cars once they had been fully developed. Compared with the ordinary 250F, the 'Piccolo' had a wheelbase 1.5 in shorter; weight was reduced by some 160lbs; the gearbox was smaller and lighter; the brakes were larger; there was modified suspension front and rear; power output was now said to be 270 bhp at 7,500 rpm; and the bodywork was rather stumpier in appearance.

The new car first appeared at the 1958 Belgian Grand Prix where it was driven for a few test laps by Masten Gregory, but whilst it was expected that Fangio would arrive to drive it, he made no appearance. The following day Stirling Moss tested both the 'Piccolo' and the new V-12 sports car at the Nürburgring. The 'Piccolo' appeared again at the French Grand Prix at Reims at the beginning of July entered by Scuderia Buell, and here it was driven by Fangio, in what was to be his last race. It was obvious that the new Maserati was no real match for the latest

Masten Gregory at the wheel of the Maserati 'Piccolo' which finished fourth on the road at Monza in 1958, but was disqualified.

Ferraris and Vanwalls, but after a pit stop to complain about gear-selector trouble when holding second place, Fangio finished fourth. Carroll Shelby drove a Buell car in the Portuguese Grand Prix and held sixth place until locking brakes caused him to spin off two laps from the end. Both Buell cars appeared at the Italian Grand Prix but only one ran in the race, driven by Masten Gregory who was racing for the first time after a crash at Silverstone in July. Gregory worked his way up to fourth place, but he was feeling the strain of racing for the first time since the accident, and stopped to hand the car over the Shelby who kept it in fourth place until the chequered flag. Unfortunately Shelby had not been approved by the scrutineers to drive the car and it was excluded from the results.

At the Moroccan Grand Prix in October the first of the Buell cars was fitted with a V-shaped nose cowling intended to take a new V radiator, but this was not ready in time for the race. The 'Piccolo' was driven by Gregory, who finished sixth. The cars were then shipped out to compete in the New Zealand Grand Prix early in 1959 in which they finished fourth (Shelby/Schell) and fifth (Jensen). The cars were sold in New Zealand and that was the end of their serious racing career.

The Tec-Mec

When Maserati had withdrawn from racing, the team's chassis and transmission engineer, Valerio Colotti, left and set up his own company known as Studio Tecnica Meccanica, and, using many of the Maserati drawings, was commissioned by amateur driver Giorgio Scarlatti to build up a new car, much lighter than the 250F, but incorporating Maserati 250F components. Colotti drew up a new space-frame chassis welded from small-diameter lightweight tubing, with new rear suspension by a transverse leaf spring and wishbones and with Girling disc brakes. The actual work on the car was carried out by Consoli, an ex-works mechanic, who built the car up in the living room of his own home until a workshop became available. The project was slow to reach completion, Scarlatti lost interest and sold the project on to an American enthusiast named Gordon Pennington. Colotti himself abandoned the project to set up, with Stirling Moss's ex-mechanic Alf Francis, a company known as Gear Speed Development Spa which was to build Colotti competition gearboxes. Consoli eventually finished the car late in 1959 and it was powered by a very tired 250F engine from a car belonging to Joakim Bonnier.

The Tec-Mec was tested at Modena by a number of drivers, but it was not running properly and in any event was completely outdated by the new breed of lightweight British cars. Tech-Mec also built up a second car on the basis of Prince Bira's old 1954 Maserati 250F chassis and installed a 4.9-litre Chevrolet Corvette engine, selling this rather nasty hybrid to Johnny Mansell in New Zealand. Pennington had entered the original Tec-Mec in the 1959 United States Grand Prix but with its hopelessly tired engine the car was completely uncompetitive; he took 17th place on the grid (there were only 19 starters) and retired after seven laps with engine failure. In early 1967 the car was acquired by Tom Wheatcroft and is now an important part of the Donington collection.

United Kingdom
Aston Martin

During the 1950s David Brown's Aston Martin team achieved a formidable record in sports car racing. Initially scoring wins only in minor British events, the team took second place at Le Mans in both 1955 and 1956, finally won that race outright in 1959 and also won that year's Sports Car World Championship. During these successful years, which some critics would argue were not as successful as they should have been, Aston Martin had toyed with the idea of building a Formula 1 car. As far back as the winter of 1951-52 the team had planned a 2-litre Formula 2 car and had built a chassis. During 1954 another attempt was made and the team built a narrower version of the DB3S sports-racing car chassis, but again the idea was taken no further. During 1955 Reg Parnell suggested to John Wyer that the single-seater should be completed so that he could take it to New Zealand for the races at the beginning of 1956. Originally it was intended that the car should be powered by a supercharged 2922cc DB3S engine, as used at Le Mans in 1954, but this broke during testing. Accordingly the car was powered by the 2493cc (83 × 76.8mm) engine used in a DB3S at Oulton Park in the British Empire Trophy in April 1953 and subsequently used at Oulton Park again the following year. The engine was somewhat down on power at 214 bhp at 7,000 rpm, but it was all Parnell had and he had to make do with it. Wyer has conceded that there should have been a unit gearbox and final drive so as to keep a lower transmission line and thereby reduce frontal area, but the CG537 unit with five speeds used in the DBR1 sports-racing car was still on the drawing board. As a result, the driver straddled a straight-line prop-shaft running from the gearbox in unit with the engine to the back axle.

The car non-started in the New Zealand Grand Prix because the engine threw a con-rod during practice, but by the time of the Lady Wigram Trophy at Christchurch a new engine had been fitted and Parnell finished fourth, not too bad considering the power handicap under which he laboured. The Lady Wigram Trophy was won by Peter Whitehead's Ferrari, with the similar 3-litre Ferrari of Tony Gaze second; third was Leslie Marr with a Jaguar-powered Connaught B-series car. Many British drivers competed in the so-called Tasman races in New Zealand and Australia where there was a 3-limit capacity with no restriction on superchargers. This Aston Martin chassis/body unit was subsequently sold to Geoff Richardson to form the basis of one of his RRA Specials and in the fullness of time it was acquired by an Aston Martin enthusiast who widened it once more to full width to produce a replica DB3S sports-racing car of somewhat inaccurate lines and obviously blurred ancestry.

It was not until Aston Martin put in hand development work on the DBR1, which first appeared in 2.5-litre form at Le Mans in 1956, that work also started on a true Formula 1 car. It was not finished until 1957 and was tested at the Motor Industry Research Association Test Centre near Rugby in late December 1957. It could have been raced in 1958, but because of the team's concentration on the Sports Car World Championship it was laid aside until 1959, a year in which the team intended to compete in sports car racing only at Le Mans, but eventually embraced in their programme sufficient races for them to win the Sports Car World Championship. The Formula 1 car was typed the DBR4/250 and used a multi-tubular space-frame chassis similar to the DBR1 sports-racing cars, but of course narrower. Originally the DBR4 featured wishbone and torsion bar front suspension, but by the time the car was raced coil springs had been substituted. As on the DBR1, there was a de Dion tube at the rear with longitudinal torsion bars, and the same five-speed gearbox/final drive unit was used. As fitted to the Formula 1 car, the 2493cc engine developed 250 bhp at 7,800 rpm. It was a pretty enough car, but not only was it outdated when it was eventually raced, but it would also have been no match for the Vanwalls and Ferraris even in 1958.

When the DBR4s first appeared, they flattered only to deceive. Roy Salvadori drove this car into second place behind Brabham's Cooper-Climax in the 1959 International Trophy at Silverstone. The race was less than Grand Prix distance and the car would probably have run its bearings if the race had been much longer. (T.C. March)

Aston Martin had signed up Roy Salvadori and, hopefully, Jack Brabham to drive the cars, but Brabham decided to stay with Cooper so his place was taken by Texan Carroll Shelby. On the cars' debut in the International Trophy at Silverstone in 1959, Salvadori took a fine second place to Brabham's Cooper, whilst Shelby retired with con-rod failure. It was an appearance that flattered only to deceive, for the race was not a full Grand Prix distance, and because of bearing trouble suffered by the team the car could not at that stage have lasted a full Grand Prix using high revs. It was only by restricting the cars to 7,000 rpm that there was any hope of reliability in Grands Prix during the year.

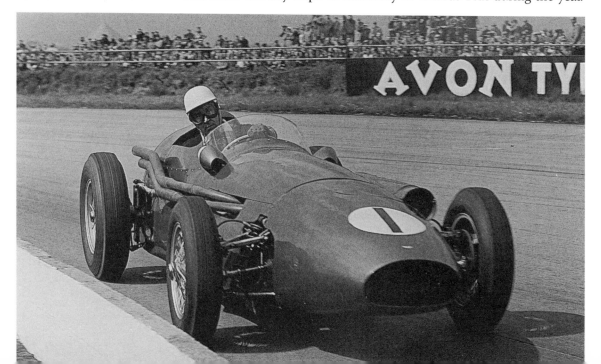

Aston Martin was still struggling in 1960 and finally withdrew after the 1960 British Grand Prix in which Maurice Trintignant brought this DBR5 across the line in eleventh place. (T.C. March)

After the 1959 season Aston Martin sold the DBR4s with 3-litre engines for Tasman racing. This car was brought back by Lex Davidson to drive in the 1961 British Empire Trophy held to the Inter-Continental 3-litre Formula at Silverstone in July 1961. The car was handling dreadfully and retired with gearbox trouble. Later these cars were very successful in Historic racing. (T.C. March)

The season proved a disaster and, in the remaining four races, both entries retired with con-rod failure at Zandvoort, Salvadori finished sixth at Aintree (Shelby retired with valve problems), and Salvadori and Shelby were sixth and eighth in the Portuguese Grand Prix; in the Italian race, Shelby was tenth, while Salvadori again retired with valve problems.

The dominance of the lightweight Cooper in 1959 made it only too clear that the Aston Martin was an outdated concept, but nevertheless the team determined to carry on in 1960. The first two cars built were sold off and the company intended to rely on the new DBR5 which was smaller and lighter than the 1959 car, featured an improved de Dion axle, torsion bar front suspension and a Maserati gearbox and final drive unit. During practice for the International Trophy at Silverstone, Salvadori's DBR5 was written off when Moss lost control of his Cooper and slid at speed into the Aston Martin which was parked in front of the team's pit. Accordingly in this race Salvadori was forced to drive DBR4/3, a slightly improved version of the 1959 car with the centre section of the body integral with the chassis and an improved improved de Dion tube. However, he retired after only four laps because of a misfiring engine, whilst Trintignant, who had joined the team for 1960, trailed round to finish tenth. The cars failed to qualify for starting money at the Dutch Grand Prix, and although they could have started without it, the team was miffed by this decision and withdrew from the race. The final outing was in the British Grand Prix when the two cars were fitted with independent rear suspension; the handling of both was appalling and Salvadori retired because of a misfiring engine while Trintignant was a hopeless 11th. One of the problems faced by Aston Martin in 1960 was that the cars were down on power compared with 1959, when they were even then not powerful enough. Aston Martin had toyed with building a rear-engine car and got as far as constructing a chassis, but after the British Grand Prix faced up to the inevitable and withdrew from racing.

Emeryson

Paul Emery was an inveterate builder of specials and his designs included a very interesting front-wheel-drive 500cc Formula 3 car, but he also built a Formula 2 car with a simple ladder-section chassis and powered initially by a 2-litre Aston Martin engine, which, it is believed, was sold through a scrap dealer who had bought it from the Aston Martin works. For 1954 the capacity of the Aston Martin engine fitted to the Emeryson was increased to 2488cc and Colin Chapman of Lotus drove it in the International Trophy at Silverstone, his only Formula 1 race. He finished 12th and last in the first heat (behind him but not classified was Horace Richards with the HAR — see below) and in the final he finished 17th and was not classified. By the Bank Holiday Monday meeting at Crystal Palace the Emeryson was fitted with

A tight-packed group of cars at the start of the final of the International Trophy at the Crystal Palace on August Bank Holiday Monday 1955. The winner, Mike Hawthorn with Moss's Maserati, has already disappeared into the distance. Here Gould (Maserati) leads Schell (Vanwall), Salvadori (Maserati) with Paul Emery's Alta-powered Emeryson to the right of the picture. Emery finished fifth.

a Grand Prix Alta engine of 2464cc. In 1955 Emery made his mark at the Crystal Palace in the London Trophy at the end of July, when he drove a stirring race to finish second to Schell's Vanwall in his heat; he also finished fifth in the final, although it was of course a very minor race. In the final he took fifth place a lap in arrears. In 1956 Emery with the Emeryson and Stirling Moss with his Maserati put on a fine display in the final of the London Trophy at the Crystal Palace. Emery led much of the way and Moss only just managed to catch him on the last lap. The Emeryson only made one appearance outside the United Kingdom, in the 1956 Caen Grand Prix in which he retired with engine trouble. In 1958 the car appeared again powered by a Jaguar 2.4-litre engine. It was a gallant shoestring effort, but obviously no serious contender in Formula 1.

HAR

The HAR was the work of a Midlands enthusiast, Horace Richards, who built for himself in 1952-53 this special, based on a chassis constructed from large-diameter steel tubing of the ladder-type with independent suspension on all four wheels using torsion bars, a 2-litre six-cylinder Riley engine and gearbox and a neat single-seater body. The car was heavy and slow, so achieved nothing worthwhile, but it was a frequent performer not only in Formula 2 but also in British Formula 1 races, often seen trailing at the tail of the field, in 1954-56. The car appeared as late as 1960 in a Formula Junior race.

JBW

Brian Wilkins was an enthusiastic amateur driver who had raced Cooper and Lotus cars before switching to a Maserati 150S. He found this too slow and heavy for British events so transferred the engine to a Lotus Eleven chassis. Subsequently he raced a Lotus with a 2-litre Maserati

Horace Richards's Riley-powered HAR was a 'hang-over' from the old Formula 2, but it was seen frequently in British events during the first couple of years of the 2500cc Grand Prix Formula. Here Richards is about to be lapped by Rosier's Ferrari in the final of the 1954 International Trophy at Silverstone. (T.C. March)

Michael Young corners his A-series Connaught inside Geoff Richardson's RRA in the 1954 International Trophy at Silverstone. Like many special builders, Richardson constantly evolved his car. As seen here it was powered by a 2-litre ERA engine with the supercharger removed. (T.C. March)

engine, but when he crashed this badly his mechanic, Fred Wilkins, built up a new sports car with the same engine and known as the JBW. There were a couple of JBW-Maserati sports cars and in addition Brian Naylor also had one powered by a Ferrari Monza engine. Naylor also built a single-seater JBW with a Maserati 2.5-litre engine which he raced in 1959-60. The JBW was basically a much-modified Cooper distinguished by its own unique styling. It achieved very little, but as only Naylor drove it, it is very difficult to assess its true potential.

RRA

Another interesting special, of which several variants were built by motor racing enthusiast Geoff Richardson, the RRA as raced in Formula 1 combined Richardson's own simple tubular ladder-type chassis frame with an ERA engine enlarged to 2 litres. In 1957 Richardson returned to Formula 1 with a new RRA which combined the ex-Parnell single-seater Aston Martin DB3S chassis with a Jaguar engine. By 1958 Richardson had moved on to a Connaught B-series car, but this was not quite the end of the line of the RRA Specials as reference will be made shortly to a Cooper-based car.

Turner

Jack Turner was another Midlands enthusiast from Wolverhampton whose main claim to fame was the series of BMC 948cc-powered glass-fibre-bodied sports cars that performed with considerable distinction during the late 1950s and 1960s, but he also built a Formula 2 car for his friend John Webb. This car, with a simple tubular ladder-section chassis, used a 1960cc Lea-Francis engine (very similar to that fitted to the A-Series Connaught) with SU fuel injection, independent suspension front and rear and cast alloy wheels with integral brake drums very similar to those fitted to Coopers. Although the car never achieved any real success, it continued to race during the early years of Formula 1 and was part of that typical and very happy scene at such circuits as Goodwood, Silverstone and the Crystal Palace. It was not raced after 1955.

Cooper variants

Cooper-BG-Bristol
F.R. (Bob) Gerard was a keen motor sport enthusiast and car dealer in Leicester with a Bristol agency. Like a number of other British drivers at the time, he was only interested in driving British cars and so this in many ways limited what could have been an internationally successful motor racing career. With venerable ERAs he finished third in the 1948 British Grand Prix behind the Maseratis of Villoresi and Ascari, and he took second place in the 1949 event behind de Graffenried's Maserati. He raced his ERA until 1953 when he acquired a Cooper-Bristol Mk II which he raced through until 1956, progressively increasing the size of the engine from the original 1971cc through 2170cc to 2246cc (the size of the production Bristol 406), and it was not until 1957 that he abandoned this immaculately prepared car, selling it to Jimmy Stuart. In 1957 Gerard acquired a Cooper T43 rear-engine Formula 2 chassis into which he installed a Bristol engine and gearbox. He drove this car in the British Grand Prix at Silverstone, finishing sixth, and he raced again in the International Trophy at Silverstone in 1957 without success. Thereafter Gerard concentrated for a while on racing Turner sports cars and subsequently in 1964 entered John Taylor with a Ford-powered T71/73 Cooper in Formula 1 events. Later that year they moved up to a Coventry Climax V-8-powered Cooper and later Gerard Racing ran a team of Formula 2 Coopers.

Cooper-BRM
On paper at least Alf Francis's project for the Cooper-BRM, built for Rob Walker to run for Stirling Moss, had everything going for it — the high standards of preparation practised by Francis and the additional power of the BRM engine had together all the makings of a world-beater. The car was based on a standard T51 Mk IV chassis, with extensive modifications, including the replacement of many of the curved tubes by straight ones, the moving of the driving position forwards to make more room for the engine, the non-standard bodywork and of course the BRM engine. Because the BRM gearbox was not suitable for accommodation in a rear-engine car, a Colotti box was fitted at Modena. Moss drove the car in the Aintree '200' race, but he was horrified to find just how difficult it was to drive and was also concerned by the violent shuddering under heavy braking. Nevertheless, after the retirement of Masten Gregory's Cooper-Climax, Moss took the lead only to retire

Above An unsuccessful Cooper variant was the Cooper-Connaught, a device put together by Paul Emery and combining the discarded chassis from Rob Walker's Cooper-BRM with a Connaught-modified Alta engine. It is seen in the Gold Cup race at Oulton Park in 1959 with Paul Emery at the wheel. (T.C. March)

with a transmission problem. The car was taken to the Monaco Grand Prix but not raced, and was thereafter sold without the engine by Rob Walker. It was a promising idea that went sadly wrong.

Cooper-Connaught

This was yet another device by Paul Emery, entered in the Gold Cup Race at Oulton Park in 1959 by Geoff Richardson, which combined the Grand Prix Connaught (ie Alta engine) with the ex-Walker Cooper-BRM chassis. At Oulton Park it was driven by Paul Emery who finished ninth and unclassified, nine laps behind the winner. The car has no other claim to fame.

Cooper-Ferrari

This was an interesting variation based on the Cooper T51 1959 chassis powered by the Ferrari *Squalo* four-cylinder, and was entered as the

Right Another variation on the Cooper theme was the Cooper-Castellotti, powered by the slightly modified Ferrari 555 SuperSqualo four-cylinder engine. This is Munaron's car in the 1960 British Grand Prix. (T.C. March)

Cooper-Castellotti by the Scuderia Castellotti with the name 'Eugenio' cast into the cam covers. Instead of the usual Cooper gearbox there was a Colotti combined gearbox and final drive unit. Because the engine was too big to accommodate the conventional sidedraught Weber carburettors, a pair of twin-choke downdraught carburettors were substituted.

At Monaco in 1960 two of these cars were entered for Scarlatti and Munaron, but both failed to qualify. Later in the year Munaron started with one in the French Grand Prix, but retired with transmission trouble. He again drove one in the British Grand Prix where he finished at the tail of the field in 16th place. In the Silver City Trophy at Brands Hatch on August Bank Holiday Monday, Munaron was 13th and Scarlatti retired with gearbox trouble. The cars' only worthwhile performance, achieved in the absence of real opposition, was in the Italian Grand Prix at Monza where Cabianca brought one car home in fourth place, but Munaron retired with engine problems. It is said that the project had the support of some financial backing from Enzo Ferrari in his attempt to find out how to make a successful rear-engine car.

Cooper-Maserati

There was likely to be a shortage of the new 2.5-litre Coventry Climax engines in 1959, so a number of small entrants opted for the four-cylinder Maserati engine; these included Tommy Atkins whose Cooper-Maserati was driven in a number of races by Roy Salvadori. Here Salvadori is seen on his way to fourth place in the 1959 Gold Cup race at Oulton Park. (T.C. March)

Because it was thought that there would be a shortage of the Coventry Climax FPF engine in 2500cc form in 1959, some entrants opted for the Maserati 250S sports car unit; this had a capacity of 2489cc (96 × 86mm), twin overhead camshafts driven by spur gears from the nose of the crankshaft, two Weber DCO3 twin-choke carburettors and a power output of 238 bhp at 7,000 rpm. To accommodate the Maserati engine a larger radiator and oil tank was needed. One of these cars was acquired by Tommy Atkins' High Efficiency Motors team for Salvadori to drive when he was not committed to Aston Martin, and this car used the standard Cooper gearbox. In 1960 Gilby Engineering ran one of these cars for Keith Greene, Sid Greene, son of *Le Patron* and a team was also run by Scuderia Centro-Sud. From the Italian team's point of view, it allowed them to go on waving the national flag but no real successes were obtained by any of the drivers of these cars,

A distinctly ugly — and unsuccessful — Cooper derivative was the Hume-Cooper. Here, driven by Ian Raby in the Gold Cup race at Oulton Park in 1959, it leads the Cooper-Climax of Stanley Hart. (T.C. March)

apart from fourth place by Salvadori in the 1959 Oulton Park Gold Cup, fourth by Menditeguy in the 1960 Argentine Grand Prix and a sixth place by Masten Gregory in the International Trophy at Silverstone in 1960.

Cooper-RRA
This was a further effort by Geoff Richardson which combined a Cooper T43 chassis with a Connaught/Alta engine and was driven by Richardson without success in minor events in 1960.

Hume-Cooper
Yet another variation on the Cooper theme, this was still Climax-powered, but was distinguished by a bulky squarish Porsche-style body and was driven by Ian Raby. Needless to say it achieved nothing in the way of success.

United States
Scarab

A visit to the European motor racing scene had convinced Lance Reventlow, heir to the Woolworth millions, that the European motor racing industry was so hopelessly inefficient that adopting an American approach would bring racing success. In August 1957, Reventlow came to a deal with an American sports car specialist, Warren Olson, to build an all-American sports-racing car which could be used to contest the 1958 Sports Car World Championship. The team planned to use the Chevrolet V-8 engine, but these plans were thwarted once it became known in September that the FIA had decided to impose a 3-litre capacity limit in the World Championship from 1958 onwards. By this time Reventlow was too committed to his project to go back and the new cars, for which he chose the name Scarab, went ahead. They were based on a multi-tubular space-frame chassis with coil spring and wishbone front suspension and a de Dion rear axle. In its initial form the Chevrolet V-8 was in 4.94-litre form, subsequently replaced by a 5.56-litre, both extensively modified by Chuck Daigh, who fitted Hilborn-Travers fuel injection and used the engine in conjunction with a modified Chevrolet Corvette production gearbox. Only three of these cars were built and enjoyed a season of immense success in racing organized by the Sports Car Club of America. Two of the cars are still raced in Historic events and one has recently been raced in the UK on a 'guest' appearance.

In 1958 Reventlow put in hand development of a new front-engine Grand Prix car, apparently ignoring the developments that had taken place in Europe and the success that Cooper had achieved in the first two Championship races of 1958. In basic concept the Scarab Formula 1 car was similar to the sports-racing cars, with a very light multi-tubular space-frame and similar suspension. The engine design was the work of Leo Goossen, closely associated with the Meyer-Drake concern that manufactured the Offenhauser engines used at Indianapolis and elsewhere. Goossen drew up a four-cylinder engine of all-alloy construction with a capacity of 2441cc (85.25 × 85.73mm), twin overhead camshafts actuating mechanically operated desmodromic valves and Hilborn-Travers fuel injection, but it would seem that power output was only around 230 bhp which obviously would be hopelessly uncompetitive when installed in such a large and bulky car. This engine was used in conjunction with a five-speed gearbox fitted in a Chevrolet Corvette casing. A change was that there was now all independent suspension front and rear by coil springs and wishbones.

Reventlow had hoped to use an American braking system incorporating aircraft-style expanding bladders in turbo-fin drums, and with a single disc brake on the back of the final drive casing with water cooling. However, because of lack of time this braking system had to be abandoned and much to Reventlow's disappointment it was necessary to fit standard Girling disc brakes front and rear. Just like the sports cars, the single-seaters were finished in a striking metallic blue and white colour scheme with a large red beetle insignia.

The new cars made their debut at the Monaco Grand Prix in 1960 and even when Stirling Moss was persuaded to test Reventlow's car, it was still hopelessly uncompetitive and neither car qualified as a starter. There was nothing to stop the cars running at the Dutch Grand Prix, although they were slow in practice, save for the fact that the organizers were prepared to pay starting money only to the first 16 qualifiers. As the Scarabs did not fall within this élite category, and so would have had to run for nothing, Reventlow scratched his team. The Scarabs eventually made the start in the Belgian Grand Prix at Spa-Francorchamps,

The American Scarabs made a hopelessly unsuccessful foray into Formula 1 in 1960 and returned, with equal lack of success, to compete in 1961 Inter-Continental races. Here is Chuck Daigh with the Scarab in the 1961 Inter-Continental Formula International Trophy at Silverstone. (T.C. March)

but both retired after a slow race. At Reims both cars ran a little better in practice, and here it was the intention that Richie Ginther should drive, but after problems in practice both were withdrawn.

Obviously Reventlow was a bitterly disappointed man, and whilst he initially planned a 1.5-litre for the new Formula starting in 1961, he decided to bring back one of the front-engine cars to run in the Inter-Continental races in the UK in 1961. After running at Goodwood and in the International Trophy at Silverstone, Chuck Daigh crashed badly in practice for the British Empire Trophy at Silverstone and the team withdrew from racing. There was planned in the United States a Formula to be known as Formula 366 for 3-litre racing engines or 5-litre production-based engines. This had great appeal to the Scarab team with its vast experience of Chevrolet engines and it decided to compete with a new Chevrolet-powered chassis with mid-mounted engine. Unfortunately the Formula never got off the ground and apart from a single race with the new car in Australia in 1962 the Scarab project was at an end. Sadly, Lance Reventlow was killed in a light aircraft crash early in 1973.

Tail-piece

Although it won only eight World Championship races, the Maserati 250F epitomized the 2500cc Grand Prix Formula; it ran in the first race to the Formula, the 1954 Argentine Grand Prix, and the last, the 1960 United States Grand Prix; it was driven by *almost* all the great drivers of the era, including Fangio, Farina, Ascari, Villoresi, Moss, Hawthorn and Collins at some time or other, but not Tony Brooks or Jim Clark (the latter came on the scene too late); and it provided the eternal workhorse of the private owner at the back of the starting grids. These two photographs were sent to the author by the photographer,

Jim Evans. On the previous page is Fritz d'Orey's 250F at the British
Grand Prix at Aintree in July 1959 (the last 250F Maserati to appear
in a UK Formula 1 race). Above is Bruce Halford's ex-Horace Gould
250F at the Gold Cup race at Oulton Park in September 1959 when
it failed to start (the last 250F Maserati to appear *at* a UK Formula 1
race).

Appendix 1

International Formula 1 results

1954-60 *(World Championship races in bold type)*

1954

Argentine Grand Prix

17 January, Buenos Aires Autodrome, 3 hours

1st, J.M. Fangio (Maserati 250), 3h 0m 55.8s, 70.16 mph
2nd, G. Farina (Ferrari Tipo 625)
3rd, J.F. Gonzalez (Ferrari Tipo 625)
4th, M. Trintignant (Ferrari Tipo 625)
5th, E. Bayol (Gordini)
6th, H. Schell (Maserati A6GCM/250F)
Fastest lap: J.F. Gonzalez, 1m 48.2s (80.70 mph)

Buenos Aires City Grand Prix

31 January, Buenos Aires Autodrome, 190 miles

Note This race is included, although it was a Formule Libre event.

1st, M. Trintignant (Ferrari Tipo 625), 2h 38m 35s, 71.80 mph
2nd, R. Mieres (Maserati A6GCM/250F)
3rd, G. Farina (Ferrari Tipo 625)
Fastest lap: Not available

Syracuse Grand Prix

11 April, Siracusa, 278 miles

1st, G. Farina (Ferrari Tipo 625), 2h 51m 37.2s, 95.32 mph
2nd, M. Trintignant (Ferrari Tipo 625)
3rd, S. Mantovani (Maserati 250F)
Fastest lap: O. Marimon (Maserati 250F), 2m 3.8s (99.30 mph)

Lavant Cup

19 April, Goodwood, 16.8 miles

1st, R. Parnell (Ferrari Tipo 625), 11m 21.4s, 88.777 mph
2nd, R.F. Salvadori (Maserati 250F)
3rd, K. McAlpine (Connaught A-series)
Fastest lap: R. Parnell and R.F. Salvadori, 1m 36.2s (89.81 mph)

Pau Grand Prix

19 April, Pau, 188 miles

1st, J. Behra (Gordini), 3h 0m 02.2s, 62.62 mph
2nd, M. Trintignant (Ferrari Tipo 625)
3rd, R. Mieres (Maserati A6GCM/250F)
Fastest lap: J. Behra, 1m 35.2s (65.06 mph)

Bordeaux Grand Prix

9 May, Bordeaux, 188 miles

1st, J.F. Gonzalez (Ferrari Tipo 625), 3h 5m 55s, 60.61 mph
2nd, R. Manzon (Ferrari Tipo 625)
3rd, M. Trintignant (Ferrari Tipo 625)
Fastest lap: J.F. Gonzalez, 1m 22.7s (66.48 mph)

BRDC International Trophy

15 May, Silverstone, two 43.9-mile qualifying heats and 102.4-mile Final

1st, J.F. Gonzalez (Ferrari Tipo 625), 1h 6m 15s, 92.78 mph
2nd, J. Behra (Gordini)
3rd, A. Simon (Gordini)
Fastest lap: J.F. Gonzalez, 1m 50s (95.79 mph)

Bari Grand Prix

23 May, Lungomare, 207 miles

1st, J.F. Gonzalez (Ferrari Tipo 625), 2h 21m 8s, 87.80 mph
2nd, M. Trintignant (Ferrari Tipo 625)
3rd, J. Behra (Gordini)
Fastest lap: O. Marimon (Maserati 250F), 2m 18.5s (89.48 mph)

Rome Grand Prix

6 June, Castelfusano, 247 miles

1st, O. Marimon (Maserati 250F), 2h 18m 48s, 104.59 mph
2nd, H. Schell (Maserati A6GCM/250F)
3rd, S. Mantovani (Maserati 250F)
Fastest lap: O Marimon, 2m 15.7s

Grand Prix des Frontières

6 June, Chimay, 136 miles

1st, 'B. Bira' (Maserati 250F) 1h 22m 16s, 98.90 mph
2nd, A. Pilette (Gordini)
3rd, D. Beauman (Connaught)
Fastest lap: J. Pollet (Gordini), 3m 51.0s

Belgian Grand Prix

20 June, Spa-Francorchamps, 315 miles

1st, J.M. Fangio (Maserati 250F), 2h 44m 42.4s, 114.99 mph
2nd, M. Trintignant (Ferrari Tipo 625)
3rd, S. Moss (Maserati 250F)
4th, J.F. Gonzalez/J.M. Hawthorn (Ferrari Tipo 625)
5th, A. Pilette (Gordini)
6th, 'B. Bira' (Maserati 250F)
Fastest lap: J.M. Fangio, 4m 25.5s (118.97 mph)

French Grand Prix

4 July, Reims, 311 miles

1st, J.M. Fangio (Mercedes-Benz W196), 2h 42m 47.9s (115.98 mph)
2nd, K. Kling (Mercedes-Benz W196)
3rd, R. Manzon (Ferrari Tipo 625)
4th, 'B. Bira' (Maserati 250F)
5th, L. Villoresi (Maserati 250F)
6th, J. Behra (Gordini)
Fastest lap: H. Herrmann (Mercedes-Benz W196), 2m 32.9s (121.46 mph)

Rouen Grand Prix

11 July, Les Essarts, 302 miles

1st, M. Trintignant (Ferrari Tipo 625), 3h 40m 34.5s, 82.37 mph)
2nd, 'B. Bira' (Maserati 250F)
3rd, R.F. Salvadori (Maserati 250F)
Fastest lap: M. Trintignant, 2m 9.9s (88.33 mph)

British Grand Prix

17 July, Silverstone, 270 miles

1st, J.F. Gonzalez (Ferrari Tipo 625) 2h 56m 14s (89.69 mph)
2nd, J.M. Hawthorn (Ferrari Tipo 625)
3rd, O. Marimon (Maserati 250F)
4th, J.M. Fangio (Mercedes-Benz W196)
5th, M. Trintignant (Ferrari Tipo 625)
6th, R. Mieres (Maserati 250F)
Fastest lap: J.F. Gonzalez, J.M. Hawthorn, S. Moss (Maserati 250F), A. Ascari (Maserati 250F), O. Marimon, J. Behra (Gordini), J.M. Fangio, 1m 50s (95.79 mph)

Circuit of Caen

25 July, La Prairie, 131 miles

1st, M. Trintignant (Ferrari Tipo 625), 1h 29m 01.1s, 88.54 mph
2nd, S. Moss (Maserati 250F)
3rd, J. Behra/J. Berger (Gordini)
Fastest lap: S. Moss, 1m 25.7s (92.40 mph)

European Grand Prix

1 August, Nürburgring, 312 miles

1st, J.M. Fangio (Mercedes-Benz W196), 3h 45m 45.8s (83.11 mph)
2nd, J.M. Hawthorn/J.F. Gonzalez (Ferrari Tipo 625)
3rd, M. Trintignant (Ferrari Tipo 625)
4th, K. Kling (Mercedes-Benz W196)
5th, S. Mantovani (Maserati 250F)
6th, P. Taruffi (Ferrari Tipo 625)
Fastest lap: K. Kling, 9m 55.1s (85.75 mph)

Gold Cup Race

7 August, Oulton Park, 99 miles

1st, S. Moss (Maserati 250F), 1h 11m 27s, 83.48 mph
2nd, R. Parnell (Ferrari Tipo 625)
3rd, F.R. Gerard (Cooper-Bristol)
Fastest lap: S. Moss, 1m 56.85s (85.11 mph)

Snetterton Formula 1 Race

14 August, Snetterton, 108 miles

1st, R. Parnell (Ferrari Tipo 625), 1h 13m 16.8s, 88.42 mph
2nd, F.R. Gerard (Cooper-Bristol)
3rd, D. Beauman (Connaught A-series)
Fastest lap: R. Parnell, 1m 48.4s (89.67 mph)

Pescara Grand Prix

15 August, Pescara, 254 miles

1st, L. Musso (Maserati 250F), 2h 55m 54.51s, 86.73 mph
2nd, 'B. Bira' (Maserati 250F)
3rd, H. Schell (Maserati A6GCM/250F)
Fastest lap: 'B. Bira', 10m 46.4s (88.45 mph)

Swiss Grand Prix

22 August, Bremgarten, 281 miles

1st, J.M. Fangio (Mercedes-Benz W196), 3h 0m 34.5s,
99.14 mph
2nd, J.F. Gonzalez (Ferrari Tipo 625)
3rd, H. Herrmann (Mercedes-Benz W196)
4th, R. Mieres (Maserati 250F)
5th, S. Mantovani (Maserati 250F)
6th, K. Wharton (Maserati 250F)
Fastest lap: J.M. Fangio, 2m 39.7s (102.91 mph)

Italian Grand Prix

5 September, Monza, 313 miles

1st, J.M. Fangio (Mercedes-Benz W196), 2h 47m 47.9s,
111.91 mph
2nd, J.M. Hawthorn (Ferrari Tipo 625)
3rd, J.F. Gonzalez/U. Maglioli (Ferrari Tipo 625)
4th, H. Herrmann (Mercedes-Benz W196)
5th, M. Trintignant (Ferrari Tipo 625)
6th, F. Wacker (Gordini)
Fastest lap: J.F. Gonzalez, 2m 0.8s (116.67 mph)

Circuit of Cadours

12 September, Cadours, 75 miles

1st, J. Behra (Gordini), 58m 49.8s, 76.32 mph
2nd, S. Moss (Maserati 250F)
3rd, L. Rosier (Maserati 250F)
Fastest lap: J. Behra/A. Pilette (Gordini), 1m 55.05 (78.12
mph)

Grosser Preis Von Berlin

19 September, Avus, 313 miles

1st, K. Kling (Mercedes-Benz W196), 3h 39m 59.8s,
132.66 mph
2nd, J.M. Fangio (Mercedes-Benz W196)
3rd, H. Herrmann (Mercedes-Benz W196)
Fastest lap: J.M. Fangio, 2m 13.4s, (137.74 mph)

Goodwood Trophy

25 September, Goodwood, 50.4 miles

1st, S. Moss (Maserati 250F), 33m 3.2s, 91.49 mph
2nd, P.J. Collins (Vanwall Special)
3rd, R.F. Salvadori (Masertati 250F)
Fastest lap: S. Moss, 1m 33.0s (92.90 mph)

Daily Telegraph Trophy

2 October, Aintree, 51 miles

1st, S. Moss (Maserati 250F), 35m 49.0s, 85.43 mph
2nd, J.M. Hawthorn (Vanwall Special)
3rd, H. Schell (Maserati 250F)
Fastest lap: S. Moss, J.M. Hawthorn, 2m 4.8s (86.54 mph)

Spanish Grand Prix

24 October, Pedralbes, Barcelona, 313 miles

1st, J.M. Hawthorn (Ferrari Tipo 553), 3h 13m 52.1s,
97.86 mph
2nd, L. Musso (Maserati 250F)
3rd, J.M. Fangio (Mercedes-Benz W196)
4th, R. Mieres (Maserati 250F)
5th, K. Kling (Mercedes-Benz W196)
6th, F. Godia-Sales (Maserati 250F)
Fastest lap: A. Ascari (Lancia D50), 2m 20.4s (100.38
mph)

Drivers' World Championship

(Best five of nine events)

1st, J.M. Fangio, 45 points
2nd, J.F. Gonzalez, 25 $^{1}/_{7}$ points
3rd, J.M. Hawthorn, 24 $^{9}/_{14}$ points
4th, M. Trintignant, 17 points
5th, K. Kling, 12 points
6th, W. Vukovich, 8 points

Note Fractions were caused partly by shared drives and
partly by the sharing of the fastest lap at Silverstone. W.
Vukovich scored his points at Indianapolis.

1955
Argentine Grand Prix

16 January, Buenos Aires Autodrome, 3 hours

1st, J.M. Fangio (Mercedes-Benz W196), 3h 0m 38.6s,
80.57 mph
2nd, J.F. Gonzalez/G. Farina/M. Trintignant (Ferrari Tipo
625A)
3rd, G.Farina/U.Maglioli/M.Trintignant(FerrariTipo625A)
4th,H.Herrmann/K.Kling/S.Moss(Mercedes-BenzW196)
5th, R. Mieres (Maserati 250F)
6th, H. Schell/J. Behra (Maserati 250F)
Fastest lap: J.M. Fangio, 1m 48.3s (80.81 mph)

Buenos Aires City Grand Prix

30 January, Buenos Aires Autodrome, aggregate of two heats totalling 175 miles

1st, J.M. Fangio (Mercedes-Benz W196), 2h 23m 18.9s, 73.40 mph
2nd, S. Moss (Mercedes-Benz W196)
3rd, J.F. Gonzalez/M. Trintignant (Ferrari Tipo 625A)
Fastest lap: S. Moss and G. Farina (Ferrari Tipo 625A), 2m 19.5s (75.44 mph)

Valentino Grand Prix

27 March, Valentino Park, Turin, 235 miles

1st, A. Ascari (Lancia D50), 2h 40m 21.25s, 87.86 mph
2nd, R. Mieres (Maserati 250F)
3rd, L. Villoresi (Lancia D50)
Fastest lap: J. Behra (Maserati 250F), 1m 44.2s (90.86 mph)

Richmond Trophy

11 April, Goodwood, 50 miles

1st, R.F. Salvadori (Maserati 250F), 33m 53.0s, 89.26 mph
2nd, F.R. Gerard (Cooper-Bristol)
3rd, D. Beauman (Connaught A-series)
Fastest lap: R.F. Salvadori, 1m 33.8s (92.11 mph)

Pau Grand Prix

11 April, Pau, 189 miles

1st, J. Behra (Maserati 250F), 3h 2m 0.6s, 62.33 mph
2nd, E. Castellotti (Lancia D50)
3rd, R. Mieres (Maserati 250F)
Fastest lap: A. Ascari (Lancia D50), 1m 35.3s (66.00 mph)

Bordeaux Grand Prix

24 April, Bordeaux, 188 miles

1st, J. Behra (Maserati 250F), 2h 54m 12.6s, 65.07 mph
2nd, L. Musso (Maserati 250F)
3rd, R. Mieres (Maserati 250F)
Fastest lap: S. Moss (Maserati 250F), 1m 20.9s (67.92 mph)

BRDC International Trophy

7 May, Silverstone, 180 miles

1st, P.J. Collins (Maserati 250F), 1h 49m 50s, 95.94 mph
2nd, R.F. Salvadori (Maserati 250F)
3rd, 'B. Bira' (Maserati 250F)
Fastest lap: P.J. Collins and R.F. Salvadori, 1m 47s (98.48 mph)

Naples Grand Prix

8 May, Posillipo, 153 miles

1st, A. Ascari (Lancia D50), 2h 13m 3s, 69.33 mph
2nd, L. Musso (Maserati 250F)
3rd, L. Villoresi (Lancia D50)
Fastest lap: J. Behra (Maserati 250F), 2m 9.4s (70.83 mph)

European Grand Prix

22 May, Monaco, 195 miles

1st, M. Trintignant (Ferrari Tipo 625A), 2h 58m 9.8s, 65.80 mph
2nd, E. Castellotti (Lancia D50)
3rd, C. Perdisa/J. Behra (Maserati 250F)
4th, G. Farina (Ferrari Tipo 625A)
5th, L. Villoresi (Lancia D50)
6th, L. Chiron (Lancia D50)
Fastest lap: J.M.Fangio (Mercedes-Benz W196), 1m 42.4s (68.73 mph)

Albi Grand Prix

29 May, Les Plânques, 195 miles

1st, A. Simon (Maserati 250F), 2h 23m 22.1s, 81.66 mph
2nd, L. Rosier (Maserati 250F)
3rd, H.H. Gould (Maserati 250F)
Fastest lap: A. Simon, 1m 17.1s (86.75 mph)

Belgian Grand Prix

5 June, Spa-Francorchamps, 315 miles

1st, J.M. Fangio (Mercedes-Benz W196), 2h 39m 29s, 118.78 mph
2nd, S. Moss (Mercedes-Benz W196)
3rd, G. Farina (Ferrari Tipo 555)
4th, P. Frère (Ferrari Tipo 555)
5th, R. Mieres/J. Behra (Maserati 250F)
6th, M. Trintignant (Ferrari Tipo 555)
Fastest lap: J.M. Fangio, 4m 20.6s (121.21 mph)

Dutch Grand Prix

19 June, Zandvoort, 260 miles

1st, J.M. Fangio (Mercedes-Benz W196), 2h 54m 23.8s, 89.62 mph
2nd, S. Moss (Mercedes-Benz W196)
3rd, L. Musso (Maserati 250F)
4th, R. Mieres (Maserati 250F)
5th, E. Castellotti (Ferrari Tipo 555)
6th, J. Behra (Maserati 250F)
Fastest lap: R. Mieres, 1m 40.9s (92.96 mph)

British Grand Prix

16 July, Aintree, 270 miles

1st, S. Moss (Mercedes-Benz W196), 2h 54m 23.8, 86.47 mph
2nd, J.M. Fangio (Mercedes-Benz W196)
3rd, K. Kling (Mercedes-Benz W196)
4th, P. Taruffi (Mercedes-Benz W196)
5th, L. Musso (Maserati 250F)
6th, J.M. Hawthorn/E. Castellotti (Ferrari Tipo 625A)
Fastest lap: S. Moss, 2m 0.4s, 89.70 mph

International Trophy

30 July, Crystal Palace, two 13.5-mile qualifying heats and 21-mile Final

1st, J.M. Hawthorn (Maserati 250F), 16m 10s, 77.38 mph
2nd, H. Schell (Vanwall)
3rd, R.F. Salvadori (Maserati 250F)
Fastest lap: J.M. Hawthorn, 1m 3.4s (78.93 mph)

Daily Record Trophy

6 August, Charterhall, two 30-mile qualifying heats and 40-mile Final

1st, F.R. Gerard (Maserati 250F) 28m 49s, 83.29 mph
2nd, H.H. Gould (Maserati 250F)
3rd, L. Rosier (Maserati 250F)
Fastest lap: F.R. Gerard and L. Rosier, 1m 23.5s (85.92 mph)

RedEx Trophy

13 August, Snetterton, 68 miles

1st, H. Schell (Vanwall), 50m 7.4s, 80.80 mph
2nd, K. Wharton (Vanwall)
3rd, S. Moss (Maserati 250F)
Fastest lap: S. Moss, 1m 56s (83.79 mph)

Daily Telegraph Trophy

3 September, Aintree, 51 miles

1st, R.F. Salvadori (Maserati 250F), 36m 33s, 83.72 mph
2nd, F.R. Gerard (Cooper-Bristol)
3rd, H.H. Gould (Maserati 250F)
Fastest lap: R.F. Salvadori, 2m 5.2s (86.26 mph)

Italian Grand Prix

11 September, Monza, 312 miles

1st, J.M. Fangio (Mercedes-Benz W196), 2h 25m 4.4s, 128.50 mph
2nd, P. Taruffi (Mercedes-Benz W196)
3rd, E. Castellotti (Ferrari Tipo 555)
4th, J. Behra (Maserati 250F)
5th, C. Menditeguy (Maserati 250F)
6th, U. Maglioli (Ferrari Tipo 555)
Fastest lap: S. Moss (Mercedes-Benz W196), 2m 46.9s (134.04 mph)

Gold Cup Race

24 September, Oulton Park, 150 miles

1st, S. Moss (Maserati 250F), 1h 44m 5.4s, 85.94 mph
2nd, J.M. Hawthorn (Lancia D50)
3rd, J.D. Titterington (Vanwall)
Fastest lap: S. Moss, 1m 53.2s (87.81 mph)

Avon Trophy

1 October, Castle Combe, 101 miles

1st, H. Schell (Vanwall), 1h 10m 32.8s, 86.07 mph
2nd, H.H. Gould (Maserati 250F)
3rd, F.R. Gerard (Cooper-Bristol)
Fastest lap: H. Schell, 1m 13.6s (90.00 mph)

Syracuse Grand Prix

23 October, Siracusa, 239 miles

1st, C.A.S. Brooks (Connaught B-series), 2h 24m 55.7s, 99.05 mph
2nd, L. Musso (Maserati 250F)
3rd, L. Villoresi (Maserati 250F)
Fastest lap: C.A.S. Brooks, 2m 0.2s (102.36 mph)

Drivers' World Championship

(Best five of seven events)

1st, J.M. Fangio, 40 points
2nd, S. Moss, 23 points
3rd, E. Castellotti, 12 points
4th, M. Trintignant, 11⅓ points
5th, G. Farina, 10⅓ points
6th, P. Taruffi, 9 points

Note Fractions of points were caused by shared drives.

1956

Argentine Grand Prix

22 January, Buenos Aires Autodrome, 3 hours

1st, L. Musso/J.M. Fangio (Lancia-Ferrari), 3h 0m 3.7s, 79.39 mph
2nd, J. Behra (Maserati 250F)
3rd, J.M. Hawthorn (Maserati 250F)
4th, F. Landi/G. Gerini (Maserati 250F)
5th, O. Gendebien (Lancia-Ferrari)
6th, A. Uria/O. Gonzalez (Maserati 250F)
Fastest lap: J.M. Fangio, 1m 45.3s (82.80 mph)

Buenos Aires City Grand Prix

5 February, Mendoza, 156 miles

1st, J.M. Fangio (Lancia-Ferrari), 1h 52m 38.9s, 85.70 mph
2nd, S. Moss (Maserati 250F)
3rd, J. Behra (Maserati 250F)
Fastest lap: J.M. Fangio, 1m 49.2s (85.72 mph)

Richmond Trophy

2 April, Goodwood, 73 miles

1st, S. Moss (Maserati 250F), 48m 50.4s, 94.35 mph
2nd, R.F. Salvadori (Maserati 250F)
3rd, L. Leston (Connaught B-series)
Fastest lap: S. Moss, 1m 30.2s (95.79 mph)

Syracuse Grand Prix

15 April, Siracusa, 273 miles

1st, J.M. Fangio (Lancia-Ferrari), 2h 48m 59.9s, 97.10 mph
2nd, L. Musso (Lancia-Ferrari)
3rd, P.J. Collins (Lancia-Ferrari)
Fastest lap: J.M. Fangio, 1m 59.8s (103.48 mph)

Aintree 200

21 April, Aintree, 201 miles

1st, S. Moss (Maserati 250F), 2h 23m 6.4s, 84.24 mph
2nd, C.A.S. Brooks (BRM P25)
3rd, J. Brabham (Maserati 250F)
Fastest lap: C.A.S. Brooks, 2m 4.6s (86.68 mph)

BRDC International Trophy

5 May, Silverstone, 176 miles

1st, S. Moss (Vanwall), 1h 44m 53s (100.47 mph)
2nd, A. Scott-Brown (Connaught B-series)
3rd, D. Titterington (Connaught B-series)
Fastest lap: J.M. Hawthorn (BRM) and S. Moss, 1m 43s (102.30 mph)

Naples Grand Prix

6 May, Posillipo, 152.5 miles

1st, R. Manzon (Gordini), 2h 20m 43.8s, 65.14 mph
2nd, H.H. Gould (Maserati 250F)
3rd, G. Gerini (Maserati 250F)
Fastest lap: L. Musso (Maserati 250F), 2m 12.3s (69.36 mph)

Monaco Grand Prix

13 May, Monaco, 195 miles

1st, S. Moss (Maserati 250F), 3h 0m 32.9s, 64.94 mph
2nd, P.J. Collins/J.M. Fangio (Lancia-Ferrari)
3rd, J. Behra (Maserati 250F)
4th, J.M. Fangio/E. Castellotti (Lancia-Ferrari)
5th, H. da Silva Ramos (Gordini)
6th, E. Bayol/A. Pilette (Gordini)
Fastest lap: J.M. Fangio, 1m 44.4s (67.39 mph)

Belgian Grand Prix

3 June, Spa-Francorchamps, 316 miles

1st, P.J. Collins (Lancia-Ferrari) 2h 40m 00.3s, 118.44 mph
2nd, P. Frère (Lancia-Ferrari)
3rd, C. Perdisa/S. Moss (Maserati 250F)
4th, H. Schell (Vanwall)
5th, L. Villoresi (Maserati)
6th, A. Pilette (Lancia-Ferrari)
Fastest lap: S. Moss, 4m 14.7s (124.01 mph)

French Grand Prix

1 July, Reims, 315 miles

1st, P.J. Collins (Lancia-Ferrari), 2h 34m 23.4s, 122.29 mph
2nd, E. Castellotti (Lancia-Ferrari)
3rd, J. Behra (Maserati 250F)
4th, J.M. Fangio (Lancia-Ferrari)
5th, C. Perdisa/S. Moss (Maserati 250F)
6th, L. Rosier (Maserati 250F)
Fastest lap: J.M. Fangio (Lancia-Ferrari), 2m 25.8s (127.37 mph)

British Grand Prix

14 July, Silverstone, 295.62 miles

1st, J.M. Fangio (Lancia-Ferrari), 2h 59m 47.0s, 98.65 mph
2nd, A. de Portago/P.J. Collins (Lancia-Ferrari)
3rd, J. Behra (Maserati 250F)
4th, J. Fairman (Connaught B-series)
5th, H.H. Gould (Maserati 250F)
6th, L. Villoresi (Maserati 250F)
Fastest lap: S. Moss (Maserati 250F), 1m 43.2s (102.10 mph)

German Grand Prix

5 August, Nürburgring, 312 miles

1st, J.M. Fangio (Lancia-Ferrari), 3h 38m 43.7s, 85.63 mph
2nd, S. Moss (Maserati 250F)
3rd, J. Behra (Maserati 250F)
4th, F. Godia-Sales (Maserati 250F)
5th, L. Rosier (Maserati 250F)
6th, O. Volonterio (Maserati A6GCM/250F) (Not officially classified)
Fastest lap: J.M. Fangio, 9m 41.6s (87.73 mph)

Caen Grand Prix

26 August, La Prairie, 153 miles

1st, H. Schell (Maserati 250F), 1h 54m 19.8s, 80.11 mph
2nd, A. Simon (Gordini)
3rd, R.F. Salvadori (Maserati 250F)
Fastest lap: R.F. Salvadori, 1m 26.2s (91.29 mph)

European Grand Prix

2 September, Monza, 311 miles

1st, S. Moss (Maserati 250F), 2h 23m 41.3s, 129.73 mph
2nd, P.J. Collins/J.M. Fangio (Lancia-Ferrari)
3rd, R. Flockhart (Connaught B-series)
4th, F. Godia-Sales (Maserati 250F)
5th, J. Fairman (Connaught B-series)
6th, L. Piotti (Maserati 250F)
Fastest lap: S. Moss, 2m 45.5s (135.50 mph)

Driver's World Championship

(Best five of eight events)

1st, J.M. Fangio, 31½ points
2nd, S. Moss, 27 points
3rd, P.J. Collins, 25 points
4th, J. Behra, 22 points
5th, P. Flaherty, 8 points
6th, E. Castellotti, 7½ points

Note P. Flaherty scored his points for his win at Indianapolis.

1957
Argentine Grand Prix

13 January, Buenos Aires Autodrome, 3 hours

1st, J.M. Fangio (Maserati 250F), 3h 0m 55.9s, 80.61 mph
2nd, J. Behra (Maserati 250F)
3rd, C. Menditeguy (Maserati 250F)
4th, H. Schell (Maserati 250F)
5th, J.F. Gonzalez/A. de Portago (Lancia-Ferrari)
6th, C. Perdisa/P.J. Collins/W. von Trips (Lancia-Ferrari)
Fastest lap: S. Moss (Maserati 250F), 1m 44.7s (81.58 mph)

Buenos Aires City Grand Prix

27 January, Buenos Aires Autodrome, aggregate of two heats, totalling 175 miles

1st, J.M. Fangio (Maserati 250F), 2h 22m 30.3s, 74.05 mph
2nd, J. Behra (Maserati 250F)
3rd, L. Musso/P.J. Collins (Lancia-Ferrari)
Fastest lap: J.M. Fangio and P.J. Collins, 2m 19.6s (75.43 mph)

Note Race held as a Formula 1 event for the first time.

Syracuse Grand Prix

7 April, Siracusa, 273 miles

1st, P.J. Collins (Ferrari Tipo 801), 2h 40m 11.9s, 102.40 mph
2nd, L. Musso (Lancia-Ferrari)
3rd, S. Moss (Vanwall)
Fastest lap: S. Moss, 1m 54.3s (107.64 mph)

Richmond Trophy

22 April, Goodwood, 74 miles

1st, S. Lewis-Evans (Connaught B-series), 50m 49.8s, 90.66 mph
2nd, J. Fairman (Connaught B-series)
3rd, R. Flockhart (BRM P25)
Fastest lap: C.A.S. Brooks (Vanwall), 1m 29.6s (96.43 mph)

Pau Grand Prix

22 April, Pau, 188.6 miles

J. Behra (Maserati 250F), 3h 0m 13.7s, 62.80 mph
2nd, H. Schell (Maserati 250F)
3rd, I. Bueb (Connaught B-series)
Fastest lap: J. Behra, 1m 35.9s (64.47 mph)

Naples Grand Prix

28 April, Posillipo, 152.8 miles

1st, P.J. Collins (Lancia-Ferrari), 2h 10m 31.2s, 70.27 mph
2nd, J.M. Hawthorn (Ferrari Tipo 801)
3rd, L. Musso (Ferrari Tipo 156F2)
Fastest lap: J.M. Hawthorn, 2m 5.6s (73.02 mph)

Monaco Grand Prix

19 May, Monaco, 205 miles

1st, J.M. Fangio (Maserati 250F), 3h, 10m 12.8s, 64.72 mph
2nd, C.A.S. Brooks (Vanwall)
3rd, M. Gregory (Maserati 250F)
4th, S. Lewis-Evans (Connaught B-series)
5th, M. Trintignant (Lancia-Ferrari)
6th, J. Brabham (Cooper-Climax)
Fastest lap: J.M. Fangio, 1m 45.6s (66.62 mph)

French Grand Prix

7 July, Les Essarts, Rouen, 313 miles

1st, J.M. Fangio (Maserati 250F), 3h 7m 46.4s, 100.20 mph
2nd, L. Musso (Ferrari Tipo 801)
3rd, P.J. Collins (Ferrari Tipo 801)
4th, J.M. Hawthorn (Ferrari Tipo 801)
5th, J. Behra (Maserati 250F)
6th, H. Schell (Maserati 250F)
Fastest lap: L. Musso, 2m 22.4s (102.87 mph)

Reims Grand Prix

14 July, Reims, 315 miles

1st, L. Musso (Lancia-Ferrari), 2h 33m 2.6s, 123.40 mph
2nd, J. Behra (Maserati 250F)
3rd, S. Lewis-Evans (Vanwall)
Fastest lap: J. Behra, 2m 27.8s (125.70 mph)

European Grand Prix

20 July, Aintree, 270 miles

1st, C.A.S. Brooks/S. Moss (Vanwall), 3h 6m 37.8s, 86.79 mph
2nd, L. Musso (Ferrari Tipo 801)
3rd, J.M. Hawthorn (Ferrari Tipo 801)
4th, M. Trintignant/P.J. Collins (Ferrari Tipo 801)
5th, R.F. Salvadori (Cooper-Climax)
6th, F.R. Gerard (Cooper-BG-Bristol)
Fastest lap: S. Moss, 1m 59.2s (90.60 mph)

Note Collins took over for four laps, insufficient to share points in the World Championship.

Caen Grand Prix

28 July, La Prairie, 188 miles

1st, J. Behra (BRM P25), 2h 1m 35s, 92.82 mph
2nd, R.F. Salvadori (Cooper-Climax)
3rd, B. Halford (Maserati 250F)
Fastest lap: J. Behra, 1m 20.7s (97.57 mph)

German Grand Prix

4 August, Nürburgring, 312 miles

1st, J.M. Fangio (Maserati 250F), 3h 30m 38.3s, 88.79 mph
2nd, J.M. Hawthorn (Ferrari Tipo 801)
3rd, P.J. Collins (Ferrari Tipo 801)
4th, L. Musso (Ferrari Tipo 801)
5th, S. Moss (Vanwall)
6th, J. Behra (Maserati 250F)
Fastest lap: J.M. Fangio, 9m 17.4s (91.54 mph)

Pescara Grand Prix

18 August, Pescara, 286 miles

1st, S. Moss (Vanwall), 2h 59m 22.7s, 95.70 mph
2nd, J.M. Fangio (Maserati 250F)
3rd, H. Schell (Maserati 250F)
4th, M. Gregory (Maserati 250F)
5th, S. Lewis-Evans (Vanwall)
6th, G. Scarlatti (Maserati 250F)
Fastest lap: S. Moss, 9m 44.6s (97.88 mph)

Italian Grand Prix

8 September, Monza, 311 miles

1st, S. Moss (Vanwall), 2h 35m 3.9s, 120.27 mph
2nd, J.M. Fangio (Maserati 250F)
3rd, W. von Trips (Ferrari Tipo 801)
4th, M. Gregory (Maserati 250F)
5th, G. Scarlatti/M. Schell (Maserati 250F)
6th, J.M. Hawthorn (Ferrari Tipo 801)
Fastest lap: C.A.S. Brooks (Vanwall), 1m 43.7s (124.03 mph)

BRDC International Trophy

14 September, Silverstone, two 44-mile qualifying heats and 102-mile Final

1st, J. Behra (BRM P25), 99.95 mph
2nd, H. Schell (BRM P25)
3rd, R. Flockhart (BRM P25)
Fastest lap: J. Behra, 1m 42s (102.30 mph)

Modena Grand Prix

22 September, Modena Autodrome, aggregate of two 57-mile heats

1st, J. Behra (Maserati 250F), 1h 24m 48.0s, 81.09 mph
2nd, L. Musso (Ferrari Dino 156/1.8-litre)
3rd, H. Schell (Maserati 250F)
Fastest lap: J. Behra and L. Musso, 1m 2.6s (82.41 mph)

Moroccan Grand Prix

27 October, Casablanca, 261 miles

1st, J. Behra (Maserati 250F), 2h 18m 23s, 112.65 mph
2nd, S. Lewis-Evans (Vanwall)
3rd, M. Trintignant (BRM P25)
Fastest lap: J.M. Fangio (Maserati 250F), 2m 25.6s (116.80 mph)

Driver's World Championship

(Best five of eight events)

1st, J.M. Fangio, 40 points
2nd, S. Moss, 25 points
3rd, L. Musso, 16 points
4th, J.M. Hawthorn, 13 points
5th, C.A.S. Brooks, 11 points
6th, M. Gregory, 8 points

1958
Argentine Grand Prix

19 January, Buenos Aires Autodrome, 194 miles

1st, S. Moss (Cooper-Climax), 2h 19m 33.7s, 83.61 mph
2nd, L. Musso (Ferrari Dino 246)
3rd, J.M. Hawthorn (Ferrari Dino 246)
4th, J.M. Fangio (Maserati 250F)
5th, J. Behra (Maserati 250F)
6th, H. Schell (Maserati 250F)
Fastest lap: J.M. Fangio, 1m 41.8s (85.96 mph)

Buenos Aires City Grand Prix

2 February, Buenos Aires Autodrome, aggregate of two heats totalling 175 miles

1st, J.M. Fangio (Maserati 250F), 2h 38m 47.3s, 66.31 mph
2nd, L. Musso (Ferrari Dino 246)
3rd, F. Godia-Sales/C. Menditeguy (Maserati 250F)
Fastest lap: J.M. Fangio, 2m 34s (68.37 mph)

Note The race was again held as a Formule Libre event.

Goodwood International 100

7 April, Goodwood, 101 miles

1st, J.M. Hawthorn (Ferrari Dino 246), 1h, 3m 44.4s, 94.96 mph
2nd, J. Brabham (Cooper-Climax)
3rd, R.F. Salvadori (Cooper-Climax)
Fastest lap: J.M. Hawthorn and S. Moss (Cooper-Climax) 1m 28.8s (97.30 mph)

Syracuse Grand Prix

13 April, Siracusa, 205 miles

1st, L. Musso (Ferrari Dino 246), 2h 2m 44.4s, 100.24 mph
2nd, J. Bonnier (Maserati 250F)
3rd, F. Godia-Sales (Maserati 250F)
Fastest lap: L. Musso, 1m 57.01s (103.30 mph)

Aintree 200

19 April, Aintree, 201 miles

1st, S. Moss (Cooper-Climax, 85.66 mph
2nd, J. Brabham (Cooper-Climax)
3rd, R.F. Salvadori (Cooper-Climax)
Fastest lap: J. Brabham, 2m 1.4s (88.96 mph)

BRDC International Trophy

3 May, Silverstone, 146 miles

1st, P.J. Collins (Ferrari Dino 246), 1h 26m 14.6s, 101.82 mph
2nd, R.F. Salvadori (Cooper-Climax)
3rd, M. Gregory (Maserati 250F)
Fastest lap: P.J. Collins and J. Behra (BRM P25), 1m 40s (105.37 mph)

Monaco Grand Prix

18 May, Monaco, 195 miles

1st, M. Trintignant (Cooper-Climax), 2h 52m 27.9s, 66.19 mph
2nd, L. Musso (Ferrari Dino 246)
3rd, P.J. Collins (Ferrari Dino 246)
4th, J. Brabham (Cooper-Climax)
5th, H. Schell (BRM P25)
6th, C. Allison (Lotus 12-Climax)
Fastest lap: J.M. Hawthorn (Ferrari Dino 246) 1m 40.6s (69.93 mph)

Dutch Grand Prix

25 May, Zandvoort, 195 miles

1st, S. Moss (Vanwall), 2h 4m 49.2s, 93.93 mph
2nd, H. Schell (BRM P25)
3rd, J. Behra (BRM P25)
4th, R.F. Salvadori (Cooper-Climax)
5th, J.M. Hawthorn (Ferrari Dino 256)
6th, C. Allison (Lotus 12-Climax)
Fastest lap: S. Moss, 1m 38.5s (94.78 mph)

European Grand Prix

15 June, Spa-Francorchamps, 210 miles

1st, C.A.S. Brooks (Vanwall), 1h 37m 6.3s, 129.92 mph
2nd, J.M. Hawthorn (Ferrari Dino 246)
3rd, S. Lewis-Evans (Vanwall)
4th, C. Allison (Lotus 12-Climax)
5th, H. Schell (BRM P25)
6th, O. Gendebien (Ferrari Dino 246)
Fastest lap: J.M. Hawthorn, 3m 58.3s (132.36 mph)

French Grand Prix

6 July, Reims, 258 miles

1st, J.M. Hawthorn (Ferrari Dino 246), 2h 3m 21.3s,
125.45 mph
2nd, S. Moss (Vanwall)
3rd, W. von Trips (Ferrari Dino 246)
4th, J.M. Fangio (Maserati 250F)
5th, P.J. Collins (Ferrari Dino 246)
6th, J. Brabham (Cooper-Climax)
Fastest lap: J.M. Hawthorn, 2m 24.9s (128.16 mph)

British Grand Prix

19 July, Silverstone, 220 miles

1st, P.J. Collins (Ferrari Dino 246), 2h 9m 4.2s, 102.05
mph
2nd, J.M. Hawthorn (Ferrari Dino 246)
3rd, R.F. Salvadori (Cooper-Climax)
4th, S. Lewis-Evans (Vanwall)
5th, H. Schell (BRM P25)
6th, J. Brabham (Cooper-Climax)
Fastest lap: J.M. Hawthorn, 1m 40.8s (104.54 mph)

Caen Grand Prix

20 July, La Prairie, 188 miles

1st, S. Moss (Cooper-Climax), 93.93 mph
2nd, J. Bonnier (Maserati 250F)
3rd, B. Halford (Maserati 250F)
Fastest lap: J. Behra (BRM P25), 1m 20.8s (97.43 mph)

German Grand Prix

3 August, Nürburgring, 212 miles

1st, C.A.S. Brooks (Vanwall), 2h 21m 15.0s, 90.35 mph
2nd, R.F. Salvadori (Cooper-Climax)
3rd, M. Trintignant (Cooper-Climax)
4th, W. von Trips (Ferrari Dino 246)
5th, C. Allison (Lotus 12-Climax)
No other Formula 1 finishers
Fastest lap: S. Moss (Vanwall), 9m 9.2s (92.90 mph)

Portuguese Grand Prix

24 August, Oporto, 230 miles

1st, S. Moss (Vanwall), 2h 11m 27.80s, 105.03 mph
2nd, J.M. Hawthorn (Ferrari Dino 256)
3rd, S. Lewis-Evans (Vanwall)
4th, J. Behra (BRM P25)
5th, W. von Trips (Ferrari Dino 246)
6th, H. Schell (BRM P25)
Fastest lap: J.M. Hawthorn, 2m 32.37s (108.74 mph)

Italian Grand Prix

7 September, Monza, 250 miles

1st, C.A.S. Brooks (Vanwall), 2h 3m 47.8s, 121.22 mph
2nd, J.M. Hawthorn (Ferrari Dino 246)
3rd, P. Hill (Ferrari Dino 246)
4th, R.F. Salvadori (Cooper-Climax)
5th, G. Hill (Lotus 16-Climax)
6th, C. Allison (Lotus 12-Climax)
Fastest lap: P. Hill, 1m 42.9s (125.00 mph)

Note The fourth, fifth and sixth place finishers were not
classified.

Moroccan Grand Prix

19 October, Casablanca, 261 miles

1st, S. Moss (Vanwall), 2h 9m 15.1s, 116.20 mph
2nd, J.M. Hawthorn (Ferrari Dino 256)
3rd, P. Hill (Ferrari Dino 246)
4th, J. Bonnier (BRM P25)
5th, H. Schell (BRM P25)
6th, M. Gregory (Maserati 250F)
Fastest lap: S. Moss, 2m 22.5s (117.80 mph)

Driver's World Championship

(Best six of eleven events)

1st, J.M. Hawthorn, 42 points
2nd, S. Moss, 41 points
3rd, C.A.S. Brooks, 24 points
4th, R.F. Salvadori, 16 points
5th, P.J. Collins, 14 points
6th, H. Schell, 14 points

Manufacturers' World Championship

1st, Vanwall, 51 points
2nd, Ferrari, 45 points
3rd, Cooper-Climax, 32 points
4th, BRM, 18 points
5th, Maserati, 7 points
6th, Lotus-Climax, 5 points

1959

Goodwood International 100

30 March, Goodwood, 101 miles

1st, S. Moss (Cooper-Climax), 1h 6m 58s, 90.31 mph
2nd, J. Brabham (Cooper-Climax)
3rd, H. Schell (BRM P25)
Fastest lap: S. Moss, 1m 31.8s (94.12 mph)

Aintree 200

18 April, Aintree, 201 miles

1st, J. Behra (Ferrari Dino 256), 2h 15m 52.0s, 88.76 mph
2nd, C.A.S. Brooks (Ferrari Dino 246)
3rd, B. McLaren (Cooper-Climax)
Fastest lap: S. Moss (Cooper-BRM), 1m 58.8s (90.91 mph)

BRDC International Trophy

2 May, Silverstone. 146 miles

1st, J. Brabham (Cooper-Climax), 1h 25m 28.6s, 102.73 mph
2nd, R.F. Salvadori (Aston Martin DBR4)
3rd, R. Flockhart (BRM P25)
Fastest lap: R.F. Salvadori, 1m 40.0s (105.37 mph)

Monaco Grand Prix

10 May, Monaco, 195 miles

1st, J. Brabham (Cooper-Climax), 2h 55m 51.3s, 66.74 mph
2nd, C.A.S Brooks (Ferrari Dino 246)
3rd, M. Trintignant (Cooper-Climax)
4th, P. Hill (Ferrari Dino 246)
5th, B. McLaren (Cooper-Climax)
6th, R.F. Salvadori (Cooper-Maserati)
Fastest lap: J. Brabham, 1m 40.4s (70.09 mph)

Dutch Grand Prix

31 May, Zandvoort, 195 miles

1st, J. Bonnier (BRM P25), 2h 5m 26.8s, 93.46 mph
2nd, J. Brabham (Cooper-Climax)
3rd, M. Gregory (Cooper-Climax)
4th, I. Ireland (Lotus 16-Climax)
5th, J. Behra (Ferrari Dino 246)
6th, P. Hill (Ferrari Dino 246)
Fastest lap: S. Moss (Cooper-Climax), 1m 36.7s (97.19 mph)

European Grand Prix

5 July, Reims, 258 miles

1st, C.A.S. Brooks (Ferrari Dino 246), 2h 1m 26.5s, 127.43 mph
2nd, P. Hill (Ferrari Dino 246)
3rd, J. Brabham (Cooper-Climax)
4th, O. Gendebien (Ferrari Dino 246)
5th, B. McLaren (Cooper-Climax)
6th, R. Flockhart (BRM P25)
Fastest lap: S. Moss (BRM P25), 2m 22.8s (130.21 mph)

British Grand Prix

18 July, Aintree, 225 miles

1st, J. Brabham (Cooper-Climax), 2h 30m 11.6s, 89.88 mph
2nd, S. Moss (BRM P25)
3rd, B. McLaren (Cooper-Climax)
4th, H. Schell (BRM P25)
5th, M. Trintignant (Cooper-Climax)
6th, R.F. Salvadori (Aston Martin DBR4)
Fastest lap: S. Moss and B. McLaren, 1m 57.0s (92.31 mph)

German Grand Prix

2 August, Avus, aggregate of two 155-mile heats

1st, C.A.S. Brooks (Ferrari Dino 246), 2h 9m 31.6s, 143.34 mph
2nd, D. Gurney (Ferrari Dino 246)
3rd, P. Hill (Ferrari Dino 246)
4th, M. Trintignant (Cooper-Climax)
5th, J. Bonnier (BRM P25)
6th, I. Burgess (Cooper-Maserati)
Fastest lap: C.A.S. Brooks, 2m 4.5s (149.13 mph)

Portuguese Grand Prix

23 August, Monsanto, Lisbon, 210 miles

1st, S. Moss (Cooper-Climax), 2h 11m 55.41s, 95.32 mph
2nd, M. Gregory (Cooper-Climax)
3rd, D. Gurney (Ferrari Dino 246)
4th, M. Trintignant (Cooper-Climax)
5th, H. Schell (BRM P25)
6th, R.F. Salvadori (Aston Martin DBR4)
Fastest lap: S. Moss, 2m 5.07s (97.30 mph)

Italian Grand Prix

13 September, Monza, 257 miles

1st, S. Moss (Cooper-Climax) 2h 4m 5.4s, 124.38 mph
2nd, P. Hill (Ferrari Dino 246)
3rd, J. Brabham (Cooper-Climax)
4th, D. Gurney (Ferrari Dino 246)
5th, C. Allison (Ferrari Dino 246)
6th, O. Gendebien (Ferrari Dino 246)
Fastest lap: P. Hill, 1m 40.4s (128.11 mph)

Gold Cup Race

26 September, Oulton Park, 152 miles

1st, S. Moss (Cooper-Climax), 1h 34m 37.2s, 96.29 mph
2nd, J. Brabham (Cooper-Climax)
3rd, C. Bristow (Cooper-Climax)
Fastest lap: S. Moss, 1m 41.8s (97.64 mph)

United States Grand Prix

12 December, Sebring, 218 miles

1st, B. McLaren (Cooper-Climax), 2h 12m 35.7s, 98.83 mph
2nd, M. Trintignant (Cooper-Climax)
3rd, C.A.S. Brooks (Ferrari Dino 246)
4th, J. Brabham (Cooper-Climax)
5th, I. Ireland (Lotus 16-Climax)
6th, W. von Trips (Ferrari Dino 246)
Fastest lap: M. Trintignant, 3m 5s (101.13 mph)

Driver's World Championship

(Best five of nine events)

1st, J. Brabham, 31 points
2nd, C.A.S. Brooks, 27 points
3rd, S. Moss, 25½ points
4th, P. Hill, 20 points
5th, M. Trintignant, 19 points
6th, B. McLaren, 16½ points

Note Half points were the result of a shared fastest lap in the British Grand Prix.

Manufacturers' World Championship

1st, Cooper-Climax, 44 points
2nd, Ferrari, 38 points
3rd, BRM, 18 points
4th, Lotus-Climax, 5 points
No other make scored Championship points.

1960

Argentine Grand Prix

7 February, Buenos Aires Autodrome, 194 miles

1st, B. McLaren (Cooper-Climax), 2h 17m 49.5s, 82.77 mph
2nd, C. Allison (Ferrari Dino 246)
3rd, M. Trintignant/S. Moss (Cooper-Climax)
4th, C. Menditeguy (Cooper-Maserati)
5th, W. von Trips (Ferrari Dino 246)
6th, I. Ireland (Lotus 18 Climax)
Fastest lap: S. Moss, 1m 38.9s (88.48 mph)

Buenos Aires City Grand Prix

14 February, Cordoba, 149 miles

1st, M. Trintignant (Cooper-Climax), 1h 53m 50.90s, 76.12 mph
2nd, D. Gurney (BRM P25)
3rd, G. Munaron (Maserati 250F)
Fastest lap: B. McLaren (Cooper-Climax), 1m 27.20s (79.52 mph)

International 100

18 April, Goodwood, 101 miles

1st, I. Ireland (Lotus 18-Climax), 1h 0m 14.8s, 100.39 mph
2nd, S. Moss (Cooper-Climax)
3rd, C. Bristow (Cooper-Climax)
Fastest lap: S. Moss, 1m 24s (102.13 mph)

BRDC International Trophy

14 May, Silverstone, 146 miles

1st, I. Ireland (Lotus 18-Climax), 1h 20m 41.1s, 108.82 mph
2nd, J. Brabham (Cooper-Climax)
3rd, G. Hill (BRM P48)
Fastest lap: I. Ireland, 1m 34.2s (111.86 mph)

Monaco Grand Prix

29 May, Monaco, 195 miles

1st, S. Moss (Lotus 18-Climax), 2h 53m 45.5s, 67.48 mph
2nd, B. McLaren (Cooper-Climax)
3rd, P. Hill (Ferrari Dino 246)
4th, C.A.S. Brooks (Cooper-Climax)
5th, J. Bonnier (BRM P48)
6th, R. Ginther (Ferrari Dino 246P)
Fastest lap: B. McLaren, 1m 36.2s (73.13 mph)

Dutch Grand Prix

6 June, Zandvoort, 195 miles

1st, J. Brabham (Cooper-Climax), 2h 1m 47.2s, 96.27 mph
2nd, I. Ireland (Lotus 18-Climax)
3rd, G. Hill (BRM P48)
4th, S. Moss (Lotus 18-Climax)
5th, W. von Trips (Ferrari Dino 246)
6th, R. Ginther (Ferrari Dino 246)
Fastest lap: S. Moss, 1m 33.8s (99.99 mph)

Belgian Grand Prix

19 June, Spa-Francorchamps, 315 miles

1st, J. Brabham (Cooper-Climax), 2h 21m 37.3s, 133.63 mph
2nd, B. McLaren (Cooper-Climax)
3rd, O. Gendebien (Cooper-Climax)
4th, P. Hill (Ferrari Dino 246)
5th, J. Clark (Lotus 18-Climax)
6th, L. Bianchi (Cooper-Climax)
Fastest lap: J. Brabham, P. Hill and I. Ireland (Lotus 18-Climax), 3m 51.9s (136.01 mph)

French Grand Prix

3 July, Reims, 258 miles

1st, J. Brabham (Cooper-Climax), 1h 57m 24.9s, 131.80 mph
2nd, O. Gendebien (Cooper-Climax)
3rd, B. McLaren (Cooper-Climax)
4th, H. Taylor (Cooper-Climax)
5th, J. Clark (Lotus 18-Climax)
6th, R. Flockhart (Lotus 18-Climax)
Fastest lap: J. Brabham, 2m 17.5s (135.06 mph)

British Grand Prix

16 July, Silverstone, 225 miles

1st, J. Brabham (Cooper-Climax), 2h 4m 24.6s, 108.69 mph
2nd, J. Surtees (Lotus 18-Climax)
3rd, I. Ireland (Lotus 18-Climax)
4th, B. McLaren (Cooper-Climax)
5th, C.A.S. Brooks (Cooper-Climax)
6th, W. von Trips (Ferrari Dino 246)
Fastest lap: G. Hill (BRM P48), 1m 34.4s (111.62 mph)

Silver City Trophy

1 August, Brands Hatch, 133 miles

1st, J. Brabham (Cooper-Climax), 1h 25m 36.6s, 92.86 mph
2nd, G. Hill (BRM P48)
3rd, B. McLaren (Cooper-Climax)
Fastest lap: J. Brabham and J. Clark (Lotus 18-Climax), 1m 40.6s (94.82 mph)

Portuguese Grand Prix

14 August, Oporto, 253 miles

1st, J. Brabham (Cooper-Climax), 2h 19m 0.03s, 109.27 mph
2nd, B. McLaren (Cooper-Climax)
3rd, J. Clark (Lotus 18-Climax)
4th, W. von Trips (Ferrari Dino 246)
5th, C.A.S. Brooks (Cooper-Climax)
6th, I. Ireland (Lotus 18-Climax)
Fastest lap: J. Surtees (Lotus 18-Climax), 2m 27.53s (112.31 mph)

European Grand Prix

4 September, Monza, 311 miles

1st, P. Hill (Ferrari Dino 246), 2h 21m 9.2s, 132.06 mph
2nd, R. Ginther (Ferrari Dino 246)
3rd, W. Mairesse (Ferrari Dino 246)
4th, G. Cabianca (Cooper-Castellotti)
5th, W. von Trips (Ferrari Dino 156 Formula 2)
6th, H. Herrmann (Porsche Formula 2)
Fastest lap: P. Hill, 2m 43.6s (136.73 mph)

Lombank Trophy

17 September, Snetterton, 100 miles

1st, I. Ireland (Lotus 18-Climax), 58m 33.8s, 102.73 mph
2nd, J. Clark (Lotus 18-Climax)
3rd, J. Bonnier (BRM P48)
Fastest lap: J. Clark, 1m 32.6s (105.36 mph)

Gold Cup Race

24 September, Oulton Park, 166 miles

1st, S. Moss (Lotus 18-Climax), 1 h 45m 54s, 93.85 mph
2nd, J. Brabham (Cooper-Climax)
3rd, G. Hill (BRM P48)
Fastest lap: J. Clark (Lotus 18-Climax), 1m 42.4s (97.07 mph)

United States Grand Prix

20 November, Riverside Raceway, 246 miles

1st, S. Moss (Lotus 18-Climax), 2h 28m 52.2s, 99.00 mph
2nd, I. Ireland (Lotus 18-Climax)
3rd, B. McLaren (Cooper-Climax)
4th, J. Brabham (Cooper-Climax)
5th, J. Bonnier (BRM P48)
6th, P. Hill (Cooper-Climax)
Fastest lap: J. Brabham, 1m 56.3s (101.38 mph)

Drivers' World Championship

(Best six of ten events)

1st, J. Brabham, 43 points
2nd, B. McLaren, 34 points
3rd, S. Moss, 19 points
4th, I. Ireland, 18 points
5th, P. Hill, 16 points
6th, O. Gendebien, 10 points

Manufacturers' World Championship

1st, Cooper-Climax, 48 points
2nd, Lotus-Climax, 34 points
3rd, Ferrari, 26 points
4th, BRM, 8 points
5th, Cooper-Maserati, 3 points
6th, Cooper-Castellotti, 3 points

Appendix 2

Specifications of Formula 1 Cars

1954-60

Make and model	Aston Martin DBR4 (UK)	BRM P25 (UK)	Connaught B-series (UK)	Cooper-Climax T45/T51/T53 (UK)	Ferrari Tipo 625 (Italy)	Ferrari Tipo 553 (Italy)	Ferrari Dino 246 (Italy)
Years raced	1959-60	1955-59	1955-57	1957-60	1954-55	1954	1957-60
Engine layout	Six cylinders in line	Four cylinders in line	Four cylinders in line	Four cylinders in line	Four cylinders in line	Four cylinders in line	65° V-6
capacity (cc)	2494	2497	2470	2495	2490	2497.56	2417
bore × stroke (mm)	83 × 76.8	102.87 × 74.93	93.5 × 90	94 × 89.9	94 × 90	100 × 79.5	85 × 71
Valve actuation	Twin overhead camshafts	Twin overhead camshafts	Twin overhead camshafts	Twin overhead camshafts	Twin overhead camshafts	Twin overhead camshafts	Twin overhead camshafts per bank of cylinders
Carburation	Three Weber 50DCO	Two Weber 58DCOE	Two Weber 58DCOE	Two Weber 58DCOE	Two Weber 52DCOA3	Two Weber 52DCOAF	Three Weber 42DCN
Power output (claimed)	250 bhp at 7,800 rpm	288 bhp at 8,250 rpm	240 bhp at 6,400 rpm	240 bhp at 6,750 rpm	250 bhp at 7,500 rpm	250 bhp at 7,500 rpm	275 bhp at 8,300 rpm
Transmission	Five-speed gearbox in unit with the final drive	Four-speed gearbox in unit with the final drive	Four-speed Armstrong-Siddeley pre-selector positioned at rear axle	Five-speed Cooper mounted behind the rear axle	Four-speed in unit with the final drive	Four-speed in unit with the final drive	Four-speed in unit with the final drive
Chassis construction	Multi-tubular spaceframe	Multi-tubular spaceframe	Tubular ladder-type with tubular cross-members	Multi-tubular	Tubular ladder-type	Multi-tubular with transverse front tubular structure	Multi-tubular with large diameter tubular lower members
Front suspension	Unequal-length wishbones and coil spring/ damper units	Unequal-length wishbones and coil spring/ damper units	Unequal-length wishbones and coil spring/ damper units	Unequal-length wishbones and coil spring/ damper units	Unequal-length wishbones, transverse leaf spring and vane-type dampers	Unequal-length wishbones, transverse leaf spring and vane-type dampers	Unequal-length wishbones, coil springs and vane-type dampers
Rear suspension	de Dion axle, torsion bars and telescopic dampers	de Dion axle, Watts linkage and coil spring/ damper units	de Dion axle, transverse link and twin radius arms	Unequal-length wishbones and coil spring/ damper units	de Dion axle, twin radius arms, transverse leaf spring and vane-type dampers	de Dion axle, twin radius arms, transverse leaf spring and vane-type dampers	de Dion axle, twin radius arms, transverse leaf spring and vane-type dampers
Brakes	Girling discs	Dunlop discs with single rear disc on gearbox output shaft	Dunlop discs	Girling discs	Hydraulic two-leading-shoe, light alloy drums	Hydraulic two-leading-shoe, light alloy drums	Hydraulic two-leading-shoe, cast iron drums
Wheelbase	7 ft 3 in	7 ft 4 in	7 ft 6 in	7 ft 7 in	7 ft 2½ in	7 ft 0 in	7 ft 1 in
Front track	4 ft 1 in	4 ft 4 in	4 ft 2 in	3 ft 10½ in	4 ft 3½ in	4 ft 1 in	4 ft 0⅞ in
Rear track	4 ft 1 in	4 ft 2 in	4 ft 2 in	4 ft 0 in	4 ft 1 in	3 ft 11½ in	3 ft 11¼ in
Notes	The team raced the lighter DBR5 in 1960, trying fuel injection and independent rear suspension.	The P25 was progressively modified. The above specification is for 1957.	Raced with aerodynamic bodywork in 1955 and early 1956. Unstreamlined bodywork from late 1955. Originally fitted with Hilborn-Travers fuel injection.	Progressively developed from 1956/7 Formula 2 car and first raced in Formula 1 with 1960cc engine.	First raced in 1951. Various engine types used. Specification relates to standard 1954 car.	Raced in 1955 in improved form as the Tipo 555.	Specification relates to 1958 car; disc brakes adopted in 1959 and irs in 1960. Also raced in 2451cc form as Dino 256.

Gordini T16 (France)	Gordini T32 (France)	Lancia D50 (Italy)	Lotus-Climax 16 (UK)	Lotus-Climax 18 (UK)	Maserati 250F (Italy)	Mercedes-Benz W196 (Germany)	Vanwall (UK)
1954-57	1955-57	1954-57	1958-59	1960	1954-60	1954-55	1954-58
Six cylinders in line	Eight cylinders in line	90° V-8	Four cylinders in line	Four cylinders in line	Six cylinders in line	Eight cylinders in line	Four cylinders in line
2473	2475	2487	2495	2495	2493	2496	2490
80 × 82	84 × 80	73.6 × 73.1	94 × 89.9	94 × 89.9	84 × 72	76 × 68.8	96 × 86
Twin overhead camshafts	Twin overhead camshafts	Twin overhead camshafts per bank of cylinders	Twin overhead camshafts	Twin overhead camshafts	Twin overhead camshafts	Twin overhead camshafts	Twin overhead camshafts
Three Weber	Four Weber	Four Solex 40 PII	Four Weber 58DCOB	Two Weber 58DCOE	Three Weber 42DCO3	Bosch fuel injection	Bosch fuel injection
230 bhp at 6,800 rpm	230 bhp at 7,000 rpm	260 bhp at 8,000 rpm	240 bhp at 6,750 rpm	240 bhp at 6,750 rpm	240 bhp at 6,500 rpm	257 bhp at 8,250 rpm	280 bhp at 7,400 rpm
Five-speed in unit with the engine	Five-speed in unit with the engine	Five-speed in unit with the final drive	Five-speed in unit with the final drive	Five-speed in unit with the final drive	Four-speed in unit with the final drive	Four-speed in unit with the final drive	Five-speed in unit with the final drive
Tubular ladder-type	Tubular ladder-type	Multi-tubular with engine as integral part of chassis	Multi-tubular spaceframe	Multi-tubular spaceframe	Multi-tubular	Multi-tubular spaceframe	Multi-tubular spaceframe
Unequal-length wishbones and torsion bars	Leading upper arm, trailing lower arm, parallel torsion bars	Equal-length wishbones, transverse leaf spring and tubular dampers	Upper and lower wishbones and coil spring/damper units	Transverse wishbones and coil spring/damper units	Unequal-length double wishbones, coil springs, vane-type dampers	Equal-length wishbones, longitudinal torsion bars, telescopic dampers	Unequal-length wishbones, coil spring/damper units
Rigid rear axle and longitudinal torsion bars	Leading upper arm, trailing lower arm, parallel torsion bars	de Dion axle, trailing arms, transverse leaf spring and tubular dampers	Independent 'strut'-type, with drive-shafts locating the wheels, radius arms and coil spring/damper units	Transverse lower wishbones, drive-shafts acting as upper wishbones, twin radius arms and coil spring/damper units	de Dion axle, twin radius arms, transverse leaf spring, vane-type dampers	Low-pivot swing-axles, Watts linkage, longitudinal torsion bars, telescopic dampers	de Dion axle, twin radius arms, Watts linkage, coil spring/damper units
Messier discs	Messier discs, mounted inboard at the rear	Hydraulic with four shoes per drum	Girling discs	Girling discs	Hydraulic two-leading-shoe, light alloy drums	Hydraulic leading/trailing shoe, mounted inboard	Vandervell/Goodyear discs
7 ft 3⅜ in	7 ft 4⅜ in	7 ft 6 in	7 ft 4 in	7 ft 6 in	7 ft 5¾ in	7 ft 8½ in	7 ft 6¼ in
3 ft 10⅜ in	4 ft 1⅜ in	4 ft 2 in	3 ft 11 in	4 ft 1 in	4 ft 3¹/₅ in	4 ft 5²/₅ in	4 ft 5¾ in
3 ft 10⅜ in	4 ft 1⅞ in	4 ft 2 in	3 ft 11 in	3 ft 11 in	4 ft 1¹/₅ in	4 ft 5 in	4 ft 3¾ in
Development of Formula 2 cars first raced in 1952.		Specification relates to 1955 car. Extensively modified by Ferrari during 1956-57.		Chapman's first rear-engine design.	Specification relates to 1954 car. Raced by the works to the end of 1957 and then by private owners.	Specification relates to 1954 car. Raced in streamlined and unstreamlined forms. 1955 cars also raced with 7 ft 3 in and 7 ft ¹/₅ in wheelbase.	Specification relates to 1957 car.

Further reading

Magazines

The best reading about Formula 1 during the years 1954-60 is the magazines of the period, *Motor Sport* for the technical accuracy and style of its Continental Correspondent, Denis Jenkinson, *Autocourse* during its heyday (that is up until about 1956) for its photography and statistical material, and the weekly *Autosport* for its spontaneity. *Autosport* usually reported a race in full on the Friday (its then publishing day) following the race, so if you want to read a race report, check the date of the race in Appendix 1 and ask Chater's Motoring Booksellers or other specialist second-hand stockist if they have the copy you want. The 'Friday following the race' rule is not 100 per cent because the Argentine races were usually reported a couple of weeks after the race, and minor Continental races were usually given a brief summary on the Friday following the race, followed by a full report the next Friday. For example, Tony Brooks' historic win with the Connaught at Siracusa took place on 23 October 1955, but was not reported in full until 4 November when his friend and entrant John Risely-Prichard, who had accompanied him to the race, wrote a detailed account.

Books

The one book that can be recommended almost without qualification is *A Record of Grand Prix and Voiturette Racing*, Volume 6: 1954-59, one of a series produced by Paul Sheldon with Duncan Rabagliatti and published by his own St Leonards Press. It contains the most detailed statistical information covering every Formula 1 and Formula 2 race of the period and the whole series is an essential *vade mecum* for serious 'motor racing students' with a propensity for facts and figures. It has to be said that the series seems more prompted by a dedicated enthusiasm for facts and figures than raw enthusiasm.

To capture the atmosphere of the period, read the book by the man who saw it all: *A Story of Formula 1* by Denis Jenkinson (Grenville Publishing, 1960).

One of the most important books is *Alf Francis, Racing Mechanic* written from Francis' diaries and memories (G.T. Foulis, 1958). It is one of the best of all motor racing books, high informative and detailed and covering Francis' years from 1948-57 as mechanic to HWM, Peter

Whitehead, Stirling Moss and Rob Walker.

The different makes in racing are in the main well covered:

Aston Martin: *Racing with the David Brown Aston Martins* is published in two volumes (Transport Bookman, 1980), both compiled by Chris Nixon. The first volume, written in collaboration with John Wyer, deals with the development and racing of the cars, while Volume 2 sets out the memories of drivers and other team personnel.

BRM: The full history by Doug Nye is awaited from Motor Racing Publications but in the meanwhile we have to make do with *BRM* by Raymond Mays and Peter Roberts (Cassell, 1962), readable, very biased (as would be expected) and surprisingly inaccurate.

Cooper: *Cooper Cars* by Doug Nye (Osprey Publishing, 2nd edition 1988) is the standard work.

Ferrari: *Ferrari* by Hans Tanner with Doug Nye (G.T. Foulis, 6th edition, 1984).

Grand Prix Ferrari by Anthony Pritchard (Robert Hale, 1974).

Ferrari, The Grand Prix Cars by Alan Henry (Hazleton Publishing, 2nd edition 1989).

Lotus: *Theme Lotus* by Doug Nye (Motor Racing Publications, 2nd Edition, 1987).

Colin Chapman: The Man and his Cars by G. Crombac (Patrick Stephens, 1986).

Maserati: *Maserati, A History* by Anthony Pritchard (David & Charles, 1976).

Mercedes-Benz: *The Mercedes-Benz Racing Cars* by Karl Ludvigsen (Bond/Parkhurst Books, 1971).

Racing the Silver Arrows by Chris Nixon (Osprey, 1986).

Vanwall: *Vanwall* by Denis Jenkinson and Cyril Posthumus (Patrick Stephens, 1975).

There are also some very worthwhile driver autobiographies:

Juan Fangio: There have been two biographies and a 1970s autobiography linked to the making of a film. Patrick Stephens published a new and definitive autobiography, *Fangio: My Racing Life*, in 1990 but the original autobiography, *My Twenty Years of Racing* (Temple Press, 1961), largely written by his manager Marcello Giambestone, remains a good read.

Mike Hawthorn: Hawthorn's two volumes of autobiography have recently been reissued by Aston Publications, *Challenge Me The Race* in 1988 and *Champion Year* in 1989.

Stirling Moss: There has been a whole series of books about and by Moss, starting with the very worthwhile *Stirling Moss* by Robert Raymond (Motor Racing Publications, 1953). Moss's deep searching book about his life, *All But My Life* (William Kimber, 1963), written with Ken Purdy, is an absorbing volume. The most important book is *Stirling Moss, My Cars, My Career* written with Doug Nye and published by Patrick Stephens in 1987.

Index

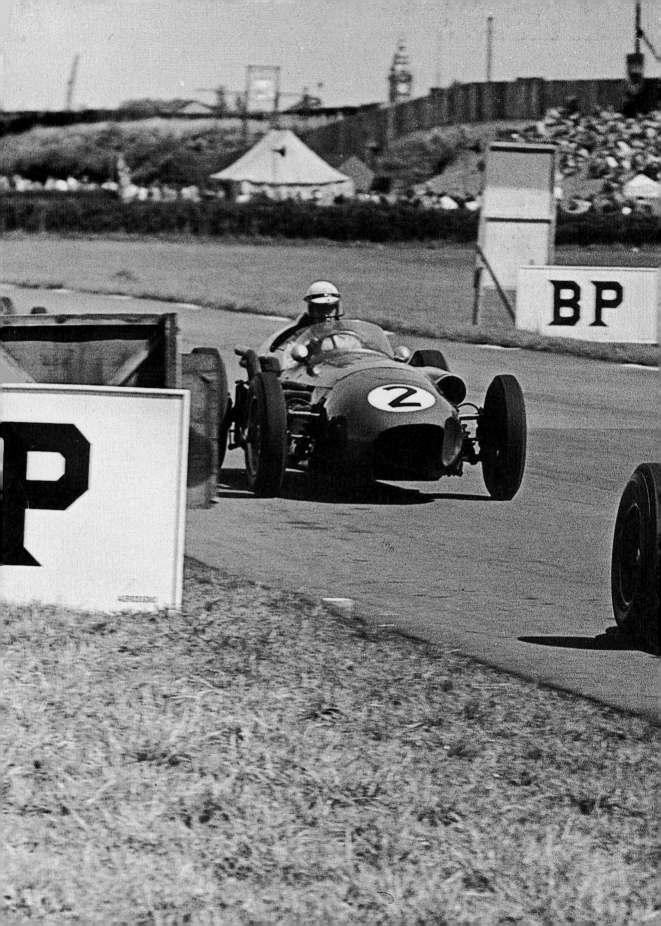